Medieval

Church Music-Dramas

A Repertory

of Complete Plays

MEDIEVAL CHURCH MUSIC-DRAMAS

A Repertory of Complete Plays

Transcribed and Edited by
Fletcher Collins, Jr.

UNIVERSITY PRESS OF VIRGINIA

CHARLOTTESVILLE

THE UNIVERSITY PRESS OF VIRGINIA
Copyright © 1976 by the Rector and Visitors
of the University of Virginia

First published 1976

The publication of
*Medieval Church Music-Dramas: A Repertory of
Complete Plays*
was sponsored by Mary Baldwin College.

Frontispiece: An *Alleluia* melisma from Paris, Bibliothèque
Nationale MS Latin 1118, p. 114, a so-called St. Martial
de Limoges tropertonarium, dated 988-996. Identification
of the sprightly melody is as uncertain as that of the
sprightly dancing girl with handbells. She may have been
Salome if the *Alleluia* was an item in the Feast of the
Beheading of St. John; or the great-grandmother of a
Limoges Wise Maiden; or merely the dancer of a *conductus*,
as in the later *Play of Daniel.*

Library of Congress Cataloging in Publication Data
Main entry under title:

Medieval church music-dramas.

   1. Liturgical dramas. I. Collins, Fletcher. M2.M2786 783 75-33896
ISBN 0-8139-0644-X

Printed in the United States of America

Contents

Preface

ONE HAVING AUTHORITY" has long been awaited to come forth with a practical edition of the medieval church music-dramas in one or another of their produceable versions—intact with words, music, and stage directions. The only major criticism of *The Production of Medieval Church Music-Drama* (1972) has been that it did not also contain the sixteen plays. To accept that criticism as a challenge, and without waiting longer for others more capable to do the job, I here offer an edition, after experience in their transcription from the original manuscripts and testing in production of about three-fourths of the repertory. Many of these are presented for the first time in modern notation as music-dramas, with their mensuralized and highly singable melodies. I have also been bold to retranscribe and reedit two of the best known of the repertory, the *Herod* and the *Daniel*, and to substitute for the already well-edited *Visit to the Sepulcher* from Fleury a quite different version of this in its time most widely used of all the music-dramas.

FLETCHER COLLINS, JR.

Mary Baldwin College
June 1975

Introduction

THERE IS ALWAYS a sense of incredulity that any work in any language cannot be well translated into English. But until a poet-translator of the caliber of William Tyndale or Richard Wilbur appears, I think it unlikely that singable English verses can be precisely fitted to the melodies of the medieval Latin music-dramas. The poet-composers of the plays created an amalgam that does not split or accept substitutions.

As a convenience to those who have no Latin, a trot in English is included under the Latin dialogue of each play. There is no thought, or even possibility, that these English phrases can be sung to the melodies. Actually, the problem of English speakers understanding the Latin is not nearly so serious as with operas in foreign languages, because the subject matter of the plays is for the most part Biblical and can be recalled by a prologue-reading of the relevant passages. I have not seen an audience hopelessly lost during a performance; rather, they have afterward confessed surprise that the play came over so clearly.

There has also been included an English translation of all the Latin rubrics (stage directions to us) from the manuscripts. Wherever necessary in order to clarify the production intent, additional stage directions in italics have been added.

In two of the plays, *The Wise and Foolish Maidens* and the St. Quentin *Visit to the Sepulcher*, a substantial quantity of verses in Old French has seemed to ask for a singable English version, since the Old French portions of the plays are least Biblical in their orientation. There is a further advantage in using a translation of medieval French in performance: a modern audience is thus placed in the same relationship to the English that a medieval audience was to its French.

In this edition of the plays I have avoided any but the most necessary duplication of material and its interpretation from my earlier volume.[1] While this method has the disadvantage, or sly device, of urging a student or director to use both works for a full consideration of the plays as produced and produceable music-dramas, it also permits the

---

[1] Fletcher Collins, Jr., *The Production of Medieval Church Music-Drama* (Charlottesville, Va., 1972), hereafter referred to as *Production.*

reader of the present volume to concentrate directly on the complete playscripts in a way never before possible. The two volumes are thus, I believe, companionable.

My ideal reader would begin with the preface and introduction to the first volume for a general orientation; read or sing through any one of the plays in the present volume; return to my interpretative treatment of ten aspects of that play in *Production*; and finally reread or begin to perform the play. A case for the plays as music-dramas was made in the earlier work, and here may need only to be corroborated by the experience of readers and audiences with the theatrical texts themselves.

Not that there can or should be one correct interpretation or one absolutely accurate transcription of the music. My hope is that this lovely repertory of high-style theater pieces will have a range of interpretation and thus production similar to what Shakespeare's now have, though I should not care to see the medieval playwright's intention ignored.

Architectural style and space, as always in theater, make a large difference to the feel of a medieval play's performance. The staging convention, described in detail in my earlier volume, usually required two *sedes*, or acting areas, with a space of at least fifteen feet between them as a *platea*, or street. The chancels of most modern churches do not have this kind of unencumbered space; yet outside the ecclesiastical environment is usually the desert. We have succeeded with a medieval play beyond the pale only at the Folger Library Theater, which has its own aura of antiquity.

The very live acoustics of most churches, old or new, are hospitable to the medieval style of melody, apparently because the medieval composer constructed melodies that would build a pattern of harmony in the intervallics, and thus would create a kind of harmony in a single voice. This phenomenon was nowhere more striking—even at first appalling—than at the twelfth-century Fleury abbey at Saint-Benôit-sur-Loire, where Theater Wagon in 1974 revived the *Lazarus* after eight centuries. But when our singer-actors got it going right in rehearsal and began what theater people call "playing the building" the result had an unearthly beauty, with harmonies and overtones reinforcing the monophonic line. Something of this effect may be found experimentally by playing a melody from this book on the piano with damper pedal down. In the *Lazarus* melody, for example, one observes a reiteration of the triadic sequences E-G-B and G-B-D, with G-B in common and E the ground to which the melody frequently returns.

The world of medieval musicological transcription is full of hazards, with transcribers seldom in agreement as to the transcription of a phrase. At one extreme are those who claim that this style of melody was not mensural after all, but was sung in a declamatory style. Other transcribers are equally certain of the accuracy of their elaborately scientific method and their complicated results, singable or not.

The principles back of my transcriptions are as simple as possible, and begin with Willi Apel's "simplification without falsification." The extravagant, the florid, and the supersubtle are unlikely in this period. More likely is something that echoes the clarity and classic simplicity of the Romanesque architecture of the edifices in which these melodies were created and sung.

Many factors influencing decisions are by degrees scientific and creative. The metric of the melodic line is determined by the meter of the verse. A melody in the manuscript is recognized as mensural, not free rhythm, like plainchant, by its being the setting for metric verse, not the free verse or prose of plainchant. The metric units of nearly all verse in the plays are either trochaic, iambic, or dactyllic, which have musical analogues in what are called rhythmic modes. In monophonic practice only the first two of these modes have meaning, and indicate

whether the basic thrust of the measure is ♩♪ or ♪♩ . Mechanical adherence to either rhythmic mode throughout a melody often produces a humdrum or jerky effect that was certainly not intended. The medieval composer-poet's metrical variations within a melodic line are similar to variations from iambic pentameter in a line of Elizabethan blank verse.

The phrases and sections of a medieval melody are dimensioned by the verse or stanza pattern, line upon line, so that this much of melodic structure can be readily determined. In fact, the perceptions and decisions of the transcriber must always be largely concerned with the phrases and sections, with what sculpts the most shapely melody in a rhythmic style recognizably medieval.

Within the measure are vexing and creative choices, subordinate to the strategy of the melody. In a 3/4 measure containing two syllables and five notes, there are theoretically many possibilities for the length of each note. This range of possibility is somewhat decreased—*Alleluia!*—by the prohibition against giving only an eighth note to a syllable when the unit of the measure is a quarter note and by having to follow the composer's clustering of notes on this or that syllable. Another prohibition, good in the credo of a songwriter of any period, is that against false accents in words. In *nó-bis*, for example, the first beat of a 3/4 measure must pick up *nó-*, not *-bis*, and a measure is unacceptable in which *domino* is accented other than *dó-mi-no*.

The medieval system of movable C and F clefs is used in the manuscripts of all the plays except the two from Limoges, which have the Aquitanian single-line staff with f^1 invariably on that line. The purpose of the movable clefs was obviously to accommodate the notation to the four-line staff, so that notation above or below did not foul the already scripted words. A literal transcription of this notation would therefore be in the key of C, F, or B-flat, never in D, G, or A. To compensate for the historical (if not hysterical) inflation of pitch-standard to A-440, however, I have frequently transcribed in the keys of D and G. In few instances have I transposed more radically, since I wish to present the melodies in approximately the pitch-range intended by their composers. There is no harm in transposing to whatever key serves the individual singer, though the pitch-range of these melodies is not great and can usually be performed as written. One must of course beware of an awkward interval from last note of one item to first of the next. The medieval composer was careful about this matter, probably because unaccompanied solo singing of dialogue had to pass an unflatted pitch from one singer to another without much, if any, instrumental cue.

Silent emendations have been eschewed. Corrections of what appear to be scribal errors in notation have been acknowledged in the notes on each play. The literary texts have been collated with Karl Young's meticulous literary edition and silently altered from his only to stand-ardize the Latin *ae* as *ae* rather than as *e*; to replace most semicolons with periods; and to treat some passages as verse which he, not having the music to guide him, printed as prose.[2]

I have been much less free with the use of a cluster of four sixteenth-notes in a 3/4 measure than have other editors of some of these plays. My custom has been to look for other medieval solutions to the rhythm of a measure or section before accepting the four sixteenths. Often an alternative solution, when discovered, has contributed to a stronger melody.

The use of duple time by medieval composers has apparently been authenticated in a few nondramatic compositions, but because of medieval reverence for the number three,[3] one finds that the bulk of melodies in the period are clearly in 3/4 or 6/8. In the playscripts I have not come on a single melody that is superior in 4/4, not even the opening of *The Lament of Mary*, which Smoldon retained in 4/4 after being dissuaded from so scoring the entire play. One would expect church composers, more than secular trouvères or troubadours, to be scrupulous about the mystique of the triple.

Indication of time for items after the first in each play is here given only for changes in tempus, whether mensural or free rhythm. My phrasing of the free-rhythm pieces is intended as an aid to the singer, and, while not always identical with the more elaborate punctuations of the modern *Antiphonale Romanum* (1949) and *Graduale Romanum* (1924), has been collated with them wherever items have been retained in the liturgy over the centuries.

Liquescent neumes, or *plicas,* which look in a medieval manuscript like a drip off the forward side of the parent note, I prefer to notate without recourse to a special symbol. Following the modern service books, many transcribers have used a miniature note to represent the drip: ♪♩ . The great pioneer Pierre Aubry was fond of ♪♪ as a solu-

---

[2]Young, *The Drama of the Medieval Church* (Oxford, 1933).

[3]See, for example, *Production*, p. 205.

tion to this and other notational problems. Dom Anselm Hughes likes
♫̂ , and Paul Evans extensively uses ♫ . Certainly Hughes is on the
right track when he writes that the liquescent is "semi-vocal,. . . is not
an ad libitum ornament, ♩♪ , but has a time value of its own." My
preference is for ♩.♪ , mainly because it is more easily realized by
singers and describes the time value of the *plica* more clearly, if not
with complete accuracy. In what I take to be a similar stylistic situation,
Cecil Sharp, recording traditional English folksong in 1917, used ♩.♪ or
♩.♪.[4] The only clues from the Middle Ages are from two theorists who
spoke of the liquescent as being formed by doing something tricky with
the epiglottis, and from another, Walter Odington, who described the
plica as a vocal sliding on one note.[5]

When in doubt about a medieval rhythm, and without an apt
medieval precedent, a knowledge of British and French folk-music style
has often put me back on the track. Noah Greenberg once told me that
when Father Rembert Weakland was transcribing the *Daniel* for the
New York Pro Musica, Weakland presented Greenberg with three possible transcriptions of the same item and asked him to choose. Greenberg
of course chose the most beautiful—and there is indeed merit in his
approach, as long as the choice is one that could conceivably have been
made in the twelfth century or in well-cured folksong, not merely by
Greenberg in New York eight centuries away. We are all surrogates in
these decisions, and no one needs to complain of another's choices
except as they are either less beautiful to sing and hear than others, or
less medieval.

A caution to those whose interest is primarily in dramatic literature
and who peruse this book more or less silently, by eye: these plays,
being music-dramas, depend for their lives on being heard and seen.
They are the only high-style drama of this sort existing in the Western
world, and are hence to the uninitiated a little strange in form. The
distinction of this form is more than that the dialogue is sung. Typically,
the dialogue of a medieval music-drama is sung to one or more melodies,
each repeated many times. The nearest comparable effect is that of a
ballad-story, in which the melody is repeated as often as there are
stanzas. A music-drama is a theater-story, its medium similarly fash-
ioned. Even the more complex of the music-dramas have a considerable
amount of melodic repetition, with variations like those in the melody
of a folk ballad. The effect is something an eye-reader will miss, and
only an audience—faced with moving, costumed, singing actors—will
fully receive.

[4]Evans, *The Early Trope Repertory of Saint-Martial De Limoges* (Princeton, N.J., 1969);
Dom Anselm Hughes, ed., *New Oxford History of Music* (Oxford, 1954), II, 325; Sharp,
English Folk Songs from the Southern Appalachians (London, 1932), II, 12 and 51.

[5]See Hughes for the Latin of all three.

1. The Visit to the Sepulcher

The Visit to the Sepulcher

THERE EXIST the manuscripts of hundreds of medieval plays on the Easter theme of the visit to the sepulcher. The version here presented is from the St. Quentin (France) Bibliothèque de la Ville MS 86, pp. 609-25. It originated in the monastery for women (that is, a nunnery) on the outskirts of St. Quentin, the Abbey of Origny-Sainte-Benôite. The play is one of six in which nuns are known to have played *Visitatio* roles. The canonesses, or sisters, of the abbey, as at five other convents in Europe and England, played the major roles of the Three Marys, while the male clergy took the male roles (See *Production*, p. 65, n. 8, and Young I, 403, 405.).

The St. Quentin playscript, moreover, has two substantial episodes in Old French, both capitalizing on the fact of women playing the Mary roles. The dialogue of these episodes I have translated into singable English.

Suggestions for the production of the play are to be found extensively in *Production*, pp. 47-84 and 283-92.

Scholars have noted that the St. Quentin version, lacking the beginning and end pages of the playscript, has no explicit liturgical setting. The Latin items are, however, so much like those of many other *Visitatio* plays that we may assume that the present play, like the others, began after the third responsory of Matins and concluded with the customary end of Matins, the *Te Deum laudamus.*

In addition I have borrowed from the great Fleury version of the *Visitatio* its last item, the "Resurrexit hodie," transcribed directly from Orléans, Bibliothèque de la Ville MS 201, p. 225. The St. Quentin lacks a final item after the Apostles' "Cernites, O socii," and could ask for no more rousing finish than the Fleury "Resurrexit hodie." The *organum* of the last measures is editorial.

The words and music of the climactic items of the St. Quentin version, as with a number of other *Visitatio*s, were lifted bodily from certain stanzas of the eleventh-century Easter hymn, the majestic *Victimae Paschali*. The substance of the climax is, therefore, liturgical. It may also have sometimes in that period been a rhythmed composition rather than the free-rhythm plainchant in which it is presented in the modern Roman *Graduale*, pp. 222-23. The borrowed stanzas have the earmarks of verse, since their lines scan (and rhyme), and are thus eligible to have measured melodies set to them from the unrhythmed notation of the manuscript. If the reader or performer prefers the more familiar plainchant version, it can be easily substituted from the *Graduale* or the *Liber Usualis*.

The last responsory of Easter Matins usually began: "Dum transisset sabbatum, Maria Magdalena et Maria Iacobi et Salome emerunt aromata . . ." (Young, I, 232-33). From this liturgical source are derived the names of the Three Marys. The Two Marys of the St. Quentin play are thus Mary Jacobi and Mary Salome. Many versions of the *Visitatio* so name them, as in Young, I, 366, 375, 381, 601, and *passim*. There is, moreover, no reason to suppose that the Two Marys always sing together.

One also observes that the Two Angels, never identified by individual names, sometimes refer to themselves in the plural, sometimes in the singular (Items 39, 41, 45). There is thus, as with the Two Marys and the Two Apostles, sanction to assign group-designated items at will to one or another individual within the group, and to alternate such assignments even within an item.

For Item 6 the manuscript clef is F, an obvious scribal error, since the melody is elsewhere written in the C clef (Items 2, 4, 24, 58). In Item 9 the present tenth measure is lacking, word and note, in the manuscript. I have inserted *bel* and have projected notation for it. The literary scribe of Item 27, measure 13, apparently added the word *positus* from the antiphon version of this piece. The music scribe followed suit and repeated three notes for the added word. I have enclosed these in brackets and suggest that they be omitted in performance.

The *incipit* of Item 65 is assigned in the manuscript to the Two Apostles, for no dramatic reason. An explanation may be that antiphons, as sung in the liturgy for centuries before the plays were composed, customarily were begun by a member of the clergy, and were continued by the Choir after the first phrase. The literary scribe, here and in Item 27, was thus behaving conventionally rather than theatrically.

The Cast

The Priest, and Archangel
The Choir
The Three Marys
   Mary Magdalene
   Mary Jacobi
   Mary Salome
The Merchant(s)
Two Angels
The Christus
The Two Apostles
   Peter
   John
Several Soldiers, nonspeaking

> The Scene: The nave of an abbey. A spice shop. A chapel. The sepulcher. Easter, at the rising of the sun.

The Visit to the Sepulcher   *Visitatio Sepulchri*

(At the back of the church, as the procession begins, each of the
Marys must have in her hand a lighted candle, and Mary Magdalene
must have a pyx in her hand and the other two none, because they
will have to buy them from the Merchant on the way. And the Priest
must go before them, and have in his hand a lighted thurible to
spread the incense. The Choir follows the Marys, and each of them
in the Choir has a lighted candle in hand. The procession moves
forward during the singing of Items 1-5.)

(1)

CHOIR   free rhythm

Ma- ri- a Mag- da- le- na et a- li- a Ma- ri- a
Mary   Magdalene   and the other Mary

fe- ré- bant di- lu- cu- lo a- ro- má- ta,
bore   at dawn   spices.

Do- mi- num quae- rén- tes in mo- nu- men- to.
The Lord   they were seeking in the tomb.

(2)

THE THREE MARYS

Iam per- cus- so, he- u! Pa- sto- re, O- ves
Now slain, alas! O Shepherd, the sheep

er- rant mi- se- re! Et ma- gi- stro di- sce- den- te tur-
wander   in misery!   And the master   having gone,

ban-   tur   di- sci- pu- li. I- ta nos,   ab-   sen-   te
confused are   the disciples.   And so we,   in His absence,

e- o do- lor te- net ni- mi- us.
    make   moan   very much.

3

CHOIR   free rhythm

Do- mi- num quae- ren- tes in   mo-   nu- men- to.
The Lord   they were seeking in   the tomb.

4

THE THREE MARYS

Sed   e- a- mus et ad e- ius Pro- pe- re- mus
But   let us go and to His   grave make haste

tu- mu- lum. Et un- guen- to li- ni- a- mus cor- pus
And with ointment let us anoint the corpse

sa- cra- tis- si- mum. Si di- le- xi- mus vi- ven- tem
most sacred. If we pleased Him living,

Di- li- ga- mus mor- tu- um.
let us honor Him dead.

⑤

CHOIR free rhythm

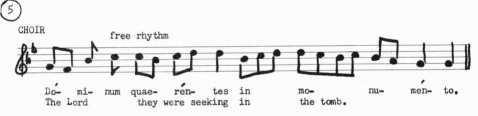

Do- mi- num quae- rén- tes in mo- nu- men- to.
The Lord they were seeking in the tomb.

(The Priest will have led the Choir into the chancel; and several
Soldiers with lances will have brought up the rear of the procession.
Then the Priest, now become the Archangel, with a palm frond in his
left hand and a branched staff-candelabrum full of lighted candles
in his right, approaches the Soldiers and brandishes his lightning
at them. Cymbals offstage. The Soldiers fall to the ground as if dead.
Then the Archangel turns to the crown light over the sepulcher, and
lights it with his candelabrum. He returns to the choir area. The
three Marys arrive at the sepulcher.)

⑥ THE THREE MARYS

Quis   re- vol-   vet er- go no- bis Ab o-   sti- o
Who   has moved aside   indeed   for us   from the entrance

la- pi- dem, Ut con- di- gnum   se- pul- tu- re a- ga-
the stone,   so that an appropriate   ceremony at the sepulcher we

mus ob- se- qui- um, Cu- ius mi- re bo- ni- ta- tis
may conduct,   from which   good deed we strangely

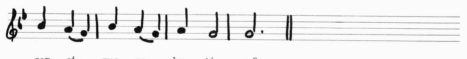

sen- si- mus so- la- ti- um?
feel   a consolation?

⑦ CHOIR
                    free rhythm

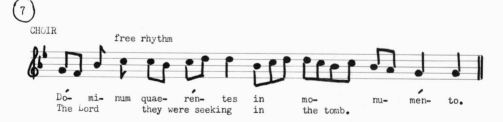

Do- mi- num quae- rén- tes in   mo-   nu- mén- to.
The Lord   they were seeking in   the tomb.

THE THREE MARYS

Pe- res tres- tous puis- sans, hau- ti- smes rois
Lord of all the fa- ther and high- est

Des an- gles, gou- vrene- res tres pi- tous,
King of an-gels, of us most mind- ful,

No- stre cuer que fe- ront mal- le- vou- rous.
What has brought this so dire e- vent upon us?

He- u las! no- stre do- lor con grans il est!
A- las, a- las! How hea- vy is our sor- row!

Nous a- vons per- du no- stre bel con- fort, Ihe- sum Chri- stum,
We have lost our on- ly com- fort, Je- sus Christ,

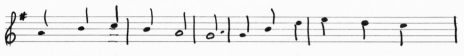

tres- tout plain de dou- cour. Il e- stoit biaus et plains
most filled with   sweet- ness. He   was   seem- ly, fair,

de bonne a- mour.   He-   las! mout nous a- moit. li vrais!
and full of kind- ness. A- las, a- las! How the true   one loved us!

THE TWO MARYS

Mais ore al- lons lon- gue- ment a- ca- ter Du- quel
But now let   us   go   a- long and buy Pre- cious

oin- dre puis- sons le cors tres bel. Il e- stoit vrai sa-lus
oint- ments for   his dear bo-   dy. He was our true sa-vior

et vraie a- mours.   He-   las! ver- rons le nous ia- mais!
and our   dear love.   A- las, a- las! We shall see Him ne-ver-more!

(Mary Magdalene remains, and the other two Marys approach the Merchant.)

10 THE MERCHANT

Ca a- proi- ches vous, qui tant fort a- mes. Cest un-
You there, now come hi- ther who so love Him. I have

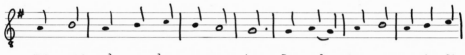

gue- ment sel vo- les a- ca- ter, Du quel oin- dre vo- stre Si-
oint- ments that you will want to buy. With them you can well a-

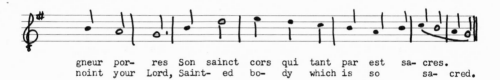

gneur por- res Son sainct cors qui tant par est sa- cres.
noint your Lord, Saint- ed bo- dy which is so sa- cred.

11 THE TWO MARYS

Di nous, Mar- chans tres bon, vrais et loi- aus, Cest un-
Tell us, Mer- chant, good and true, ho- nest, This fine

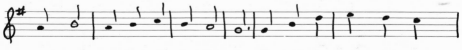

gue- ment se tu ven- dre le veus, Di tost du pris que tu
oint- ment that you would sell to us, Say for what price you would

a- voir en veus.   He-   las! ver-rons le nous ia- mais!
let us   have it. A- las,a- las! We shall see Him ne-ver-more!

⑫ THE MERCHANT

Cest oin- gue- ment se mout le con- voi- ties, Cinc be- sans dor
This fine oint- ment that you do che- rish, Five gol-den coins

don- ner vous en con- vient, Ne au- tre- ment ia no len-por- te- res.
will make it all for you. O-ther-wise I just can't let it go,no,I can't.

⑬ THE TWO MARYS

He-   las! ver- rons le nous ia-   mais!
A- las, a- las! We shall see Him ne- ver- more!

⑭ THE MERCHANT

Jou- ai un au- tre mout bon oin- gue- ment Pour mains la- res,
I have still an- o- ther fine oint- ment For less mo- ney,

sil vous vient a ta- lent. As au- tres est de mout
if it meets your needs. And I have o- thers that

plus chier piu- ment.
cost a good deal more.

(15)
THE TWO MARYS

Gen- tius Mar- chans, du mil- lour bien nous vent, Tant que
Gen- tle Mer- chant, give to us now the best. All you

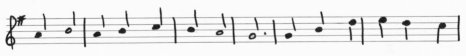

tu veus de l'ar- gent, plus em prent. No grant Si- gnour du ciel
want of mo- ney, well, take it. Our ho- ly Lord we are

oin- dre en vo- lons. He- las! ver- rons le nous ia- mais!
bound to a- noint with it. A- las, a-las! We shall see Him ne-ver-more!

(16) THE MERCHANT

Vous a- vez bien pal- le, da- mes vail- lans. Iel vous don- rai
You have spo- ken no- bly, my va- liant dames. Two golden coins

pour mainz bien deuz be- sans Pour le Si- gneur cui vous pa-ra-mes tant.
is all I'll ask of you For that great Lord whom you so a- dore.

(17) THE TWO MARYS

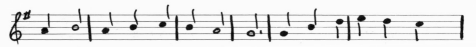

Sai- ges Mar- chans, pour Dieu nous te pri- ons Que tu
Wise young Mer- chant, for God we beg of you That you will

nous li- vres as- ses du plus bon, Que bon- ne o- dor en
give us some of the ve- ry best, With a sweet o- dor that

aient tout li bon.   He-   las! ver-rons le nous ia-mais!
will make all fine and good. A- las, a-las! We shall see Him ne-ver-more!

THE MERCHANT

Te- nes ces- tui, ou sie- cle n'a mil- lor. Oin- dre por- res
Take this oint-ment; it is the best there is, Fit to a- noint

vo- stre tres grant Si- gneur. Mer- ci que- res a lui,
your great and ho- ly Lord. Mer- cy ask of Him, dear

da- mes, pour moi.
la- dies, for you, for me.

THE TWO MARYS

Mer- ci te fa- ce li vrais Diex glo- ri- ous. Et nous os- si
Mer- cy you ask of the true God glo- ri- ous. And for us al- so

en- sam- ble toi tres- tous. Veus tu ve- nir ou fu mis li sains
who live a- mong you. Won't you come and see where the sa- cred

cors?   He-   las! ver- rons le nous ia- mais!
corpse is ly- ing?   A-las, a- las! We   shall see Him   ne-ver- more!

20

THE MERCHANT

Dou- ce da- mes, ne de- man- des mais ce. Cer- tes
Gen- tle la-dies, you need but   on- ly ask. Sure-ly I

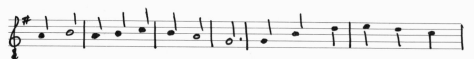

ie voil a- ler a- pres Ihe- su. Tout cils   sont sot qui   ne
will fol-low af- ter this Je- sus. All those   are fools who do

vont a- pres   lui.
not fol- low   af- ter Him.

21

THE TWO MARYS

A- mis, tu as mout tres bien dit le voir. De- ceu   sont   cil
Dear friend, you have ve- ry   well spo-ken true. De- ceived are those

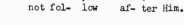

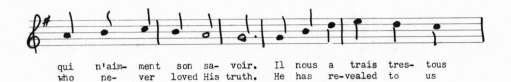

qui n'aim- ment son sa- voir. Il nous a trais tres- tous
who ne-   ver   loved His truth. He has re-vealed to   us

a son a- mour.   He-   las! ver- rons le nous ia- mais!
tru- ly His love.   A- las, a- las! We shall see Him   ne-ver- more!

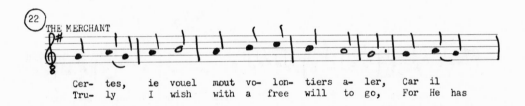

THE MERCHANT

Cer- tes,   ie vouel mout vo- lon- tiers a- ler, Car il
Tru- ly   I   wish   with a   free will to go, For He has

nous a mout vo- lon- tiers a- mes. Il nous a de la mort
gi- ven so free- ly   of His love. He has saved us from the

d'en- fer ge- tes.
tor- ment of death in Hell.

Jove- nes Mar- chans, en- samble o nous en vien. Nous te
Kind young Mer- chant, do come a- long with us. We shall

mer- rons ou le sains cors fu mis. No- stre Si- gnour vo-lons
lead you to where the corpse is laid. Let us hope to see and

ve- oir et te- nir. He- las! ver- rons le nous ia- mais!
touch our dear sa- vior. A- las, a- las! We shall see Him ne-ver- more!

(Now the Two Marys go back to Mary Magdalene, and all three go to the sepulcher.)

㉔

THE THREE MARYS

Il-　　　le　quip- pe　qui　fe- ren- tem　su- sci-　ta- vit
It was He　　of course　who　　　　　　revived the dead

La- zar-　rum, E-　ius　et　so-　ro- res　flen- tes　re- du-
Lazarus,　　　He,　　and　the sisters　sorrowing,　led back

xi- sti ad　gau- di- um,　Pot- e- rit　no- bis　op- ta- tum
　　sti　to　joy.　　　He should be able　on us　the most

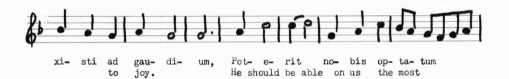

con- fer-　re so-　la- ti- um. E-　y- a!　Con- so- la- tor,
consolation to confer.　Hey!　Ee- ya!　The consoler,

Je- su　bo- ne, re- spi- ce. E- y- a!　Nunc　vul- tu　se-
Jesu　　the good, have in mind. Hey! Eeya!　Now,　with face

re- no   men- tes no- stras   re- fo- ve.   E- y- a! San- cte
serene   our spirits   please revive. Eeya!   Holy

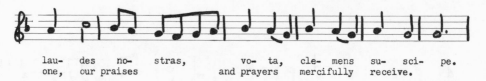

lau- des no-   stras,   vo- ta, cle- mens su-   sci-   pe.
one,   our praises   and prayers mercifully receive.

(At this point the Three Marys have arrived at the sepulcher.)

Quis   re- vol- vet no-   bis   ab o-   sti-   o
Who   has removed   for us   from the door

La- pi- dem quem te- ge- re san- ctum   Cer-
the stone   which covering   the holy sepulcher

ni-   mus   se- pul-   crum?
we noticed?

(Then the Two Angels appear at the sepulcher and seat themselves,
  one at the head, one at the foot, clothed in trimmed white.)

㉕ THE TWO ANGELS

O   vos   Chri-   sti-   co-   lae,   quem quae- ri- tis   es- se do-
O   you   Christ- followers,   whom do you seek,   being so

len-   tes?   Un- guen- tis-   que sa-   cris   un- ge-   re
sorrowful?   And with holy ointments   to anoint

quem   cu- pi- tis?
whom   do you want?

㉖ THE THREE MARYS

Quae-   ri- mus, O   su- pe- ri ci- ves,   Ihe-   sum
We seek,   O   citizens,   Jesus

cru- ci- fi- xum. Di- ci- te   quis   no- bis
who was crucified.   Tell us,   who   upon us

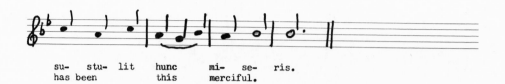

su- stu- lit hunc   mi- se- ris.
has been   this   merciful.

(Then the Angels open the sepulcher a little, and point.)

27
THE TWO ANGELS

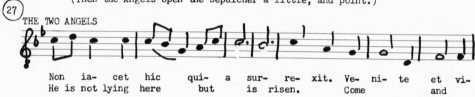

Non ia- cet hic   qui- a sur- re- xit. Ve- ni- te   et vi-
He is not lying here   but   is risen.   Come   and

de- te!
see!

(The Angels now expose the sepulcher fully, and the Three Marys
approach and kiss the sepulcher.)

En   ec- ce lo- cus quo [po- si- tus] fu- e- rat Do- mi- nus.
Behold   the place in which [placed] was   the Lord.

(The Angels close the sepulcher, and the Three Marys are together.)

28
THE THREE MARYS

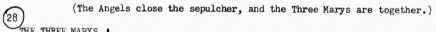

He- u, in- fe- li- ces! Quid a- gi- mus Qui- a
Alas, we are unfortunate!   what can we do   Unless

Do- mi- num no- strum mi- ni- me re- pe- ri- mus?
our Lord at least we locate?

(29) THE TWO ANGELS Free rhythm

Re- cor- da- mi- ni qua- li- ter lo- quu- tus sit no- bis
Remember that as He said to us

cum ad- huc es- set in Ga- li- lae- am, di- cens
when still He was in Galilee, saying

qui- a o- por- te- bat Fi- li- um ho- mi- nis
that it was necessary for the Son of man

pa- ti et di- e ter- ti- a re- sur- ge- re.
to suffer and on the third day to rise again.

(The Two Marys leave, and Mary Magdalene remains alone at the sepulcher.)

(30) MARY MAGDALENE

free rhythm

In- fe- lix é- go, mí- se- ra! Iu- re fle- o qui- a
Unfortunate　　I,　　miserable!　Justly　I weep,　　because

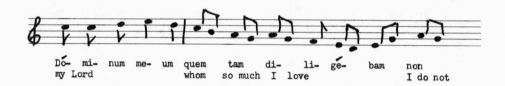

Do- mi- num me- um quem tam di- li- gé- bam non
my Lord　　　　　　whom　so much　I love　　　　I do not

in- ve- ni-　　　　o.
find.

(31) THE TWO ANGELS

Mu- li- er, quid plo-　　　　ras?
Woman,　　why do you weep?

(32) MARY MAGDALENE

Qui- a tu- le- runt Do- mi- num me- um, et ne- sci- o
Because I dont know　what they have done with my Lord,　and

u— bi po— su— e— runt e— um.
where they have taken Him.

33 THE TWO ANGELS   **34** CHOIR

No— li fle— re, Ma— ri— a. A— le— lu— ia!
Do not weep, Mary.

35 THE TWO ANGELS   **36** CHOIR

Re— sur— re— xit Do— mi— nus! Al— le— lu— ia!
Risen is the Lord!

37 MARY MAGDALENE

free rhythm

Ar— dens est cor me— um; de— si— de— ro
Ardent is my heart; I desire

vi— de— re Do— mi— num me— um. Quae— ro
to see my Lord. I seek

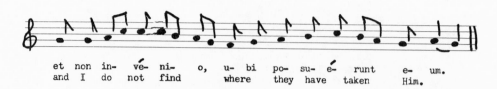

et non in- vé- ni- o,   u- bi po- su- é- runt   e- um.
and I do not find   where they have taken   Him.

(38)

CHOIR

Al- le- lu- ia!

(39)

THE TWO ANGELS

Dou- ce da- me,   qui si   plou-   res, Di- tes nous ou
Gen- tle la- dy,   who so   la-   ment, Tell us where you

vo- les   a- ler. Ie croi mout bien, se Diex   nous gart,
long for   to go. I think it true, if God   keeps us,

de vraie a- mour   li cuers   vous art.
With tru- est love your heart will flame.

MARY MAGDALENE

Las- se do- lan- te, que fe- rai De mon Si- gnour
Let me still la-ment.What else can I do For my dear Lord

sic

que per- du ai? Ie cuit de duel me tu- e- rai.
whom I have lost? I think with grief I shall soon die.

Do- lan- te! Ta mors au cuer grant duel me plan- te.
Woe is me! Your death plants grief deep- ly in my heart.

THE TWO ANGELS

Dou- ce da- me, qui ci ve- neis, Qui si tres fort
Gen- tle la- dy, you who come here, Who so strong- ly

vous gra- men- tes, Bien sai Ihe- sum a- les que- rant,
are la- men- ting, I know that Je- sus you seek to find,

Pour cui souf- fres si grant tor- ment.
For Him suf- fer such great tor- ment.

(42) MARY MAGDALENE

Iai le cuer de duel a- bu- vre. Tost m'ont de mon
Now my heart is with grief o-ver- flow-ing. Now I have from my

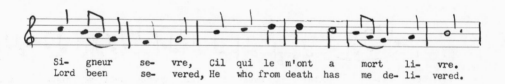

Si- gneur se- vre, Cil qui le m'ont a mort li- vre.
Lord been se- vered, He who from death has me de-li- vered.

Do- lan- te! Ta mors au cuer grant duel me plan- te.
Woe is me! Your death plants grief deep- ly in my heart.

(43) THE TWO ANGELS

Dou- ce da- me, ne plou- res plus. Par tampz ver- res
Gen- tle la- dy, do not weep more. In good time you

le Roi   Ihe- su,   Proi- chain- ne- ment ver- ra   a   toi,
will see King Je- su, So ve- ry   short-ly He'll come to   you

Sa- li- ge- ra   ta   grant   do- lour.
To re- lieve you of your so great sor- row.

44 MARY MAGDALENE

Cer- tes sor cui doi ie trou- ver, Ce- lui qui tant
Tell me   tru- ly where I may find Him, He who made Him-self

fait a   a- mer. Quer- roi- e le de- la   la mer?
so   much be- lo- ved. Must I   now seek Him far be-yond the sea?

Do- lan-   te! Ta mors au cuer grant duel me plan-   te.
Woe   is me! Your death plants grief deep- ly   in   my   heart.

THE TWO ANGELS

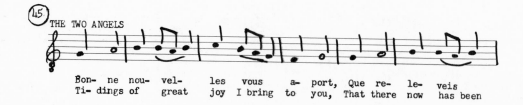

Bon- ne nou- vel-   les vous   a- port, Que re- le-   veis
Ti- dings of   great   joy I bring to   you, That there now   has been

est de   la mort Ihe- sus Cris, li dous   fiex   Ma- ri-   ae.
raised up from the dead Je- sus Christ, dear sweet   son   of Ma-   ry.

Ne plou- res plus,   ma   dou- ce   a- mi-   e.
Do not   weep anymore,   my   gen- tle sweet-ing.

MARY MAGDALENE

N'est pas mer- veil- le se   ie pleur, Car i'ai per-   du
It's   no won- der if   I still la- ment, For I   have lost

mon douc Si-   gnour. C'a- voit pi- tie de   mes   do- lours.
my gen-tle, dear Lord. You may then pi- ty these my com-plaints.

Do- lan- tel Ta mors au cuer grant duel me plan-   te.
Woe   is mel Your death plants grief deep- ly in my   heart.

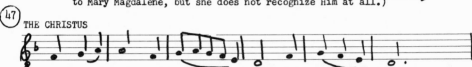

(The following words Our Sire [The Christus, dressed as a gardener] sings
to Mary Magdalene, but she does not recognize Him at all.)

47 THE CHRISTUS

Mu- li- er, quid plo-   ras? Quem quae-   ris?
Woman,   why do you weep? Whom do you seek?

(Mary Magdalene curtsies to Him.)

48 MARY MAGDALENE   free rhythm

Do- mi- ne, si tu su- stu- li- sti e- um, di- ci- te mi- chi,
Kind sir,   if you have taken   Him,   tell   me

49 CHOIR   **50** MARY MAGDALENE

u- bi po- su- i- sti e- um. Al- le- lu- ia! Et e- go e- um
where you have put   Him.   And I will Him

51 CHOIR   **52** THE CHRISTUS

tol- lam.   Al- le- lu- ia! Ma- ri- al
take up.   (Mary Magdalene kneels to
                            our Lord.)

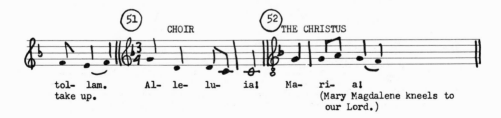

Ra- bo- ni!   No- li me tan-   ge- re! Non-dum
Master!   Do   not   touch me!   I am not yet

(They remain here while
He sings:)

a- scen- di ad pa- trem me- um.   A-
ascended   to   my father.

(Mary Magdalene goes alone to the sepulcher, while the Christus
goes to the other two Marys, who kneel at his feet while He sings:)

ve- te, vos mi- chi di- le- cte, Et me de mor- te sur- re-
Rejoice, you who to me are so dear,   for that I from death   have

xis- se fi- de- li- ter cer- tum ha- be- te.
risen,   absolutely   a certainty you may have.

(The Two Marys rise, and are before the Lord as He continues.)

free rhythm

I- te, nun- ti- á- te   fra- tri- bus me- is ---
Go,   tell   my brethren ---

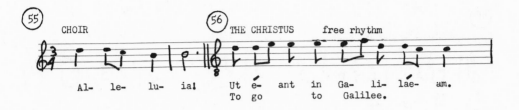

Al- le-   lu-   ia!   Ut é-   ant   in   Ga- li- lae- am.
                     To go   to   Galilee.

I- bi me vi- de- bunt.   Al- le- lu- ia! Al- le- lú- ia!
There they will see me.

Al- le- lú- ia!

(After these things, The Lord leaves Mary Magdalene and goes to
the other Two Marys, and all three begin to sing together:)

58

THE CHRISTUS & THE TWO MARYS

E-   y-   a!   No- bis in- ter-   nas   men-   tes
Hey!   Eeya!   Into the depths   of our souls

pul-   sat gau- di-   um   Pro no-   stro   con-   so-   la-
strikes   joy   because of our   consolator,

to-   re,   Quem gau-   de-   mus   ho-   di-   e.
                  whom   we praise   today.

Cum tri- um-   pho   vi- cto- ri- ae   a mor-   tu-
With his triumphant   victory   over death

is   re-   sur- ge-   re.
He has risen.

Ad mo- nu- men- tum ve- ni- mus plo- ran- tes,
To the tomb we came, weeping,

an- ge- lum Do- mi- ni se- den- tem vi- di- mus, et
and angel(s) of the Lord seated we saw, and

di- cen- tem qui- a sur- re- xit Ihe- sus.
saying that risen is Jesus.

De- o gra- ti- as!
To God thanks!

(And the Two Apostles, Peter and John, come before the Marys, and,
taking Mary Magdalene aside by the sleeve, they ask:)

Dic no- bis, Ma- ri- a, Quid vi- di- sti in vi- a?
Tell us, Mary, what saw you on the way?

(And the Two Apostles let go the sleeve of Mary Magdalene. She
points to the sepulcher, and sings, forte:)

(62)

MARY MAGDALENE

Se- pul- chrum Cri- sti vi- ven-   tis, Et glo- ri- am
The sepulcher   of the living Christ,   And the glory,

(63) THE TWO MARYS

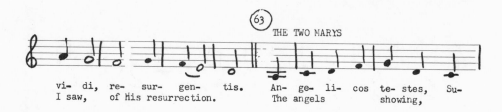

vi- di, re- sur- gen- tis. An- ge- li- cos te- stes, Su-
I saw,   of His resurrection.   The angels   showing,

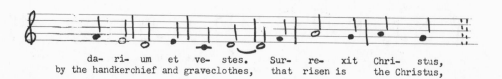

da- ri- um et ve- stes.   Sur- re- xit Chri- stus,
by the handkerchief and graveclothes,   that risen is   the Christus,

(64)

MARY MAGDALENE (her hand at her breast)

Spes   no-   stra. Prae- ce- det vos in Ga- li- lae- am.
Our   hope.   He goes before   you into Galilee.

(The Two Apostles run to the sepulcher while the Choir narrates.)

(65)

CHOIR

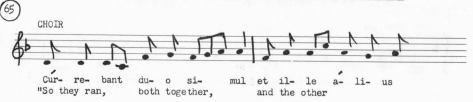

Cur- re- bant du- o si- mul et il- le a- li- us
"So they ran,   both together,   and the other

di- sci- pu- lus prae- cu- cúr- rit cí- ti- us Fe- tro,
disciple (John)   did outrun   Peter,

et ve- nit ad mo- nu- men- tum. Al- le- lu- ia!
and came first to the sepulcher."

(The Two Apostles at the sepulcher, or inside the tomb, find the
graveclothes and appear with them.)

⟨66⟩ THE TWO APOSTLES

Cre- den- dum est ma- gis so- li Ma- ri- ae ve- ra- ci
More to be believed is   solely Mary's   veracity

Quam Iu- de- o- rum tur- be fal- la- ci.
Than the Jews'   wild   deceptions.

⟨67⟩ THE THREE MARYS

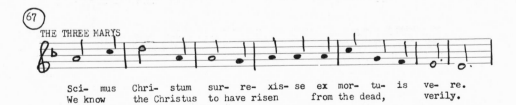

Sci- mus Chri- stum sur- re- xis- se ex mor- tu- is ve- re.
We know the Christus to have risen from the dead,   verily.

Tu no- bis, vi- ctor Rex,   mi- se- re- re!
You upon us, O victor   King,   have mercy!

THE TWO APOSTLES

Cer- ni- tes, O so- ci- i! Ec- ce lin- te- mi- ni- a et
Look,   O friends! Behold the graveclothes   and

su- da-   ri- um, Et   cor- pus non   est
handkerchief,   And   the body   is   not

in se- pul- chro in- ven- tum.
in the sepulcher   found.

(The Two Apostles replace the graveclothes inside the
tomb or sepulcher, while the Three Marys and the Apostles sing:)

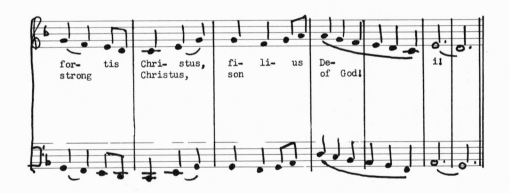

(The "Te Deum laudamus" follows, sung as a recessional by the company.)

(The complete "Te Deum" begins on p. 491.)

2. The Lament of Mary

The Lament of Mary

A SINGLE-EPISODE PASSION PLAY, *The Lament of Mary* is so identified by its content and full title, "The Lament of Mary and of Others on Good Friday." The play has been preserved in a manuscript (C 1, fols. 74^r-76^v) in the National Archeological Museum near the Cividale (Italy) basilica in which this music-drama presumably was performed. The action of the play, at the cross, immediately follows the Crucifixion and precedes the events of *The Visit to the Sepulcher*.

The playscript lacks a concluding page. The words of the last item (No. 22) have been supplied by previous editors from a contemporary religious song, *Flete, fideles animae* (Young, I, 499). The *Flete* music has not survived but can be reconstructed for our Item 22 from the melody of Item 20.

Editors of this play have observed several inappropriate assignments of items. The following reassignments have here been made: Item 6 to Mary Jacobi, in order to remove John from what seems to be women's talk; Item 10 restored to John, where the manuscript is only two words short of getting it right anyway; and Item 19 to Mary Magdalene, the probable "Maria sola" of the manuscript.

As possible processional and closing humns for the play, one notes that in the Regensberg version of the play the hymn *Crux Fideles*, to be found in the modern *Graduale Romanum*, p. 204, follows on the heels of the play. With its partner, the famous *Pange lingua gloriosi*, there is material for processional and recessional. The equally famous *Stabat Mater* is also available in the *Graduale*, p. 445.

An itemized discussion of the seventy-nine stage directions that are written into the music staves of the manuscript along with the neumes is in *Production*, pp. 293-301. There the item references must be corrected for the present edition.

The Cast

Mary Magdalene
Mary Major
John
Mary Jacobi

The Scene: At the cross. Good Friday.

The Lament of Mary *Planctus Mariae*

THE LAMENT OF MARY Planctus Mariae

(1)

(Here begins "The Lament of Mary and of Others on Good Friday.")

MARY MAGDALENE (turning to the congregation with arms outstretched)

O fra- tres et so- ro- res, U- bi est spes me- a?
O brothers and sisters, where is my hope?

(Gesturing to them) (Beating her breast)

U- bi con- so- la- ti- o me- a? U- bi to- ta
Where is my consolation? Where my whole

(Raising her hands) (Bowing her head)

sa- lus, O ma- gi- ster mi?
security, O my Master?

(Kneeling at the crucifix)

(2)

MARY MAJOR

O do- lor! Pro do- lor! Er- go qua- re
O sorrow! Ah sorrow! Now why,

fi- li ca- re, Pen- des i- ta, Cum sis
son so dear, do you hang there, when you are

(Here she gestures to the Christ with open hands.)

vi-   ta Ma- nens an-   te   sae-   cu-   la?
life   leading   to   eterni-ty?

(Here she gestures to the Christ with open hands.)

③ JOHN

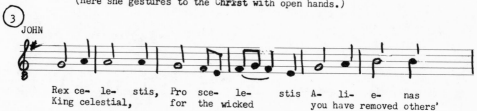

Rex ce- le- stis, Pro sce-   le-   stis A- li- e-   nas
King celestial,   for the wicked   you have removed others'

(Here, with hands extended, he gestures to the Christ.)

Sol- vis   poe- nas, A- gnus si- ne   ma- cu-   la.
         guilt,   Lamb   without   spot.

④ MARY JACOBI

Mun- da ca- ro, mun-   do   ca- ra, Cur in cru- cis
Clean   of flesh,   for the world caring,   why on the cross

(Gesturing to the cross with open hands)

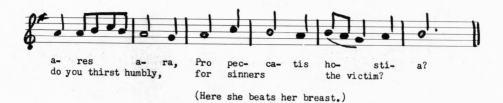

a- res   a- ra, Pro pec- ca- tis ho-   sti- a?
do you thirst humbly,   for   sinners   the victim?

(Here she beats her breast.)

Fle-   ant   ma- ter- na   vi- sce- ra Ma-   ri- ae
Weeping   the maternal, visceral   Mary

(Turning toward Mary, and pointing to her tears)

ma-   tris vul- ne-   ra.
the mother,   for the wounds.

Ma- ter- nae   do- le- o   Que di- ci   so- le-   o,
Motherhood   I mourn,   that which I used to say was

(Here she beats herself.)

Fe- lix pu- er- pe-   ra.
happy   childbearing.

(Here she greets Mary Major.)

Fle-   te, Fi- de- les a- ni-   mae, Fle-
Weep,   faithful   souls,

(Here she puts her arm around the neck of one of the Marys.)

te,   so-   ro-   res   o-   pti-   mae,   Ut sint mul- ti- pli-
         sisters   best,   that there may be multiplied

(Here around the neck of the other Mary.)

ces Do- lo-   ris   in- di- ces,   Plan- ctus et la- cri-   mae.
     sorrow's   signs,   lamenting   and tears.

(Here she beats herself.)

⑧

BOTH MARYS (Magdalene and Jacobi)

Cur me-   ro- re de- fi- cis,   Ma- ter cru- ci- fi-   xi?   Cur do-
Why do you faint   for grief,   mother of the crucified one?   Why

(Here Both Marys rise, with hands outstretched to Mary Major and to Christ.)

lo-   re con- su- me- ris,   Dul- cis   so- ror no-   stra?   Sic o-
does sorrow consume you,   sweet   sister   of ours?   Thus

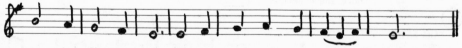

por- tet fi- e- ri,   Ut prae- di- xit psal- mi-   sta.
it had   to happen,   as was predicted   by the Psalmist.

(Here they curtsey to Mary Major as a salutation.)

MARY MAJOR

Tri-   ste spec- ta- cu-   lum Cru- cis et lan-   ce-   ae!
Sad   spectacle   of the cross and the spear!

(Here she beats herself.)   (Here she points to the Christ.)

Clau-   sum si- gna- cu-   lum Men-   tis   vir-   gi-
The secret   token   of the soul's purity

(Here she points to the side of Christ.)

ne-   ae Pro- fun- de me vul-   ne-   rat.
    profoundly   wounds me.

(Here she beats herself.)

JOHN

Hoc est quod di- xe-   rat, Quod pro- phe- ta- ve-   rat
This is what was said,   what was prophesied

Il-   le prae- nun- ci-   us. Hic il- le gla-
by that same one who foretold it.   This is the sword

(Here he points to the angel.)   (Here he beats himself.)

di- us Qui me trans- ver- be-   rat.
          that   transfixes me.

⑪

MARY MAJOR

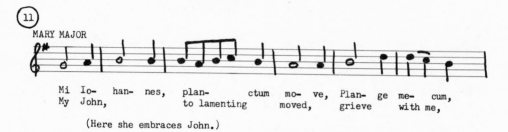

Mi Io- han- nes, plan-   ctum mo- ve, Plan- ge me- cum,
My John,   to lamenting   moved,   grieve   with me,

(Here she embraces John.)

fi- li   no- ve, Fi- li no- vo fe- de-   re Ma- tris et ma-
son   so new,   son   of a new compact   between a mother

(Here she points to the Christ.)

ter-   te- rae. Tem- pus est   la- men-   ti. Im- mo-
and the maternal.   It is time   to lament.   Let us

(Here she lowers her hands.)

le- mus in- ti- mas La- cri- ma-   rum vi- cti-   mas Chri- sto
immolate ourselves, his intimates, with tears   overcome   for the Christ

(Here she beats herself.)   (Here she lowers her hand.)

mo-   ri- en-   ti.
dying.

(12)

JOHN

O   Ma- ri- a,   ma-   ter me- a,   Sem- per tu   mi-   chi
O   Mary,   mother   mine,   always   you   to me

(Here he turns to Mary <u>Major</u> with open hands.)

e- ris   ca- ra,   Et the- sau- rum con- ser- va-   bo
will be   dear,   and as a treasure   will I protect you,

Qui mo- do   mi- chi   est   com- mis-   sus.
who now   to me   is   committed.

(Here he gestures to the Christ.)

(13)

MARY MAGDALENE

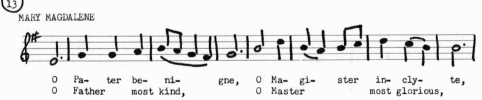

O   Pa- ter be- ni-   gne, O Ma- gi-   ster in- cly-   te,
O   Father   most kind,   O Master   most glorious,

(She kneels before the crucifix.)

No-   li   me   de- re- lin-   que- re.   Pec- ca- tri-   cem
do not   me   foresake.   On this sinner

(Here she points to herself.)   (Here she beats herself.)

re-   spi-   ce,   Tu   qui me sal- va-   sti.
cast a glance,   You   who me   have redeemed.

⑭

MARY MAJOR

O   Ma- ri- a   Mag- da-   le-   na,   Fi- li- i
O   Mary   Magdalene,

(Here she gestures to <u>Mary</u> Magdalene.)   (Here to the Christ.)

me- i   dul- cis di-   sci- pu-   la, Plan- ge   me- cum,
of my son   a sweet   disciple,   weep   with me,

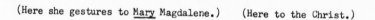

so- ror   me-   a,   Plan- ge   me- cum   cum do-
sister   mine,   weep   with me   in

(Here she embraces <u>Mary</u> Magdalene with both arms around the neck.)

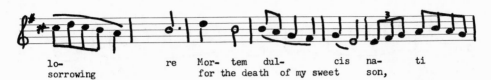

lo-   re Mor- tem dul-   cis na-   ti
sorrowing   for the death of my sweet   son,

(Relaxing with one arm her embrace,   (She gestures to the Christ.)
she half turns to John.)

me-   i,   Et mor-   tem   ma- gi- stri   tu-
and for the death   of your Master,

(Here she gestures to <u>Mary</u> Magdalene.)

i,   Mor- tem il- li- us Qui te tan- tum   a-
and for the death of Him   who   so much

(Here she gestures to the Christ.)

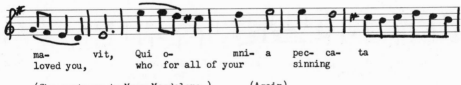

ma-   vit, Qui o-   mni- a   pec- ca-   ta
loved you,   who for all of your   sinning

(She gestures to <u>Mary</u> Magdalene.)   (Again)

tu- a Ti- bi re- la-   xa-   vit,   Dul-
he forgave you,

(Here she drops her gesturing arm.)

cis- si-   ma   Mag- da- le-   na.
dearest   Magdalene.

(Here she embraces <u>Mary</u> Magdalene, as at first, and finishes the verse.)

⑮

MARY MAGDALENE

Ma- ter Ihe-   su   cru- ci- fi-   xi,   Te- cum
Mother of the Jesus   crucified,   with you

(Here she salutes Mary <u>Major</u> with her hands only.)

plan- gam   mor-   tem Chri-   sti, Et mor-   tem
I lament   the death   of Christ,   and the death

(She brushes away her tears.)   (She kneels before
                                              the crucifix.)

me-   i   ma- gi-   stri. Et ex do- lo-   re
of my   master.   And by sorrow

(Here she beats her breast.)

cru- ci- a-   ta, Sum in cor-   de   vul-
being anguished,   I am in my heart   wounded.

(Here she beats herself with both hands.)

ne-   ra- ta.

(16)
MARY MAJOR

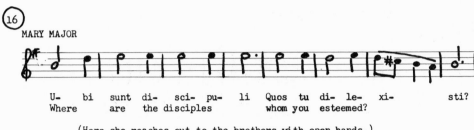

U- bi   sunt di- sci- pu- li   Quos tu di- le-   xi-   sti?
Where   are   the disciples   whom you esteemed?

(Here she reaches out to the brothers with open hands.)

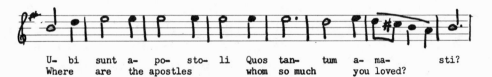

U- bi   sunt a-   po- sto- li   Quos tan-   tum   a- ma-   sti?
Where   are   the apostles   whom so much   you loved?

(Here she reaches out to the sisters with open hands.)

(Pointing to the Christ)

Qui ti- mo- re ter- ri- ti, O- mnes fu- gi- e-   runt.
Those who were with fear terrified, all   fled.

(Here she turns to the people, the congregation.)

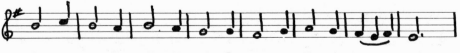

Et te so- lum, fi- li mi, In cru- ce di- mi- se-   runt.
and you alone,   my son,   on the cross they have left.

(Here she points to the crucifix.)

He-   u me! He-   u me! Mi- se- ra Ma- ri-   a!
Alas   for me! Alas   for me! Miserable   Mary!

(Here she beats her breast.)

MARY JACOBI

Quis est hic qui non   fle- ret, Ma- trem Chri- sti
Who   is   there who   would not weep,   the mother of Christ

(Looking about her at Mary Magdalene and John, and with her hands
to her eyes, she then says.)

si vi-   de- ret In tan- ta tri- sti- ti- a?
so to see   in such   sadness?

(Here she beats herself.)

MARY MAJOR

O   vos o- mnes qui tran- si- tis   per vi- am Si- mul me-
O   all you   who pass si-   by this way, along   with

Here she gestures to the people with outstretched hands.)

cum   fle- te, Et me- um dul- cem fi- li-   um Pa- ri-
me   weep,   and for my dear   son   um also

(Hand to eyes)   (Here she gestures to the Christ.)

ter lu- ge-   te et vi-   de- te Si   est do-   lor
lament,   and see   if there is any sorrow

(Here she beats herself.)

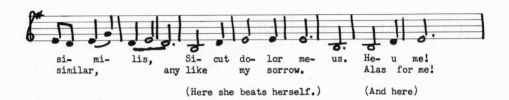

si- mi- lis,   Si- cut do- lor me- us. He- u me!
similar,   any like   my sorrow.   Alas for me!

(Here she beats herself.)   (And here)

He- u me! Mi- se- ra   Ma- ri-   a!
Alas for me! Miserable Mary!

(19)
MARY MAGDALENE

Con- so- la- re, Do- mi- na, ma- ter et re- gi-   na.
Console yourself,   lady,   mother and queen.

(Here she turns to Mary Major.)

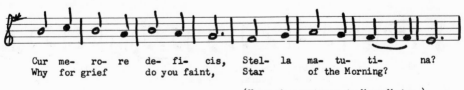

Cur me- ro- re de- fi- cis, Stel- la ma- tu- ti-   na?
Why for grief   do you faint, Star   of the Morning?

(Here she gestures to Mary Major.)

Tu- us le- vat fi- li- us Mun- dum a ru- i- na.
Your son raises   the world   from its ruin.

(Here she lowers her hand.)

20 MARY MAJOR

Fi- li mi ca- ris- si- me, Dul- cis a- mor me- us,
Son   of mine most dear,   my sweet   love,

(Here she gestures to the Christ.) (She kneels before the crucifix.)

Cur te mo- do vi- de- o In cru- ce pen- den- tem
Why   now   do I see you   on the cross   hanging,

(She gestures to the crucifix.)

In- ter la- tro- nes po- si- tum, Spi- nis co- ro-
between   thieves   placed,   with a crown of thorns,

(She gestures to the thieves.)   (And to the crown of thorns)

na- tum, La- tus tu- um, fi- li mi, Lan- ce-
the side of yours,   my son,   by a lance

(And to His side)

a   per-   fo-   ra-   tum?   He-   u   me!   He-   u   me!
pierced   Alas   for me! Alas   for me!

(Here she beats herself.)

Mi-   se-   ra   Ma-   ri-   a!
Miserable   Mary!

(21) JOHN

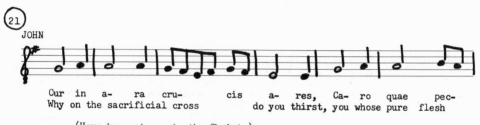

Cur in a-   ra   cru-   cis   a-   res, Ca- ro   quae   pec-
Why on the sacrificial cross   do you thirst, you whose pure flesh

(Here he gestures to the Christ.)

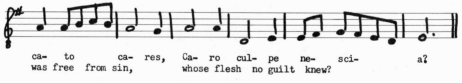

ca-   to   ca-   res, Ca- ro   cul- pe   ne-   sci-   a?
was free from sin,   whose flesh no guilt knew?

(Here he beats himself.)

(22) MARY MAJOR

O   men- tes   per- fi-   das,   Et lin- guas   du-   pli- ces,
O   minds   perfidious,   and double-talkers

(Here she turns to the people and stands as far as the words
"Ferre stipendium," and then she . . . .)

O   te- stes sub- do- los Et fal-   sos iu-   di- ces,
O   witnesses sly,   and false   judges,

Se- nes cum iu- ni- o-   ri- bus So- lent ma- io-
old   and young alike   usually, though of

ri-   bus Cri- mi- ni- bus da-   mna- ti Fer-   re
greater   crimes   guilty,   they require

sti- pen- di- um Su- spen- di- um pec- ca-   ti!
payment   by hanging   for sins!

(She makes a final gesture to the Christ.)

3. The Pilgrim

The Pilgrim

A BEAUVAIS COMPOSITION like the *Daniel, The Pilgrim* was performed in the twelfth century during Easter Monday Vespers. In commenting on the formal intent of the playwright in *Production,* pp. 105-6, I mention the creative use of liturgical antiphons at many moments of the play. As an indication of the distribution and extent of this use, the following items in the present edition are verbally and musically similar or identical to free-rhythm antiphons in the modern service books, the *Antiphonale Romanum* and *Graduale Romanum*: 1, 2, 3, 11, 14, 15, 22, 24, 33, and 35. Most of these are also in the tenth-century *Antiphonale* of Hartker.

Other items are mensuralized and are thus attributable to the playwright as original compositions, though all are steeped in the verbal narrative of Luke 24 and in the verbal and musical antiphons. In fact there is one item, (No. 33) which was apparently sung in the first rhythmic mode in the play, yet which appears in the modern *Antiphonale* (p. 595) with practically identical words and melody, the notation in free rhythm of course.

I have mensuralized the first item, the "Jesu nostra redemptio," since it is in stanza form with repeated melody. If one prefers the free-rhythm version, as did W. L. Smoldon, it may be found in his edition of the *Peregrinus* (1965) and in the *Graduale Romanum*, p. 140*.

There are many similarities between Smoldon's and my transcriptions of the mensural items. These likenesses are often owing to our intensive collaboration on a production score for my modern premiere in 1965. In reviewing our voluminous correspondence on this project, I note that some of our later ideas about the melody of items did not make the publication deadline, though they were afterward incorporated in my production, and were noticeable in such an item as No. 9.

In other items the similarity is probably an indication of melodic inevitability. For this edition I have worked directly from the Beauvais manuscript (Bibliothèque Nationale, Nouvelles Acquisitions, MS Latin 1064, fols. 8ʳ-11ᵛ), with a minimum recall of the production of ten years ago. New solutions have often been mere variations of those found before. In other instances my new transcriptions reflect ten additional years of experience with medieval playscripts, as well as second guesses and Monday-morning quarterbacking.

An addition to the present edition is the use of the *Christus resurgens* as the recessional, for which the Beauvais playscript calls but does not offer notation. I have transcribed it from the twelfth-century Sicilian version of the play (Madrid, Biblioteca Nacional MS C. 132, fol. 109^r), and have collated its melody with similar notations in such other musical texts as Rouen (Bibliothèque Nationale MS Latin 904, fol. 102^v), Dublin (Oxford, MS Rawlinson Liturg. d. iv, fol. 85^v), and the modern *Antiphonale Romanum,* pp. 164*-65*. What is here presented may be termed a common version of the well-known hymn.

After Item 5 the assignment of characters to items is often of necessity editorial and may be compared with the manuscript assignments as printed in Young, I, 467-69.

The Cast

Cleopas, a Disciple
Peter, a Disciple
The Christus
Thomas, a Disciple
The Choir

The Scene: On the road. The Inn at Emmaus. Easter Monday, toward nightfall.

The Pilgrim *Peregrinus*

THE TWO DISCIPLES (in procession)

Je- su   no- stra re- dem-   pti- o,   A- mor et de- si-
Jesu,   our   savior,   our love and desire.

de- ri- um. De- us, cre- a- tor   o- mni- um, Ho- mo in
             God,   creator   of all,   created a man in

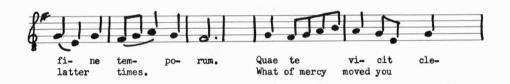

fi- ne tem- po- rum.   Quae te   vi- cit   cle-
latter   times.   What of mercy moved you

men- ti- a, Ut fer- res no- stra cri- mi- na, Cru- de- lem
         to bear   our   sins,   pains

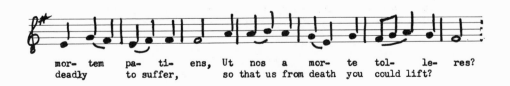

mor- tem pa- ti- ens, Ut nos a mor- te tol- le- res?
deadly   to suffer,   so that us from death you could lift?

In- fer- ni clau- stra pe- pe- ne- trans, Tu- os
Hell's gates penetrating, your

cap- ti- vos re- di- mens, Vic- tor tri- um- pho no- bi-
prisoners releasing, victor in triumph noble,

li Ad dex- tram Pa- tris re- si- dens, Ip- sa
to the right hand of the Father sitting, this same

te co- gat pi- e- tas, Ut ma- la no- stra su- pe-
mercy, may it lead you, our sins to rise

res Par- cen- do, et vo- ti com- po- tes Nos tu- o
above, sparing us, and our wish grant your

vul-   tu   sa-   ti-   es.
face   to see.

② CHRISTUS (approaching)
                  free rhythm

Qui sunt hi ser- mo- nes   quos con- fer- tis ad in- vi- cem
What are these communications that you have,   one to another,

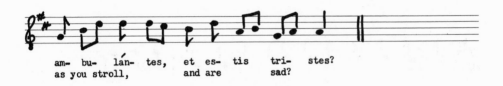

am- bu- lan- tes, et es- tis   tri-   stes?
as you stroll,   and are   sad?

③ CLEOPAS

Tu so- lus pe- re- gri- nus es in Ie- ru- sa- lem   et   non
Are you the only pilgrim   in Jerusalem   who has not

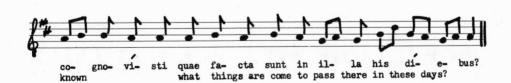

co- gno- vi- sti quae fa- cta sunt in il- la his di- e- bus?
known   what things are come to pass there in these days?

CHRISTUS

Quae?
What things?

THE TWO DISCIPLES

De Ihe- su Na- za- ré- no, qui fu- it vir pro- phé- ta, pó-
Concerning Jesus of Nazareth,   who was   a manly prophet, powerful

tens in ó- pe- re et sér- mo- ne co- ram De- o   et
in deed   and word   in the court of God and

o- mni   pó- pu- lo.
all   the people.

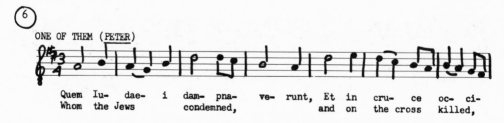

ONE OF THEM (PETER)

Quem Iu- dae- i dam- pna-   ve- runt, Et in cru- ce oc- ci-
Whom the Jews   condemned,   and on the cross killed,

de- runt, Et nos qui- dem spe- ra- ba- mus Quod nos es- set
but we indeed trusted that us He should

re- dem- ptu- rus.
have redeemed.

⑦
THE OTHER (CLEOPAS)

Iam tres di- es a- bi- e- runt, Fa- cta i- sta quod fu-
Now three days have passed since these things

e- runt. Et nos quae- dam ter- ru- e- runt, Quae se-
happened. And us some women astonished, who the

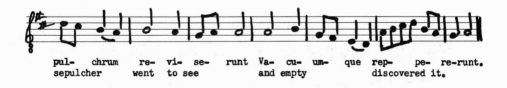

pul- chrum re- vi- se- runt Va- cu- um- que rep- pe- re-runt.
sepulcher went to see and empty discovered it.

Se vi- dis- se nar- ra- ve- runt An- ge- lo- rum vi- si- a
They told what they saw,   of angels   a vision,

o- nem, Qui et e- is in- di- xe- runt E- ius re- sur-
who   to them indicated   His   resurrection.

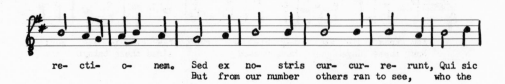

re- cti- o- nem. Sed ex no- stris cur- cur- re- runt, Qui sic
But from our number others ran to see, who the

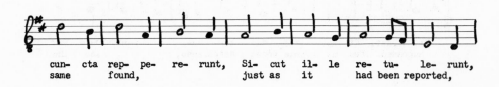

cun- cta rep- pe- re- runt, Si- cut il- le re- tu- le- runt,
same   found,   just as it   had been reported,

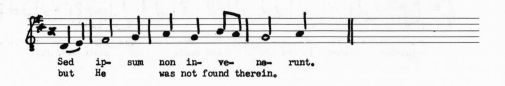

Sed ip- sum non in- ve- ne- runt.
but He   was not found therein.

CHRISTUS

O cum si- tis e- ius di- sci- pu- li! Cur tam stul- ti,
O what studious disciples of His! Why are you so stupid,

tar- di, in- cre- du- li? I- gno- ra- tis ab or- tu sae-cu-li
slow, unbelieving? Don't you know what from earliest times

Quae pro- phe- tae di- xe- re sin- gu- li? Non- ne Chri-stum
the prophets said severally? Ought not Christ

pa- ti o- por- tu- it Et in- tra- re glo- ri- am de- cu- it?
to have suffered and to enter into His glory?

Haec Mo- y- ses si- gni- fi- ca- ve- rat, Cum Pas- cha- lem
All this Moses signified when the Pascal

a- gnum oc- ci- de- rat. I- sa- i- as i- dem prae- di- xe-
lamb   was sacrificed.   Isaiah   the same predicted,

rat, Cum ut a- gnum il- lum cla- ma- ve- rat Fla- gel- la- ri et
when of the lamb he   spoke   of its being whipped and

ob- mu- te- sce- re, Et oc- ci- sum pec- ca- ta tol- le- re. Ob-
silenced,   and being slain, the sins of all to bear. This

la- tus est in- quit cum vo- lu- it, Et pec- ca- ta no- stra sus-
oblation He is said   to make willingly, and our sins   to

ti- mu- it. Sic et cunc- tis pro- phe- tis te- sti- bus, "Chri-stus,
sustain.   And thus, all   prophecies   testifying,   "Christ,

mor- tis so- lu- tis ne- xi- bus, Quod sit vi- vus et hoc per-
the bonds of death   breaking,   because He is alive   and will be

hen- ni- ter." Iam de- be- tis cre- de- re fir- mi- ter.
forever."   Now you should   believe   firmly.

Ne mo- re- mur, fra- tres, di- u- ti- us. Iam o- por- tet nos
Let us not linger, brethren,   any longer.   Now we must

(As if about to leave them)

i- re lon- gi- us.
move   along.

(Then they detain Him, and one <u>of them</u> says:)

(10)

CLEOPAS

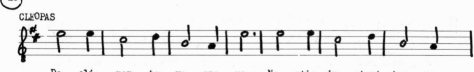

De- cli- nan- te ve- spe- ra. No- ctis in- stant tem- po-
Coming on is   evening.   Night is drawing nigh,

ra, Nec pa- tent i- ti- ne- ra.   Sub- si- ste!
and the road can't be seen.   Stay here with us!

(11)

PETER   free rhythm

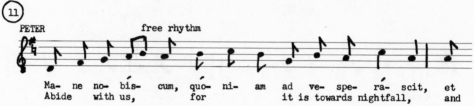

Ma- ne no- bis- cum, quo- ni- am ad ve- spe- ra- scit,   et
Abide   with us,   for   it is towards nightfall,   and

in- cli- na- ta   est iam   di- es.
far spent is   now   the day.

(12)   (Now the Two lead Him, as if urging Him toward the inn <u>at Emmaus</u>.)

CLEOPAS

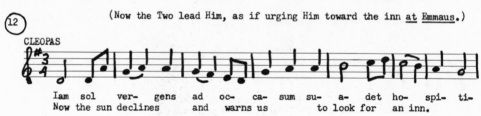

Iam sol ver- gens   ad oc- ca- sum su- a- det ho- spi- ti-
Now the sun declines   and   warns us   to look for   an inn.

um. No- strum, Pa- ter, ob- se- cra- mus, in- tres ha-   bi-
     Padre,   we beg you,   enter   as our guest.

ta- cu- lum.

PETER

Pla- cent e- nim tu- i no- bis ser- mo- nis col- lo- qui-
Pleasing   indeed   has been to us   our conversation,

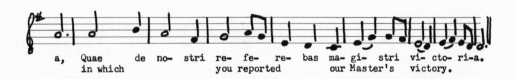

a,   Quae   de no- stri re- fe- re- bas ma- gi- stri vi- cto- ri- a.
in which   you reported   our Master's   victory.

(They lead Him to a table <u>in the inn</u>, while the Choir sings:)

CHOIR   free rhythm

Et co- e- ge- runt il- lum di- cén- tes, "Ma- ne no- bis- cum,
But they restrained   Him   saying,   "Abide   with us,

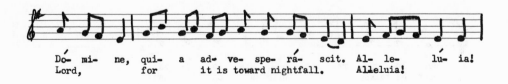

Do- mi- ne, qui- a ad- ve- spe- rá- scit. Al- le- lu- ia!
Lord,   for   it is toward nightfall.   Alleluia!

Et in- tra- vit cum il-   lis, et fa- ctum est dum re- cum-
And He entered   with them,   and it happened   as He sat

be- ret cum   e- is: Ac- ce- pit pa-   nem, be- ne- di- xit,
with   them: He took   bread,   and blessed it,

(Making the sign of
the cross)

(Bell)   ac fre- git, (Bell) et por- ri- ge- bat e- is.
and broke it,   and passed it   to them.

(Breaking it)   (Let Him give it to them - and then disappear.
The Two by turns rise up from the table and look for Him, and run about
the church as if searching for Him, and sing:)

(15)

CLEOPAS

Non- ne cor no- strum ar- dens e- rat in no- bis de Ie- su,
Wasn't   the heart of us burning   in us   about Jesus,

dum lo- que- re- tur no- bis in vi- a?
when He talked   with us on the road?

PETER

Quo in- tel-   lec- tus a- bi- é- rat?
Our minds   have left us, haven't they?

CHOIR

Sur- ré- xit   Do-   mi- nus,   et ap- pá-
Risen is   the Lord,   and has appeared

ru- it Pe-   tro, Al-   le-
to Peter,   Alleluia!

lu-   ia!

(Suddenly then the Lord appears in another outfit, and
    says to them:)

CHRISTUS

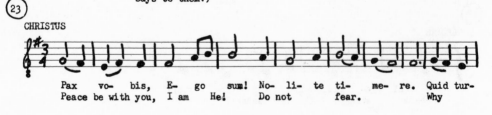

Pax vo- bis, E- go sum! No- li- te ti- me- re. Quid tur-
Peace be with you, I am He! Do not   fear.   Why

ba- ti es- tis,   Et co- gi- ta- ti- o-   nes   A-
afraid   are you,   and why do misgivings   well up

scen- dunt in cor-   da ve- stra? Vi- de- te ma- nus
       in   your hearts?   Examine   my hands

(Now he points to his hands
and feet.)

me- as Et pe-   des me- os, Qui- a e-   go ip- se
and my   feet,   for   I am   indeed

sum. Pal- pa- te et vi- de- te, Qui- a spi- ri- tus car-nem et
He.   Touch   and see,   for   the spirit has no flesh

os- sa non ha- bet si- cut me vi- de- tis ha- be- re.
and bones   as   you see me   to have.

(And then, as He disappears, let the Choir sing:)

Sur- re- xit Do- mi- nus de se- pul- chro, qui pro
Risen is   the Lord   from the sepulcher, who for

no- bis pe- pén- dit in li- gno. Al- le- lú- ia,
us   was hung   on the tree. Alleluia,

al- le- lú- ia, al- le- lú- ia!
alleluia,   alleluia!

(Now let Thomas, who has not been seen,
appear, and the Two, standing in the
middle of the choir, say to him:)

THE TWO DISCIPLES

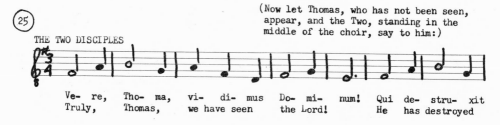

Ve- re, Tho- ma, vi- di- mus Do- mi- num! Qui de- stru- xit
Truly,   Thomas,   we have seen   the Lord!   He has destroyed

mor- tis im- pe- ri- um.
death's   empire.

THOMAS (to them)

Ni- si fi- xu- ram cla- vo- rum vi- de- ro, Et di- gi- to
Unless the print of the nails in his hands I see, and with my finger

vul- nus pal- pa- ve- ro, At- que ma- num in la- tus mi- se-
the wound touch, and my hand in His side thrust,

ro, Hoc, sci- a- tis, nun- quam cre- di- de- ro.
This, know you, never will I believe.

(Then in the midst of them appears the Lord, and says to all:)

CHRISTUS

Pax vo- bis, E- go sum!
Peace be with you, I am He!

CHOIR (and Disciples)

Al- le- lu- ia!
Alleluia!

CHRISTUS

No- li- te ti- me- re.
Do not fear.

CHOIR (and Disciples)

Al- le- lu- ia!
Alleluia!

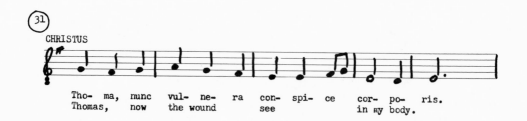

(31) CHRISTUS

Tho- ma, nunc vul- ne- ra con- spi- ce cor- po- ris.
Thomas, now the wound see in my body.

In- fer et di- gi- tum in lo- cum vul- ne- ris,
Reach in with your finger in the place of the wound,

(He shows it to him.)

Et iam in- cre- du- lus in me ne fu- e- ris, Ex-
for then unbelieving in me you won't be, but an

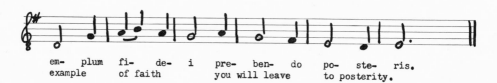

em- plum fi- de- i pre- ben- do po- ste- ris.
example of faith you will leave to posterity.

(32)   (Thomas falls prostrate at His feet.)

THOMAS (rising)

O Ihe- su Do- mi- ne, coe- lo- rum con- di- tor, Te cre- do
O Jesu, Lord, of the heavens the maker, You I believe

vi- ve- re,   cre- dens et fa- te-   or.   Quod fu- i   du- bi- us,
are alive,   I believe and acknowledge.   Because I have had doubts,

i-   gno-   sce, de- pre- cor,   De- us me-   us, et Do- mi-
forgive me,   I pray,   my God,   and my Lord!

nus me- us!

⟨33⟩

CHRISTUS

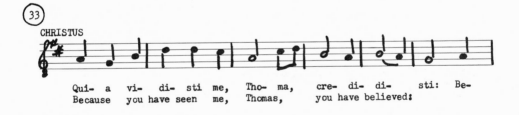

Qui- a vi- di- sti me,   Tho- ma,   cre- di- di-   sti: Be-
Because you have seen me,   Thomas,   you have believed:

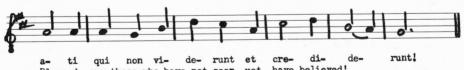

a- ti qui non vi- de- runt et cre- di- de-   runt!
Blessed are those who have not seen yet have believed!

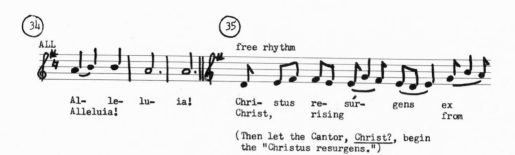

Al- le- lu- ia!   Chri- stus re- sur- gens ex
Alleluia!   Christ,   rising   from

(Then let the Cantor, <u>Christ?</u>, begin
the "Christus resurgens.")

mor- tu- is,   iam   non mó- ri- tur.
the dead,   now   has not died.

Mors il- li   ul- tra non do- mi- ná- bi-   tur,
Death over Him   has no dominion,

quod é-   nim   vi- vit, vi-   vit De-   o.
for   indeed   He lives, lives   with God.

Al-   le-   lú- ia, al- le- lú- ia!
Alleluia,   alleluia!

4. The Shepherds

The Shepherds

THE DIALOGUE AND MUSIC are transcribed from a Rouen Cathedral manuscript of the thirteenth century, now in the Bibliothèque Nationale (MS Latin 904, fols. 11^v-14^r). The stage directions have been translated from that manuscript and from a somewhat later service book from the same cathedral (Bibliothèque de la Ville MS 384, fols. 22^r-23^r).

The play was performed at the beginning of Lauds, early Christmas morning. It thus followed the predawn service, Matins, which had concluded with the *Te Deum laudamus,* as the first stage direction indicates.

As with other plays of the repertory, the score for the five Shepherds may be distributed among them for Items 3 and 9. While my transcription does not attempt to distinguish between tenor Shepherds and baritones, there certainly were some of each.

The movement and blocking for the play, as well as such other production concerns as the curtained image of the Mother and Child, are considered in *Production,* pp. 117-27 and 310-12.

Space limitations prevent the inclusion of the other choric piece, which the Rouen Shepherds were accustomed to sing after the conclusion of their play: the *Nato canunt.* It is a longer and more elaborate composition than the *Benedicamus* here transcribed, but for a modern production the latter has more appropriate dimensions.

The Cast

The Archangel
The Heavenly Host
Five Shepherds
First Midwife
Second Midwife
Choir

The Scene: A pasture. The manger. Christmas Day.

The Shepherds *Officium Pastorum*

OFFICIUM PASTORUM

(When the "Te Deum laudamus" is finished, let the Office of the Shepherds
be set forth in accordance with the Rouen use. Let the manger be prepared
behind the altar, and let the Image of the Holy Mary be placed on it. At
opening, some choirboy before the choir and high up, in the likeness of an
Angel announcing the birth of the Lord to five canons who as Shepherds
enter and cross the choir area, and the Angel saying this to them:)

(1)

ARCHANGEL   free rhythm

No- li- te ti- me- re! Ec- ce e- nim e- van- ge- li-
Do not fear!   For behold   I bring

zo vo- bis gau- di- um ma- gnum quod e- rit o- mni po-
you   great joy   which shall be to all

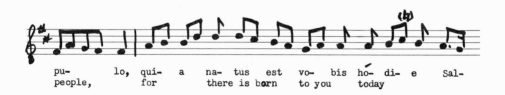

pu- lo, qui- a na- tus est vo- bis ho- di- e Sal-
people,   for   there is born to you today

va- tor mun- di, in ci- vi- ta- te Da- vid, et hoc vo-
the Savior of the world, in the City of   David,   and this to

bis   si- gnum: In- ve- ni- é- tis in- fán- tem pan- nis
you   is a sign: shall find   the child in swaddling clothes

in- vo- lu- tum, et   po- si- tum in   prae- se- pi-   o.
wrapped,   and   lying   in   a manger.

(Hearing this, let seven choirboys, as the Heavenly Host, standing in a
high place, say:)

HEAVENLY HOST

Glo- ri- a in ex- cel- sis De-   o, et in ter- ra   pax
Glory   on high,   and on earth   peace

ho- mi- ni- bus bo- nae vo- lun-   ta- tis!
to men   of good will!

(This hearing, the Shepherds sing:)

SHEPHERDS

Pax in ter- ris nun- ci- a- tur, In ex-   cel- sis
Peace on earth   is now proclaimed, and on high   glory.

glo- ri- a. Ter- ra cae- lo fe- de- ra- tur, Me- di- an- te
Earth with heaven is joined, by the means of

gra- ti- a. Me- di- a- tor, ho- mo De- us
grace. As mediator, to man God

de- scen- dit in pro- pri- a Ut a- scen- dat ho- mo
descends in person so that may ascend man,

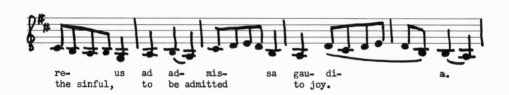

re- us ad ad- mis- sa gau- di- a.
the sinful, to be admitted to joy.

E- y- a! E- y- a! Tran- se- a- mus,
Hey! Eeya! Eeya! Let us go forth,

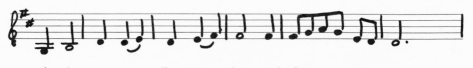

vi- de- a- mus   Ver- bum hoc quod fac-   tum est.
let us see   this thing   which has come to pass.

Tran-   se- a-   mus ut sci- a-   mus Quod an-
Let us go forth   so that we may know   what

nun- ci- a-   tum   est.
has been announced.

In Iu- de- a   pu- er va- git,   pu- er sa- lus po- pu- li.
In Judea   a boy   is crying,   a boy   who saves   all people.

Quo bel- lan-   dum se   prae- sa- git Ve- tus ho- spes
For whom striving   as   was prophesied   of old,   a friend

sae- cu-   li. Ac- ce- da-   mus, ac-   ce-   da-
forever.   Let us go on,   let us go on

mus ad prae- se-   pe Do- mi- ni,   Et di- ca-   mus,
to   the manger   of the Lord,   and   let us sing,

"Laus fe- cun-   dae Vir- gi- ni."
"Praise to the birthing   by the Virgin!"

(This having been sung, the Shepherds move to the place where
the manger has been prepared.)

free rhythm

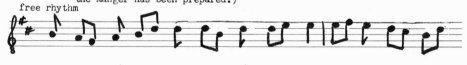

Tran- se- á- mus us- que Beth- le- em et vi- de- á-
Let us go forth   to   Bethlehem   so that we can see

mus hoc ver- bum quod fac- tum est,   quod fe-   cit Do- mi-
this thing   that has come to pass,   which the Lord has done

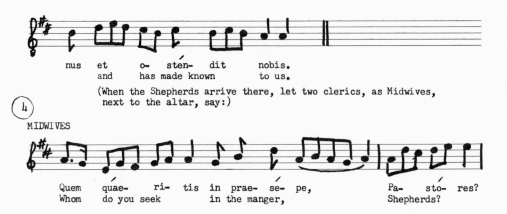

nus   et   o- sten- dit   nobis.
and   has made known   to us.

(When the Shepherds arrive there, let two clerics, as Midwives,
next to the altar, say:)

④
MIDWIVES

Quem   quae-   ri- tis in prae- se- pe,   Pa-   sto-   res?
Whom   do you seek   in the manger,   Shepherds?

Di- ci- te!

⑤
SHEPHERDS

Sal- va- to- rem, Chri- stum Do-   mi-   num, in-   fan-
The Savior,   Christ   the Lord,   as a child

tem pan- nis in- vo-   lu- tum, se- cun- dum ser- mo-
in swaddling clothes wrapped,   according   to the

nem an- ge- li- cum.
teaching of the angel.

6 (The Midwives reveal the Image of the Holy Mary and Child.)

FIRST MIDWIFE

Ad- est hic par- vu- lus, cum Ma- ri- a
Here is this little one, with Mary

ma- tre su- a. De quo du- dum va- ti- ci- nan- do
His mother. Of His coming, long ago, prophesying

Y- sa- i- as di- xe- rat pro- phe- ta:
Isaiah said:

7 SECOND MIDWIFE

"Ec- ce vir- go con- ci- pi- et et pa- ri- et fi-
"For behold a virgin shall conceive and shall bear a

li- um!"
son!"

(8) MIDWIVES

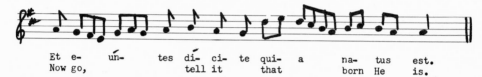

Et e- un- tes di- ci- te qui- a na- tus est.
Now go,   tell it   that   born He is.

(Then, seeing Him, the Shepherds, bowing, adore the Child, and sing:)

(9) SHEPHERDS

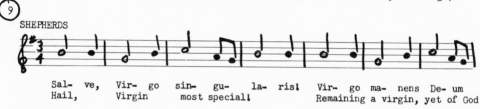

Sal- ve, Vir- go sin- gu- la- ris! Vir- go ma- nens De- um
Hail,   Virgin most special!   Remaining a virgin, yet of God

pa- ris! An- te sae- cla ge- ne- ra- tum Cor- de Pa- tris.
the bride! Before all ages   was He created   in the heart of the Father.

A- do- re- mus nunc cre- a- tum Car- ne ma- tris.
Let us adore Him now embodied   in the flesh of His mother.

Nos, Ma- ri- a, tu- a   prae- ce A pec- ca-   ti pur- ga fae-ce
We, Mary,   to you pray,   Of our sins   to purge   the shit

No- stri cur- sum in- co- la- tus; Sic di- spo- ne
during   our life's length,   and so grant

Ut det su- a fru- i na- tus vi- si- o- ne.
that your son may show us   His face.

(The Shepherds return to the choir.)

⑩ CHOIR

Al- le- lu- ia! Al-   le- lu- ia!

⑪ SHEPHERDS

Iam ve- re sci- mus Chri- stum na-   tum   in ter- ris,
Now verily we know that Christ   is born   on earth,

de quo ca- ni- te o- mnes　cum pro- phe- ta di- cen-tes:
of Whom sing　all,　with the prophet　saying:

ALL

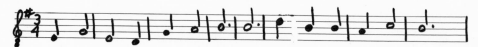

Ver- bum Pa- tris ho- di- e　Pro- ces- sit ex Vir- gi- ne.
This Thing from the Father today　issues　from the Virgin.

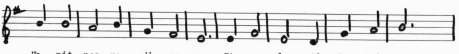

Ve- nit nos re- di- me- re, Et cae- le- sti Pa- tri- e
It comes　to redeem us,　and to our heavenly Father

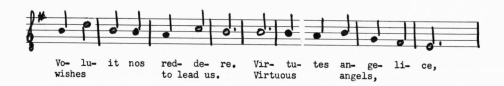

Vo- lu- it nos red- de- re. Vir- tu- tes an- ge- li- ce,
wishes　to lead us.　Virtuous　angels,

Cum ca- no- re iu- bi- lo Be- ne- di- cant Do- mi- no!
with singing　jubilant,　bless　the Lord!

Re- ful- gens pa- sto- ri- bus   Nun- ci- a-   vit   an- ge- lus
Radiant,   to the shepherds   the angel   announced

Pa- cem,   pa- cis nun- ci- us.   Tu, Pa- stor ec- cle- si- ae,
peace,   he of peace the herald.   You, Shepherd of the flock,

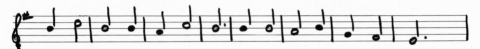

Pa- cem tum et di- ri- ge   Fi- li- os et   in- stru-   ae
in Your way of peace now direct   Your people, and   teach   them

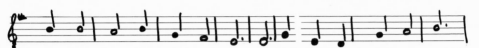

Re- dem- pto- ri de- bi- tas.   Iu- bi- lan- do   gra- ti- as!
redemption's   debt.   Joyful   thanks!

5. The Play of Herod

The Play of Herod

THIS FLEURY PLAY and its sequel, *The Slaughter of the Innocents,* have already been published in a lavish performing edition: full musical transcriptions, copious stage directions from the Greenberg production, photographs of the manuscript, a "black semi-breve" literal transcript of the notation, an orchestral score as developed by the Pro Musica for their performances, and editorial notes by the coeditor, W. L. Smoldon.[1] The intention was not only to encourage performance of the two plays but also to offer a model for the editing of medieval music-drama for scholars and performers.

Justification for the present new edition of the *Herod,* from the same manuscript (Orléans, Bibliothèque de la Ville MS 201, pp. 205-20) can only be on the basis of significant differences, which are outlined as follows:

Many items transcribed by Smoldon as free-rhythm plainchant appear here in mensural transcription. These items in the *Herod* are, in the present numbering, 19, 25, 29-48, 53, and 74, of which 25, 29-48, and 53 are unrhymed hexameters. The total amounts to 30 percent of the items in the play manuscript and markedly alters the musico-dramatic expression. The proportions are now only twenty-seven plainchant items out of a total of seventy-five items. This balance is typical of many of the sophisticated music-dramas of the period.

Except for Item 74, all of the twenty-one newly mensuralized items are in the Herod-Magi court scenes, where there was little traditional service-book material available. There was, moreover, small likelihood that plainchant melodies would be invented by a twelfth-century play-wright, who as a fashionable composer in the trouvère style was ipso facto a mensuralist. It is also true of the present edition that a liturgical source can be located for most of the bona fide plainchant items. Where such a source has not been found, the Latin statement is always in prose and cannot therefore have been set to a mensuralized melody.

A further comment which explains the major difference between the present transcription of the *Herod* and Smoldon's is that he did not in

[1] *The Play of Herod: A Twelfth-Century Musical Drama,* ed. Noah Greenberg and William L. Smoldon (New York: Oxford University Press, 1965).

the *Herod* allow mensuralization of hexameters unless they rhymed. On the other hand, in the sequel (in such Items as Nos. 18-23) he is not dissuaded from mensuralizing hexameters for want of rhymes; and yet in Item 25 of the *Herod* he refuses to mensuralize even when the hexameter is rhymed. Since the rhyming only indirectly affected the rhythm by indicating the ends of verse-lines, rhyme had much less authority over musical metricality than had the meter of the verses. Mensuralization seems therefore not only feasible but also preferable for the transcription of versified dialogue in the plays, and thus rhyme is in these instances to be regarded as an optional ornament, not a prerequisite for mensural interpretation. A rather boggling corollary is that blank verse—here meaning blank of rhyme—was apparently permitted in the twelfth century.

Another indication of the extent to which the present transcription differs from Smoldon's is that we have treated identically only Items 27 and 28, short mensural phrases. Elsewhere the significant differences in our interpretations arise not from a wish to be different but from honest preference, my first draft being made from the manuscript without sight or conscious recall of Smoldon's musical text.

There are no interpolated items in the present edition, while the Greenberg-Smoldon edition interpolates three vocal items and seven instrumental ones.

Suggestions for appropriate production are in *Production,* pp. 129-42 and 313-16.

The Cast

Archangel
Multitude of the Heavenly Host (Angels)
First Shepherd
Second Shepherd
Third Shepherd
First Midwife
Second Midwife
First King
Second King
Third King
Armiger
Herod
Courtiers
Scribes
Choir (of Angels)
Archelaus
(Mary and Christ Child, in tableau)

The Scene: A field. Herod's court. The Bethlehem manger. The Christmas season.

(Herod and others of the cast being ready, let then a certain Archangel
with a multitude of Angels appear on high. Whom being seen, the Shepherds
fall to the ground. Let the Archangel thus announce the greeting to them
while the others are silent:)

ARCHANGEL · free rhythm

No- li- te ti- mé- re vos! Ec- ce e- nim e- van- gé-
Do not   fear!   For behold   I bring

li- zo vo- bis gau- di- um ma- gnum quod e- rit o- mni
     you   great joy   which shall be to all

po- pu- lo, qui- a na- tus est no- bis hó- di- e
people,   for   there is born to us   today

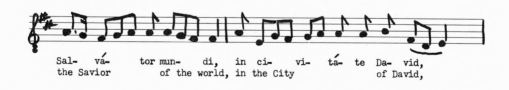

Sal- vá- tor mun- di, in ci- vi- tá- te Da- vid,
the Savior   of the world, in the City   of David,

et hoc   vo- bis si- gnum: In- ve- ni- é-   tis in- fán-
and this to you is a sign: You shall find   the Child

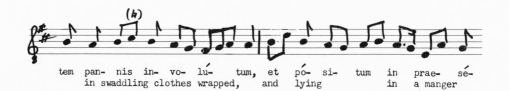

tem pan- nis in- vo- lú- tum, et pó- si- tum in prae- sé-
in swaddling clothes wrapped,   and lying   in   a manger

pi- o in mé- di- o du- um a- ni- má- li-   um.
     between   two   animals.

② HEAVENLY HOST (with Archangel, suddenly)

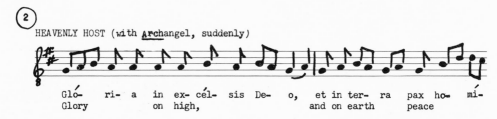

Gló-   ri- a   in ex- cél- sis De- o, et in ter- ra pax ho- mi-
Glory   on high,   and on earth peace

ni- bus bo- nae vo- lun- tá- tis. Al- le- lú- ia, al- le- lú- ia!
to men   of good will.   Alleluia,   alleluia!

③ SHEPHERDS (rising and leaving)

Tran- se- a- mus us- que Beth- le- em et vi- de- a- mus
Let us go forth   to   Bethlehem   so that we can see

hoc   ver- bum quod fa- ctum est, quod fe- cit Do- mi- nus et
this thing   that has come to pass, which the Lord has done   and

o- sten- dit no- bis.
has made known   to us.

(And so they proceed to the Manger, which has been prepared at the church
doors. Then let two women, _Midwives_, guarding the Manger, question the
④ Shepherds, saying:)

MIDWIVES

Quem quae- ri- tis, Pa- sto- res? Di- ci- te!
Whom do you seek,   Shepherds?   Tell us!

⑤

SHEPHERDS

Sal- va- to- rem Chri- stum Do- mi- num, in- fan- tem
The Savior,   Christ   the Lord,   as a child

pan- nis in- vo- lu- tum, se- cun- dum ser- mo- nem
in swaddling clothes wrapped, according to the teaching

an- ge- li- cum.
of the angel.

6 FIRST MIDWIFE

A- dest [hic] par- vu-lus, cum Ma- ri- a ma- tre
Here is this little one, with Mary His mother.

7 SECOND MIDWIFE

e- ius. De quo du- dum va- ti- ci- nan- do Y- sa- i- as
Of whose coming, long ago prophesying Isaiah

pro- phe- ta di- xe- rat:
said:

8 MIDWIVES

"Ec- ce vir- go con- ci- pi- et et pa- ri- et fi- li-um!"
"For behold a virgin shall conceive and shall bear a son!"

(Then the Shepherds, throwing themselves down, worship the Child, saying:)

9 SHEPHERDS

Sal- ve, Rex sae- cu- lo- rum!
Hail, King of eternity!

(After this, rising, let them invite the people standing around, the
audience, to worship the Child, saying to those nearest:)

10 FIRST SECOND THIRD SHEPHERD ALL

Ve- ni- te! Ve- ni- te! Ve- ni- te! A- do- re- mus De- um,
O come! O come! O come! Let us adore the Lord,

qui- a ip- se est Sal- va- tor no- ster.
for He Himself is our Savior.

(Meanwhile the Magi, coming forward, each at his own angle, as if from
his country, meet before the altar or at the source of the Star, and
while they are approaching let the First King say:)

11 FIRST KING

Stel- la ful- go- re ni- mi- o ru- ti- lat.
The Star with brightness extraordinary shines.

12. SECOND KING

Quem ven- tu- rum o- lim pro- phe- ta si- gna- ve- rat.
Of whose appearance, in olden days the prophets spoke.

13. THIRD KING (to Second)   **14. SECOND KING (to Third)**

Pax ti- bi, fra- ter. Pax quo- que ti- bi. (And they kiss.)
Peace to you, brother. Peace also to you.

15. FIRST KING (to Second)   **16. SECOND KING (to First)**

Pax ti- bi, fra- ter. Pax quo- que ti- bi. (And they kiss.)
Peace to you, brother. Peace also to you.

17. (Now they see the Star.)

THIRD KING   FIRST KING   SECOND KING

Ec- ce stel- la! Ec- ce stel- la! Ec- ce stel- la!
Behold the star! Behold the star! Behold the star!
(The Star then moves forward and leads them, while they say:)

18. THREE KINGS

free rhythm

E- á- mus er- go et in- qui- rá- mus e- um of- fe- rén- tes
Let us go, therefore, and seek Him, we offering

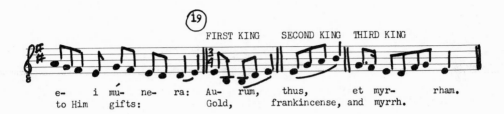

FIRST KING   SECOND KING   THIRD KING

e- i mu- ne- ra: Au- rum, thus, et myr- rham.
to Him gifts: Gold, frankincense, and myrrh.

THREE KINGS

free rhythm

Qui- a scri- ptum di- di- ci- mus: "A- do- ra- bunt e- um
For Scripture tells us: "They shall adore Him,

o- mnes re- ges, o- mnes gen- tes ser- vi- ent e- i."
all kings shall, and all people shall serve Him."

(Coming to the entrance to the choir area, let them ask of those
standing there:)

FIRST KING

Di- ci- te no- bis, O Ie- ro- so- li- mi- ta- ni ci- ves,
Tell us, O Jerusalem citizens,

SECOND KING

U- bi est ex- pe- cta- ti- o gen- ti- um?
Where is the One expected by all people?

(23) THIRD KING

U- bi est qui na- tus est rex Iu- de- ó- rum,
Where   is He who is born   king of the Jews,

(24) THREE KINGS

quem si- gnis cae- lé- sti- bus á- gni- tum ve- ni- mus a- do- rá- re?
Whom, by signs celestial   shown,   we come   to adore?

(Whom seeing, let Herod send to them an Armiger, who says:)

(25) ARMIGER (to the Kings)

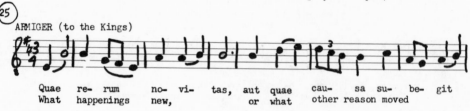

Quae   re- rum   no- vi- tas, aut quae   cau- sa su- be- git
What   happenings   new,   or what   other reason moved

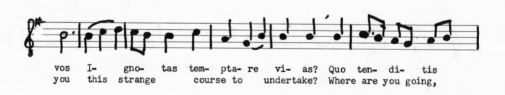

vos I-   gno- tas tem- pta- re vi- as? Quo ten- di- tis
you this strange   course to undertake? Where are you going,

er- go, quod ge- nus? Un- de do-   mo? Pa-   cem ne huc
therefore, what is your race? And from what home? Peace   do you

fer- tis, an ar- ma?
bring us, or war?

26 THREE KINGS

Cal- de- i su- mus. Pa- cem fe- ri- mus. Re- gem re- gum
Chaldeans we are. Peace we bring. The King of Kings

quae- ri- mus, Quem na- tum es- se stel- la in- di- cat, quae
we seek, Who to be born the star is indicating, whose

ful- go- re ce- te- ris cla- ri- or ru- ti- lat.
light more than any others brighter shines.

(Let the Armiger, returning, salute the king. Bending his knee,
let him say:)

27 ARMIGER (to Herod, ceremonially)

Vi- vat, Rex, in ae- ter- num.
Live, O King, forever.

28 HEROD (ceremonially)

Sal- vet te, gra- ti- a me- a.
Let you be greeted, and my thanks.

29 ARMIGER

Ad- sunt no- bis, Do- mi- ne, tres vi- ri i- gno- ti.
There are come to us, my lord, three men unknown.

Ab o- ri- en- te ve- ni- en- tes. No- vi- ter na- tum
From the east they are coming. A certain newborn

quen- dam re- gem quae- ri- tan- tes.
king seeking.

(Then let Herod send his <u>Courtier</u> Spokesmen or Interpreters to
the Magi, saying:)

30 HEROD

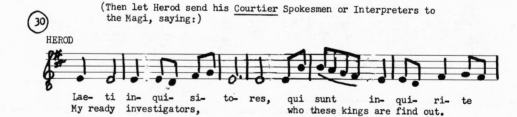

Lae- ti in- qui- si- to- res, qui sunt in- qui- ri- te
My ready investigators, who these kings are find out.

re- ges. Af- fo- re quos no- stris iam fa- ma re-
Question   them about One whom already rumor

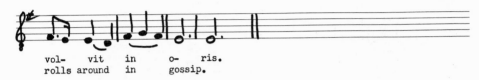

vol- vit in o- ris.
rolls around in gossip.

(The Courtiers go to the Magi.)

31 COURTIERS

Prin- ci- pis e- di- ctu, Re- ges, pre- sci- re ve- ni- mus
By our master   sent,   O Kings,   to find out   we come

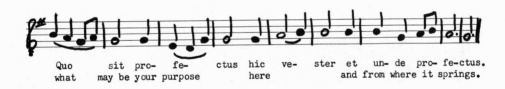

Quo   sit pro- fe- ctus hic ve- ster et un- de pro- fe-ctus.
what may be your purpose here   and from where it springs.

32 THREE KINGS

Re- gem quae- si- tum, Du- ce stel- la si- gni- fi-
A king   we seek,   led   by a star   as was

ca-   tum.   Mu- ne-re pro- vi-   so   Pro- pe- ra- mus e-   um
prophesied.   With gifts provided,   we hurry   Him

ve- ne-   ran-   do.
to venerate.

(The <u>Courtier</u> Spokesmen return to Herod.)

③③ COURTIERS (to Herod)

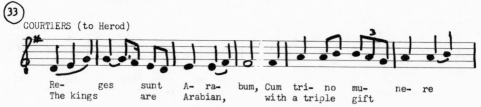

Re-   ges   sunt   A- ra-   bum, Cum tri- no   mu-   ne- re
The kings   are   Arabian,   with a triple   gift

na- tum, Quae-   runt in- fan-   tem, Quem mon-strant si-de-ra re-gem.
to the newborn, and they seek the Child,   whom   the stars show to be King.

③④ HEROD (to the Armiger)

An-   te ve- ni-   re   iu- be,   quo pos- sim sin- gu- la
Before us   to come   command them,   that I may be able specific things

sci- re: Qui sunt?   **Cur** ve- ni- ant?   Quo   nos ru-
to find out: Who they are? Why   they come here?   About what   rumor

mo-   re   re-   qui-   rant?
are they asking us?

(35) ARMIGER (to Herod)

Quod man- das, ci- ti-   us, Rex in- cli- te, per-fi- ci- e-tur.
What you command, quickly,   O King renowned,   shall be done.

(The Armiger goes to the Magi.)

Re-   gi- a vos man- da- ta vo- cant: Non se-gni- ter i- te!
By royal   order   you are called: Without delay,   go!

(The Armiger leads the Magi to Herod, saying to his king:)

En,   Ma- gi ve- ni-   unt! Et re-   gem na- tum,
See, the Magi are come!   And the King   newborn,

stel-   la   du- ce, re- qui- runt.
by the Star   led,   they seek.

(36)
HEROD (to the Three Kings)

Quae   sit   cau- sa vi- ae? Qui vos? Vel un-   de   ve-
What is the   cause of your journey? Who are you? And from whence

         ni- tis? Di- ci- te!
do you come?   Speak!

(37)   (38)
FIRST KING   SECOND KING

Rex   est   cau- sa vi- ae. Re- ges   su- mus ex A-
A King is   the cause of our journey. Kings   we are from

ra- bi- tis huc   ve- ni-   en- tes.
Arabia   here come.

THIRD KING

Quae ri- mus, en, re- gem re- gnan- ti- bus im- pe- ri- tan- tem,
We seek, lo, a King above all kings the Emperor,

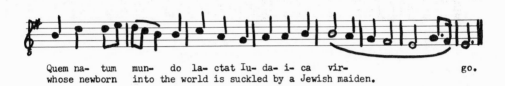

Quem na- tum mun- do la- ctat Iu- da- i- ca vir- go.
whose newborn into the world is suckled by a Jewish maiden.

HEROD

Re- gem quem quae- ri- tis na- tum es- se quo si- gno
This King whom you seek, of His birth-to-be what sign

di- di- ci- stis?
has revealed it to you?

FIRST KING

Il- lum na- tum es- se di- di- ci- mus in o- ri-
His birth- to-be we have learned in the East,

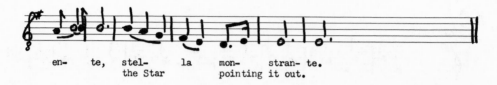

en- te, stel- la mon- stran- te.
the Star pointing it out.

(42) HEROD

Si il- lum re- gna- re cre- di- tis, di- ci- te no- bis.
If He is to reign believably, explain it to us.

(43) THREE KINGS

Il- lum re- gna- re fa- ten- tes, cum mi- sti- cis mu-
He to reign acknowledging, with holy gifts

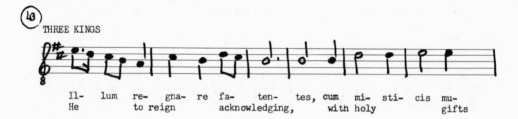

ne- ri- bus De ter- ra lon- gin- qua, a- do- ra- re
from lands afar, to adore

ve- ni- mus, Tri- num De- um ve- ne- ran- tes
we come, the Trinity venerating

tri- bus cum mu- ne- ri- bus.
with triple gifts.

(And let them show their gifts:)

44

FIRST KING   SECOND KING   THIRD KING

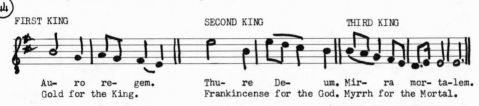

Au- ro re- gem.   Thu- re De- um. Mir- ra mor- ta-lem.
Gold for the King. Frankincense for the God. Myrrh for the Mortal.

(Then let Herod order the Symmiste Courtiers, who are sitting with him,
in the dress of young men, to lead in the Scribes who, as outsiders,
are bearded.)

45

HEROD

Vos me- i Si- mi- ste, le- gis pe- ri- tos a- sci-te ut
You, my Courtiers, from the legal experts brief me as to

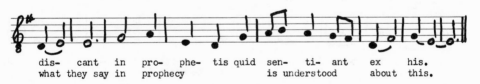

dis- cant in pro- phe- tis quid sen- ti- ant ex his.
what they say in prophecy is understood about this.

(The Courtiers bring in the Scribes with their book of prophets.)

46

COURTIERS (to the Scribes)

Vos le- gis pe- ri- ti ad re- gem vo- ca- ti.
You, in law expert, to the king are called.

Cum pro- phe- ta- rum li- bris, pro- pe- ran- do ve- ni- te.
With your prophecies   book,   speedily   come.

(47) HEROD (interrogating the Scribes)

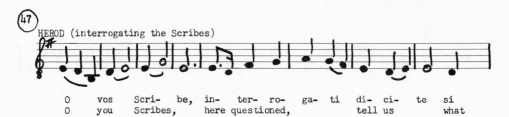

O vos Scri- be, in- ter- ro- ga- ti di- ci- te si
O you Scribes, here questioned,   tell us   what

quid de hoc Pu- e- ro scri- ptum vi- de- ri- tis in li- bro.
about   this Boy   written   you find   in the book.

(Then let the Scribes turn the pages of the book tediously, and finally,
as if finding the prophecy, let them say this, as pointing with their
fingers <u>to the place</u> they pass the book to the incredulous King Herod:)

(48) SCRIBES

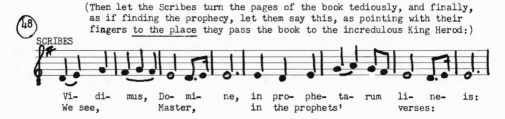

Vi- di- mus, Do- mi- ne, in pro- phe- ta- rum li- ne- is:
We see,   Master,   in the prophets'   verses:

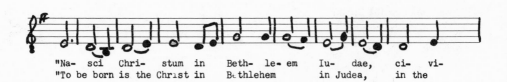

"Na- sci Chri- stum in Beth- le- em Iu- dae, ci- vi-
"To be born is the Christ in Bethlehem   in Judea,   in the

ta- te Da- vid." Pro- phe- ta sic va- ti-ci-
City of David." The prophets so prophesy.

nan- te.

"Beth- le- em non es mí- ni- ma in prin- cí- pi- bus
Bethlehem, you are not the least among the princes

Iu- da. Ex te é- nim é- xi- et dux, qui re- gat
of Juda. From you indeed will come a leader, who shall rule

pó- pu- lum me- um Is- ra- hel."
my people Israel."

(Then let Herod, seeing the prophecy and in a towering rage, throw down the
book. But let his son, Archelaus, hearing the tumult, proceed to pacify
his father, and standing beside Herod, let him say:)

ARCHELAUS

Sal- ve,   Pa- ter,   in- cli- te! Sal- ve,   Rex e- gre- gi- e!
Hail,   Father,   renowned!   Hail,   King most excellent!

Qui u- bi- que   im- pe- ras, Sce- ptra te- nens   re- gi- a.
Who everywhere   rules,   the scepter holding   of the kingdom.

HEROD

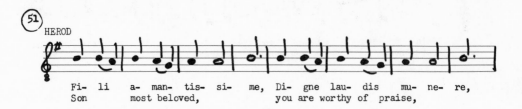

Fi- li a- man- tis- si- me, Di- gne lau- dis mu- ne- re,
Son   most beloved,   you are worthy of praise,

Lau- dis pom- pam re- gi- ae Tu- o ge- rens   no- mi- ne.
of praise's pomp   royal   bearing in your name.

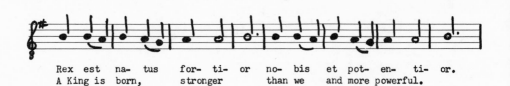

Rex est na- tus   for- ti- or no- bis et pot- en- ti- or.
A King is born,   stronger   than we and more powerful.

Ve- re-   or ne so- li-   o Nos ex- tra- het   re- gi- o.
Have a care   lest from our royal throne He may tumble us.

(52) ARCHELAUS

Con- tra   il- lum re- gu- lum, Con- tra na- tum par- vu- lum,
Against   this   little king,   against this newborn little one,

Iu- be, Pa- ter, fi- li- um Hoc i- ni- re   proe- li- um.
order,   Father,   your son   to begin   the battle.

(Then finally let Herod dismiss the Magi so that they may search for
the Boy, and let Herod, pledging allegiance to the newborn King, say:)

(53) HEROD

I-   te et de pu- e-   ro di- li- gen-   ter in- ve- sti-
Go,   and for the Boy   diligently   search,

ga-   te, Et in- ven- to re- de- un- tes mi- chi
and having found Him, come back   to me

re- nun- ci- a- te,   Ut et e-   go ve- ni-   ens a-
and tell me,   so that I too   may come

do- rem   e- um.
and adore   Him.

(The Magi leave, and the Star leads them, which is not yet in Herod's
sight. They point it out to each other as they proceed. When Herod
and his son see the Star, let them brandish their swords at it.)

THREE KINGS

Ec- ce stel- la in o- ri- en- te prae- vi- sa. I- te-
Behold   the Star in the East,   already seen.   Even

rum prae- ce- dit nos lu- ci- da.
now it precedes   us   with its light.

(Meanwhile let the Shepherds, returning to the Manger, come in,
rejoicing and singing:)

SHEPHERDS   free rhythm

O Re- gem cae-   li, cu- i ta- li- a   fa- mu-
O King   of heaven,   who with such   ceremony

lan- tur   ob-   se- qui-   a!   Stá- bu- lo
is served!   In a stable

po- ni- tur   qui con- ti- net   mun-   dum.
He is placed,   who owns   the world.

Ia- cet in prae- se- pi-   o   et in nu-
He lies in a manger,   yet in the

bi-   bus   to-   nat.
clouds   thunders.

56 THREE KINGS (to the Shepherds)

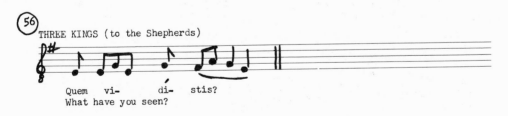

Quem vi- di- stis?
What have you seen?

Se- cun- dum   quod di- ctum est no- bis ab
Following   what was told to us by

an- ge- lo de pu- e- ro i- sto, in- ve- ni- mus
the Angel   about this Boy,   we found

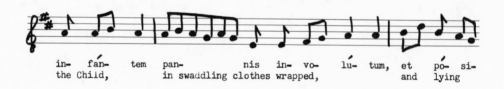

in- fan- tem pan-   nis in- vo- lu- tum, et po- si-
the Child,   in swaddling clothes wrapped,   and lying

tum in prae- se- pi- o in me- di- o du- um
in a manger   in between two

a- ni- ma- li- um.
animals.

(After the Shepherds have left, let the Magi follow after
the Star as far as the Manger, singing:)

THREE KINGS

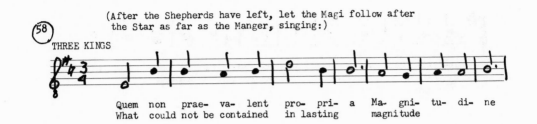

Quem non prae- va- lent pro- pri- a Ma- gni- tu- di- ne
What could not be contained in lasting magnitude

Coe- lum, ter- ra at- que ma- ri- a La- ta ca- pe- re,
by sky, earth, and sea,

De vir- gi- ne o na- tus u- te- ro Po- ni- tur in prae-
from the Virgin's womb born, is laid in a

se- pi- o. Ser- mo ce- ci- nit quem va- ti- di- cus,
manger. As was foretold by the prophets,

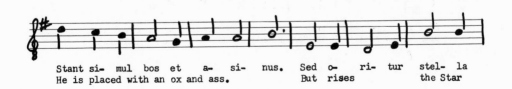

Stant si- mul bos et a- si- nus. Sed o- ri- tur stel- la
He is placed with an ox and ass. But rises the Star

lu- ci- da,   Prae- bi- ta   Do- mi- no   ob- se- qui- a.
so bright,   offering   to the Lord   homage.

Quem   Ba- la- am   ex Iu- da- i- ca   Na- sci- tu- rum di- xe-
Whom   Balaam   from Jewish stock   prophesied would be born.

rat pro- sa- pi- a.   Haec no- stro- rum   o- cu- los
                      Our   eyes

Ful- gu- ran- ti lu- mi- ne Prae- strin- xit lu- ci- da,
this shining light   by its brilliance has blinded us,

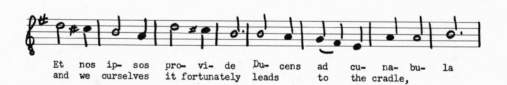

Et   nos ip- sos   pro- vi- de Du- cens ad   cu- na- bu- la
and   we ourselves   it fortunately leads   to   the cradle,

Re- splen- dens ful- gi- da.
by light resplendent.

(Now the Midwives seeing the Magi, let them call out:)

59 MIDWIVES

Qui sunt hi- i qui, stel- la du- ce, nos a- de-
Who are these who, by the Star led, approaching us,

un- tes in- au- di- ta fe- runt?
strange things bring?

60 THREE KINGS

Nos su- mus quos cer- ni- tis, re- gem Thar- sis et
We are, whom you see, kings of Tarsus and

A- ra- bum et Sa- ba, do- na fe- ren- tes Chri- sto
Arabia and Saba, gifts bearing to Christ

na- to Re- gi, Do- mi- no,   quem, stel- la du- cen-
the newborn King,   the Lord,   Whom, by the Star led,

te, a- do- ra- re ve- ni- mus.
to adore   we come.

61 MIDWIVES (showing the Boy)

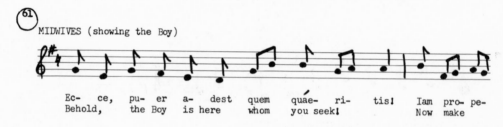

Ec- ce, pu- er a- dest quem quae- ri- tis!   Iam pro- pe-
Behold,   the Boy is here   whom   you seek!   Now make

ra- te et a- do- ra- te,   qui- a ip- se est re- dem-
haste   and adore,   for   He indeed is the

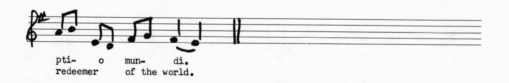

pti- o mun- di.
redeemer of the world.

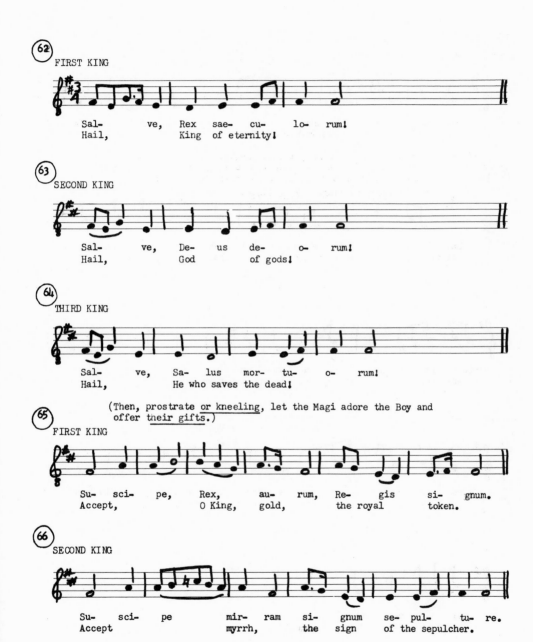

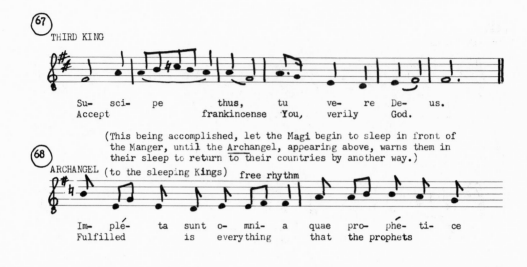

67 THIRD KING

Su - sci - pe   thus,   tu   ve - re   De -   us.
Accept   frankincense You,   verily   God.

(This being accomplished, let the Magi begin to sleep in front of
the Manger, until the Archangel, appearing above, warns them in
their sleep to return to their countries by another way.)

68 ARCHANGEL (to the sleeping Kings)   free rhythm

Im - plé - ta   sunt o - mni - a   quae pro - phé - ti - ce
Fulfilled   is   everything   that   the prophets

scri - pta   sunt. I - te, vi - am re - me - án - tes á - li - am,
have written.   Go,   by another road   go back,

nec de - la - tó -   res tan - ti re - gis pu - ni - en -
and so you will not be informers   so great   a king   to

di   é - ri -   tis.
punish.

(69) THREE KINGS

De- o gra- ti- as!
To God thanks!

(70) FIRST KING free rhythm

Sur- gá- mus, er- go, vi- si- ó- ne mo- ni- ti an-
Let us rise up, therefore, by the angelic vision warned.

gé- li- ca.

(71) SECOND KING

Et, cal- le mu- tá- to, lá- te- ant He- ró- dem,
And, by a shrewd manouever, conceal from Herod,

(72) THIRD KING

Quae ví- di- mus de pú- e- ro.
What we have seen about this boy.

(Then the Magi, leaving by another way, and Herod not seeing them, sing:)

(73)

THREE KINGS

O ad- mi- ra- bi- le com- mer- ci- um! Cre- a- tor
O   admirable   fellowship!   The Creator

ge- ne- ris hu- ma- ni, a- ni- ma- tum cor- pus
of the race of humans, a living   body

su- mens, de Vir- gi- ne na- sci di- gna- tus est. Et
assuming,   from the Virgin to be born permitted   himself. And

pro- ce- dens ho- mo si- ne se- mi- ne, lar- gi- tus
became   a man   without (her) being inseminated, and bestowed

est no- bis su- am de- i- ta- tem.
on us His   divinity.

(Then, coming into the choir area, the Magi say:)

(74)

THREE KINGS (to the Fratres, audience)

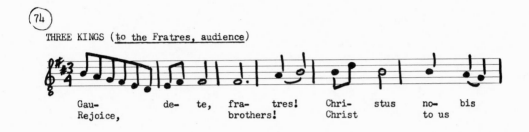

Gau- de- te, fra- tres!   Chri- stus no- bis
Rejoice,   brothers!   Christ   to us

na- tus est!   De- us ho- mo fa- ctus est!
is born!   God   a man   is made!

(75)

ALL   free rhythm

Te Dé- um lau- dá- mus; Te Dó- mi- num con - fi-
You God   we praise;   You the Lord   we acknowledge....

té- mur. . . .

(And so it ends.)

(Unless "The Slaughter of the Innocents" is to follow without
intermission, in which case the "Te Deum" is postponed.)

(The complete "Te Deum" begins on p. 491.)

The Slaughter of the Innocents

MUCH OF WHAT has been remarked above on the *Herod* also applies to its sequel.

There are five items in the *Innocents* which Smoldon transcribed in the Greenberg-Smoldon edition as free-rhythm plainchant and which the present editor identifies as mensural compositions: Items 3, 5, 24, 29, and 30, or 16 percent of total items. There are in addition eight traditional plainchant pieces that both editors necessarily present as such. The proportions of mensural and free-rhythm items in the two editions are thus: Smoldon 18 mensural, 13 free rhythm; Collins 23 mensural, 8 free rhythm. The proportions in the present edition are similar to those for his edition of the *Herod* and to those for many other sophisticated plays of the repertory.

Two items are interpolated in the Pro Musica edition: an organ version of the *Alleluia psallite* motet and an extension of their Item 30 by Greenberg's Gregorian invention. The present edition, following the manuscript, interpolates nothing. Instrumental interpolation was limited by the Pro Musica to organ, drums, and bells, unmentioned in the manuscript. The use of bells, however, is frequent in medieval liturgy and may have been appropriate at moments of this play. For other suggestions as to its interpretation and production, and that of the *Herod,* see *Production,* pp. 129-42 and 313-16.

Seven of the eight plainchant items have only the *incipit* in the manuscript and have been completed from either the modern *Antiphonale Romanum* or the medieval Sarum *Antiphonary*. Only free-rhythm Item 3 is given completely in the play manuscript.

The Cast

The Innocents (Choirboys)
The Bearer of the Lamb
Armiger
Herod
Archangel
Joseph
Mary
The Christ Child
First Mother (Consoler)
Second Mother (Consoler)
Third Mother (Consoler)
Rachel

The Scene: Herod's court. The Manger. Egypt. The Christmas season.

The Slaughter of the Innocents   *Ad Interfectionem Puerorum*

(At "The Slaying of the Boys," let the Innocents be costumed in
white stoles, and singing joyfully through the church, let them
pray to God, saying:)

1

INNOCENTS   free rhythm

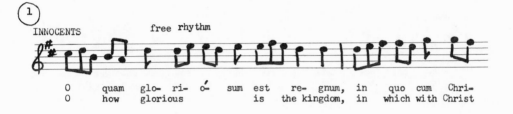

O   quam   glo- ri- ó-   sum est   re- gnum,   in   quo cum Chri-
O   how   glorious   is   the kingdom,   in   which with Christ

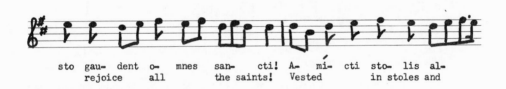

sto gau- dent o- mnes   san-   cti! A- mi- cti sto- lis al-
rejoice   all   the saints! Vested   in stoles and

bis,   se- quun- tur A-   gnum quo- cúm- que   i-   e-   rit.
albs, they follow   the Lamb   wherever   He   goes.

(Then the Lamb appears suddenly, carrying a cross, and goes before
them, hither and yon, and they follow, singing:)

INNOCENTS (continuing)

E- mit- te A- gnum, Do- mi- ne, Do- mi- na- tó- rem ter- rae,
Send forth   the Lamb, O Lord,   Ruler   of the earth,

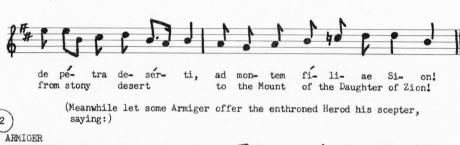

de pé- tra de- sér- ti,   ad mon- tem fí- li- ae Si- on!
from stony   desert   to the Mount of the Daughter of Zion!

(Meanwhile let some Armiger offer the enthroned Herod his scepter,
saying:)

ARMIGER

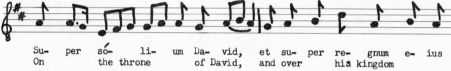

Su- per só- li- um Da- vid,   et su- per re- gnum e- ius
On   the throne   of David,   and over   his kingdom

se- dé- bit in ae- tér- num.   Al- le- lú- ia!
He will preside forever.   Alleluia!

(Meanwhile let the Archangel, appearing above the manger, warn Joseph
to flee into Egypt with Mary. The Archangel thrice calls "Joseph.")

ARCHANGEL   free rhythm

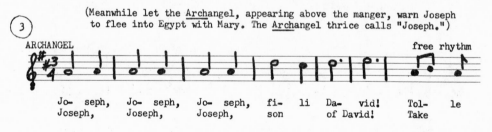

Jo- seph,   Jo- seph,   Jo- seph,   fi- li Da- vid!   Tol- le
Joseph,   Joseph,   Joseph,   son   of David!   Take

pú- e- rum et ma- trem e- ius,   et va- de in Ae-
the Boy   and his Mother,   and go   into Egypt,

gy- ptum, et e- sto i- bi us- que dum di- cam
and stay there until the time I tell

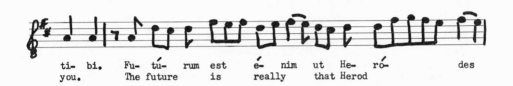

ti- bi. Fu- tú- rum est é- nim ut He- ró- des
you. The future is really that Herod

quae- rat pú- e- rum ad per- dén- dum é- um.
searches for the Boy to destroy Him.

(Not being seen by Herod, Joseph as he leaves, with Mary carrying
the Boy, says:)

④

JOSEPH

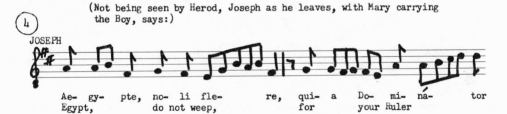

Ae- gy- pte, no- li fle- re, qui- a Do- mi- ná- tor
Egypt, do not weep, for your Ruler

tu- us ve- ni et ti- bi, an- te cu- ius
comes to you, before whose

con- spe-   ctum mo- ve- bun- tur a-   bys- si, Li- be-
face   shudders   the abyss (of Hell), comes to

rá- re pó- pu- lum su-   um de má- nu
liberate His people   from the hands

pot- én- ti-   um.   Ec- ce   Do- mi- ná- tor Do- mi- nus
of the powerful.   Behold,   the omnipotent   Lord

cum vir- tú- te   vé- ni-   et!
with His strength   comes!

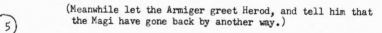

(Meanwhile let the Armiger greet Herod, and tell him that
the Magi have gone back by another way.)

ARMIGER

Rex,   in ae- ter- num vi-   ve! De- lú- sus   es,
O King,   forever   live!   Deluded   you are,

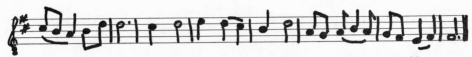

Do- mi- ne! Ma- gi vi- am re- di- e- runt a- li- am.
my lord! The Magi by another road have gone home.

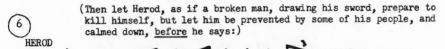

(Then let Herod, as if a broken man, drawing his sword, prepare to
kill himself, but let him be prevented by some of his people, and
calmed down, <u>before</u> he says:)

6 HEROD

In- cen- di- um me- um ru- i- na re- stin- guam!
My flaming rage only my death can put out!

(Meanwhile let the Innocents, still in a line behind the Lamb, sing:)

7 INNOCENTS

A- gno sa- cra- to pro no- bis mor- ti- fi- ca- to Splen-
To the Lamb so holy, for us slaughtered, the

do- rem Pa- tris splen- do- rem vir- gi- ni- ta- tis Of-
splendor of the Father, the splendor of virginity, we

fe- ri- mus Chri- sto sub si- gno lu- mi- nis i- sto.
offer to Christ under this banner of light.

Mul- tis i- ra mo- dis ut quos in- qui- rit He- ro- dis
In many ways the wrath of Herod that has sought us,

A- gno sal- ve- mur cum Chri- sto con- mo- ri- e- mur.
by the Lamb we'll be saved from, in Christ we'll die.

⑧

ARMIGER (prompting Herod)

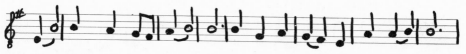

Di- scer- ne, Do- mi- ne, vin- di- ca- re i- ram tu- am,
Decide, my lord, whether to show your wrath,

Et stri- cto mu- cro- ne iu- be oc- ci- di pu- e- ros.
or by the strict sword's point to order the slaughter of these boys.

For- te in- ter oc- ci- sos oc- ci- de- tur et Chri- stus.
Perchance among the slaughtered may be killed the Christ.

HEROD (bestowing on the Armiger a <u>two-edged</u> sword)

Ar- mi- ger, ex- i- mi-   e! Pu- e- ros fac en- se pe- ri-   re.
Armiger   most excellent!   Do you the boys make thus to perish.

(Meanwhile, as the killers are approaching, the Lamb leaves,
while the Innocents hail him:)

INNOCENTS

Sal- ve, A- gnus De- i! Sal- ve, qui tol- lit pec- ca- ta
Hail,   Lamb   of God! Hail, you who take away   the sins

mun- di! Al- le-   lu- ia!
of the world! Alleluia!

(Then let the Mothers of the victims beg the killers:)

MOTHERS

O- re- mus, te- ne- re na- to- rum par- ci- te vi-   tae.
We pray that   the tender lives of our children you spare.

(After this, <u>and</u> when the Innocents have fallen dead, let the
Archangel from on high admonish them:)

ARCHANGEL

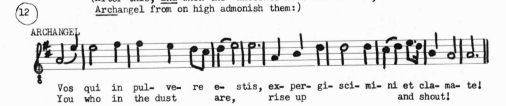

Vos qui in pul- ve- re e- stis, ex- per- gi- sci- mi- ni et cla- ma- te!
You who in the dust   are,   rise up   and shout!

(13) INNOCENTS (still fallen)

Quae- re non de- fen- dis san- gui- nem no- strum,
Why did you not defend our blood,

De- us no- ster?
God of ours?

(14) ARCHANGEL

free rhythm

Ad- huc su- sti- né- te mo- di- cum tem- pus, do- nec
Here stay for a little while, until

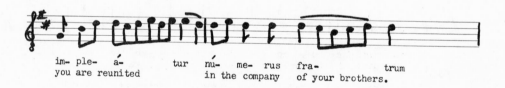

im- ple- á- tur nú- me- rus fra- trum
you are reunited in the company of your brothers.

ve- stró- rum.

(Then let Rachel and two [three] Mother-Consolers come in, and
standing over the Innocents, let her [Rachel], sometimes faint, lament:)

(15)

RACHEL

He- u, te- ne- ri par- tus, la- ce- ros quos cer- ni-mus
Alas, tender babes, in you such wounds we see!

ar- tus! He- u, dul- ces na- ti, so- la ra- bi- e
Alas, sweet children, by an act of madness

iu- gu- la- ti! He- u, quem nec pi- e- tas nec ve- stra co-
your throats slit! Alas, that neither your piety nor your

er- cu- it ae- tas! He- u, ma- tres mi- se- re, quae
age could prevent it! Alas, mothers miserable, that

co- gi- mur i- sta vi- de- re! He- u, quid nunc a- gi- mus?
we have had this to see! Alas, what now shall we do?

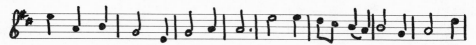

Cur non haec fac- ta su- bi- mus? He- u, qui- a me- mo- res no-
How can we bear this reality?   Alas, these recollections of

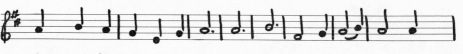

stros- que le- va- re do- lo- res! Gau- di- a non pos- sunt,
ours   only stir   our grief!   Joys   are not possible,

nam dul- ci- a pi- gno- ra de- sunt.
now that our dear   sweet ones   are gone.

(16)

MOTHERS (supporting her as she faints)

No- li, vir- go Ra-   chel, no- li, dul- cis- si- ma
Do not, pure   Rachel,   do not, dearest

ma- ter, Pro ne- ce par- vo- rum fle- tus re- ti- ne- re do-
mother, for   the killing of the children your tears of woe stop,

lo- rum, Si quae tri- sta- ris e- xul- ta quae la- cri-
but as you bewail exult in your tears,

ma- ris, Nam- que tu- i na- ti vi- vunt su- per
because your children live above

a- stra be- a- ti.
the stars, and are blessed.

(17)

RACHEL (rallying in response to them)

He- u, he- u, he- u! Quo- mo- do gau- de- bo dum mor- tu- a
Alas, alas, alas! How can I rejoice when these dead

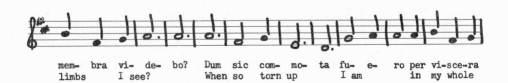

mem- bra vi- de- bo? Dum sic com- mo- ta fu- e- ro per vi-sce-ra
limbs I see? When so torn up I am in my whole

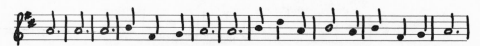

to- ta? Me fa- ci- ent ve- re   e- ri si- ne fi- ne do- lo-
body?   For me, in truth, they create, these boys, without end   grief.

re.   O   do- lor! O   pa-
      O   sorrow! O

trum mu- ta- ta- que   gau-   di- a ma-   trum Ad lu- gu- bres
how changed   is the joy   of the parents to sad

lu- ctus! La- cri- ma-   rum fun- di- te fle- tus, Iu- dae- ae
lamenting! Of tears   in floods   pour out, Juda's

flo- rem, pa- tri- ae la- cri- man- do do- lo- rem.
flower,   the country's sorrow, bewailing.

RACHEL

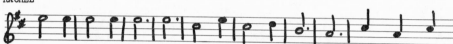

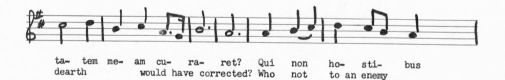

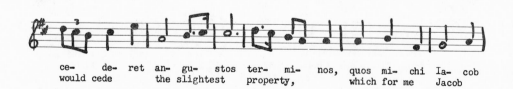

ad- qui- si- vit?   Qui-   que   sto-   li-   dis   fra- tri-   bus.
had accumulated?   And to the   **stolid**   brethren

quos   mul-   tos   pro   do-   lor   ex- tu-   li,   es-   set
what   cause   for   grief   were he borne to the grave

pro-   fu-   tu-   rus?
anytime?

(Then the Mothers, raising up the Innocents, say:)

25

MOTHERS

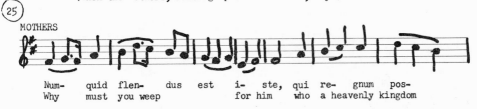

Num-   quid flen-   dus   est   i-   ste,   qui re-   gnum   pos-
Why   must you weep   for him   who   a heavenly kingdom

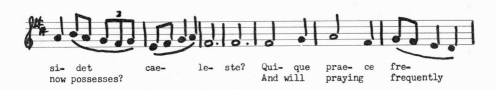

si-   det   cae-   le- ste?   Qui- que   prae-   ce   fre-
now possesses?   And will   praying   frequently

quen- ti mi- se- ris fra- tri- bus a- pud De- um
by the grieving brethren,   with   God

au- xi- li- e- tur?
be of any help?

(26)

RACHEL (staggering toward the Innocents)   free rhythm

An- xi- a- tus est in me spi- ri- tus me- us. In me
Anxious   is in me my spirit.   In me

tur- ba- tum est cor me- um.
turbulent   is   the heart of me.

(27)   (Then let the Mother-Consolers lead Rachel off, and let the
         Archangel meanwhile from above sing this antiphon:)

ARCHANGEL

Si- ni- te par- vu- los ve- ni- re ad me, ta- li- um est
Suffer   little children to come   unto me, for such   is

e- nim re- gnum cae- lo- rum.
in fact the kingdom of heaven.

(At the voice of the Archangel let the Innocents, rising up,
enter the choir area, singing:)

(28)

INNOCENTS

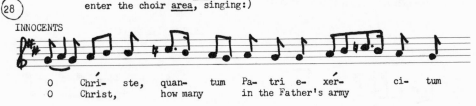

O Chri- ste, quan- tum Pa- tri e- xer- ci- tum
O Christ, how many in the Father's army

iu- ve- nis do- ctus ad bel- la ma- xi- ma! Po-
of youth learned in battles the most! To the

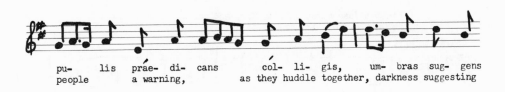

pu- lis prae- di- cans col- li- gis, um- bras sug- gens
people a warning, as they huddle together, darkness suggesting

cum tan- tum mi- se- ris.
by so much misery.

(While this was being performed, let Herod die and his son Archelaus
be put on the throne and be exalted as king. Meanwhile let the Archangel order Joseph in Egypt, where he had earlier gone, saying:)

(29)

ARCHANGEL   free rhythm

Jo- seph, Jo- seph, Jo- seph, fi- li Da- vid. Re- ver- te- re
Joseph,   Joseph,   Joseph,   son of David!   Go back

(Joseph appears.)

in ter-   ram Iu- dam. De- fun- cti sunt e-
to the land   of Juda.   Dead   are those in

nim qui quae- re-   bant a- ni- mam pu- e- ri.
fact who sought   the life   of the Boy.

(30)   (Then let Joseph return with Mary and the Boy, and going to
        the Galilee set, let him say:)

JOSEPH (to Mary)

Gau- de, gau-   de, gau- de, Ma- ri- a Vir-   go!
Rejoice, rejoice,   rejoice,   Mary   the Virgin!

JOSEPH (as Cantor)   free rhythm

Te De- um lau- da- mus;   Te Do- mi- num con- fi- te- mur...
You God   we praise;   you the Lord   we acknowledge...

(And so it ends.)

(The complete "Te Deum" begins on p. 491.)

6. The Procession
of the Prophets

The Procession of the Prophets

THE ELEVENTH-CENTURY LIMOGES version is here transcribed from Bibliothèque Nationale MS Latin 1139, fols. 55^v-58^r, a manuscript that is verbally and musically superior to the other extant versions, while lacking stage directions and the opening processional item of the others. Rubrics from the Laon and Rouen versions clarify the production requirements, which are interpreted in *Production,* pp. 143-49 and 317-19. An eleventh-century version from Einsiedeln uniquely supplies music for the processional hymn, *Gloriosi et famosi* (Stiftsbibliothek MS 366, p. 54). Inasmuch as the verbal text of the Limoges version is close to that of other versions and is identical in the first speech of the Presentor, there is reason for positing the use of the *Gloriosi* at Limoges. If more stanzas are required for the processional, nine additional stanzas from Einsiedeln are in Young, II, 458-60.

At the end of the playscript occurs its only stage direction: "Hic incoant Benedicamus" (Here let them begin the Benedicamus). Thereafter is written out, words and music, a handsome *Benedicamus* in three stanzas. My assumption, not completely shared by Young (II, 144), is that this piece is the recessional for *The Prophets* and that therefore its first stanza should be included in the transcript of the play. The second and third stanzas are musically more florid, but their words (from Young, II, 456-57) can be fitted to the melody of the first stanza. Another *Benedicamus,* printed at the end of the present edition of the Rouen *Shepherds,* may be considered as an alternate if more length is needed, though it has no direct connection with the *Prophets* play.

Another possibility for expansion of the Limoges playscript is that while the Augustinian sermon on which the play versions are based gives twenty-seven hexameter lines to Sybil, the Limoges text uses only three of these. The Sybil role, a colorful one, can therefore be extended ad lib, the melody being capable of repetition. This tune, incidentally, is closely related to that of the Saintes version (Bibliothèque Nationale MS Latin 16309, fol. 41^r).

As noted in *Production,* pp. 147 and 149, Habakkuk is traditionally a comic character. Not there remarked is the pun in his first line: "expectavi . . . expavi."

The Limoges manuscript lacks music for the two items concerning Simeon, Nos. 16 and 17, though space was provided for the musical scribe to write it in above the words. Since these items were intended by the playwright and we have his verbal text, which cannot be performed without its melodies, I have ventured to invent these settings out of melodic material from the same playscript. They are enclosed in brackets to make clear that they are optional and not authentic.

The Cast

Presentor (Augustine?)
Israel
Moses
Isaiah
Jeremiah
Daniel
Habakkuk
David
Simeon
Elizabeth
John the Baptist
Virgil
Nebuchadnezzar
Sybil

The Scene: A witness stand. The Christmas season.

The Procession of the Prophets   *Ordo Prophetarum*

1a

CHOIR (at beginning of procession and after each stanza)

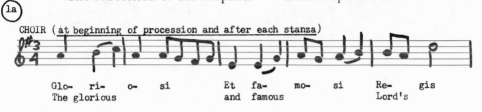

Glo- ri- o- si   Et fa- mo- si   Re- gis
The glorious   and famous   Lord's

fe- stum   Ce- le- bra-   mus.   Gau- de- a-   mus.
feastday   let us celebrate.   Let us rejoice!

1b

PROPHETS (in procession)

1. Cu- ius or- tum,   Vi- tae por- tum   No- bis
   Whose   birth,   as life's portal,   to us

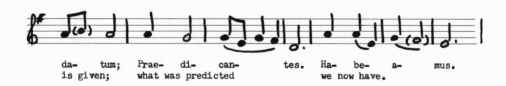

da- tum;   Prae- di- can-   tes.   Ha- be- a-   mus.
is given;   what was predicted   we now have.

2. Ec- ce,   re- gem   No- vam   le- gem   Dan- tem
   Behold,   that the king   will new   law   give

or- bis Cir- cu- i- tu, Prae- di- ca- mus.
to the universe around, we predict.

3. Quem fu- tu- rum re- gna- tu- rum pro- phe-
What future kingdom was prophesied

ti- co Am- mo- ni- tu Nun- ci- a- mus.
with joy we now announce.

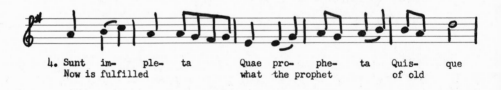

4. Sunt im- ple- ta Quae pro- phe- ta Quis- que
Now is fulfilled what the prophet of old

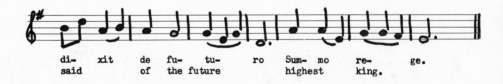

di- xit de fu- tu- ro Sum- mo re- ge.
said of the future highest king.

O- mnes gen- tes, Con- gau- den- tes Dent can- tum Lae-
All you people, rejoicing together, let be given a song of

ti- ti- ae. De- us ho- mo Fit de do- mo Da- vid
joy. God as man, sprung from the house of David,

na- tus ho- di- e! O Iu- dae- i, Ver- bum De- i
is born today! O Jews, the Word of God

(Gesturing somewhere offstage)

Qui ne- ga- tis ho- mi- nem, Ve- strae le- gis,
which you denied mankind, your true law,

Te- stem re- gis, Au- di- te per or- di- nem.
your lordly rule, now hear as it should be.

Et vos gen- tes,   Non cre- den-   tes   Pe- pe- ris- se
And your people,   not believing   the power of

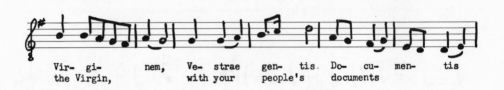

Vir- gi-   nem,   Ve- strae   gen- tis. Do- cu- men-   tis
the Virgin,   with your   people's   documents

Pel- li-   te ca- li- gi-   nem. Is- ra-   el,   vir
you spread   gloom.   Israel,   man

(To Israel)

le- nis   in- que De Chri-   sto   no-   sti
of leniency,   tell   about the Christ   what you know

fir-   me.
for sure.

③ ISRAEL

Dux de Iu- da non tol- le- tur Do- nec ad- sit
The leader of Juda was not exalted until He arrived

qui mit- te- tur Sa- lu- ta- re De- i Ver- bum
who was sent. To greet God's Word

Ex- spec- ta- bunt gen- tes me- cum.
were expecting people along with me.

④ PRESENTOR (to Moses)

Le- gis- la- tor huc pro- pin- qua, Et de Chri- sto
Legislator, come near, and of Christ's

pro- me di- gna.
merit tell.

⑤ MOSES

Da- bit De- us vo- bis va-   tem. Hu- ic ut
God gave   to you   a prophet.   To him as to

mi- hi   au- rem da-   te Qui non au-   dit hunc au-di-
me   give ear.   Who does not listen   to this

en-   tem Ex- pel- li- tur   su- a   gen-   te.
hearing   is to be expelled from   his   tribe.

⑥ PRESENTOR (to Isaiah)

I- sa- y- as, ve- rum qui   scis, Ve- ri- ta- tem
Isaiah,   you who know the truth,   the truth

cur non di-   cis?
why do you not say?

(7)

ISAIAH

Est ne- ces- se   Vir- gam   Ies-   se
It is necessary   for the rod   of Jesse

De ra- di- ce pro- ve-   hi. Flos de- in- de
from the roots   to prove it.   The flower of it

Sur- get   in- de   Qui est spi- ri- tus De-   i.
budded   there   which is   the spirit   of God.

(8)

PRESENTOR (beckoning)

Hoc ac- ce- de, Ie- re- mi-   as. Dic de Chri- sto
Approach,   O Jeremiah.   Tell us of Christ

pro- phe- ti-   as.
your prophecy.

(9)

JEREMIAH

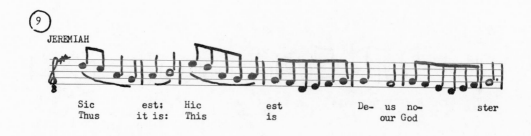

Sic   est: Hic   est   De- us no-   ster
Thus   it is: This   is   our God

Si-   ne   quo   non e- rit al-   ter.
without   whom   there could not be other.

(10)

PRESENTOR (<u>calling</u>)

Da-   ni- el, in-   di   ca Vo- ce pro- phe-
Daniel,   indicate   orally   your

ti- ca Fa- cta Do- mi- ni- ca.
prophecy concerning the Lord.

(11)

DANIEL

San- ctus San- cto- rum   ve- ni-   et, Et un- cti- o de- fi-ci-et.
The Holy of Holies   comes,   and unction   is lacking.

(12)

PRESENTOR (<u>calling</u>)

A- ba- cuc, re- gis cae- le- stis Nunc o- sten- de
Habakkuk, about the King of Glory now show

quod sis te- stis.
what you can witness.

(13)

HABAKKUK

Et ex- pec- ta- vi, Mox ex- pa- vi Me- tu mi- ra-
And I waited for, and suddenly was terrified and astounded by the

bi- li- um, O- pus tu- um In- ter du- um Cor- pus
marvel: Your birth between the bodies of two

a- ni- ma- li- um.
animals.

PRESENTOR (beckoning)

Dic tu, Da- vid, de ne- po- te Cau- sas
Speak, David, about your descendant what point of view

que sunt ti- bi no- te.
you take.

DAVID

U- ni- ver- sus Grex con- ver- sus A- do- ra- bit
The universal company of the faithful will adore

Do- mi- num, Cu- i fu- tu- rum Ser- vi- tu- rum
the Lord, who is the future servant

O- mne ge- nus ho- mi- num. Di- xit Do- mi- nus,
of all kinds of men. Said the Lord

Do- mi- no me- o, "Se- de a dex- tris me- is."
my God, "Sit at my right hand."

16

PRESENTOR

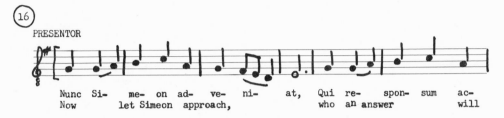

Nunc Si- me- on ad- ve- ni- at, Qui re- spon- sum ac-
Now let Simeon approach, who an answer will

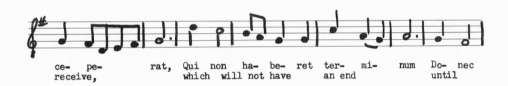

ce- pe- rat, Qui non ha- be- ret ter- mi- num Do- nec
receive, which will not have an end until

vi- de- ret Do- mi- num.
he sees the Lord.

17

SIMEON

Nunc me di- mit- tas, Do- mi- ne, Fi- ni- re vi- tam in
Now let me depart, O Lord, to finish my life in

pa- ce. Qui- a me- i mo- do   cer- nunt   o- cu- li
peace.   For my eyes   have seen

Quem mi- si- sti Hunc mun- dum pro sa- lu- te po- pu- li.
whom   you have sent into this world for the salvation of all people.

(18)

PRESENTOR

Il- lud, He- li- sa- bet, in me- di- um De Do- mi- no
Here,   Elizabeth,   in public   about the Lord

pro-   fer e- lo- qui- um.
profer   some   expression.

(19)

ELIZABETH

Quid est re- i Quod me me-   i Ma- ter he- ri
Whence is this thing, that to me   the mother lately

vi- si- tat? Nam ex e- o Ven- tre me- o Lae- tus
should come? For at that moment in my womb for joy

in- fans pal- pi- tat.
the baby leaped.

(20)

PRESENTOR

Dic, Bab- ti- sta, Ven- tris ci- sta Clau- sus
Say, O Baptist, inside your closed book (Gospels)

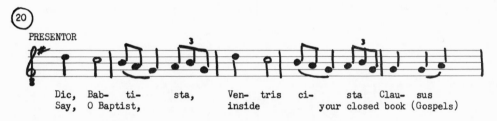

Qua de- di- sti Cau- sa Chri- sto Plau- sus? Cu- i de-
what you gave to the cause of Christ most plausibly? He to whom

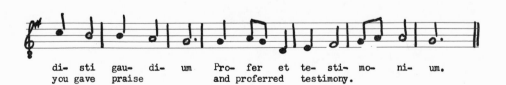

di- sti gau- di- um Pro- fer et te- sti- mo- ni- um.
you gave praise and proferred testimony.

JOHN THE BAPTIST

Ve- nit ta- lis   So- tu- la-   ris Cu- ius non sum
He comes as such   a savior   that I am not

e- ti- am Tam be- ni- gnus   Ut sim au-   sus
even   so worthy   or could be so brash

Sol- ve- re   cor- ri- gi- am.
as to loosen   his shoe-latchet.

PRESENTOR

Va- tes, Ma- ro gen- ti- li- um, Da Chri- sto te-   sti-
Tell us,   gentle Maro.   Give us about Christ your

mo- ni- um.
testimony.

(23)

VIRGIL

Ec- ce po- lo De- mis- sa so- lo No- va pro-
Lo, by heaven sent from what a lineage

ge- ni- es est.
He is.

(24)

PRESENTOR (to Nebuchadnezzar)

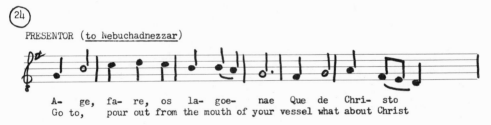

A- ge, fa- re, os la- goe- nae Que de Chri- sto
Go to, pour out from the mouth of your vessel what about Christ

no- sti ve- re, Na- bu- co- do- no- sor, pro- phe- ti- za,
you know to be true, Nebuchadnezzar, prophet,

Au- cto- rem o- mni- um au- cto- ri- za.
authority above all authorities.

25 NEBUCHADNEZZAR

Cum re- vi- si   Tres quos mi- si   Vi- ros in in-
When I looked again at those three men whom I sent   into the

cen- di- um,   Vi- di iu-   stis   In- con-   bu-   stis Mix-tum
fiery furnace, I saw   completely   unburned   one very like

De- i   fi- li- um.   Vi- ros   tres   in i- gnem   mi- si,
God's   Son.   Three   men   into the fire   I sent,

Quar- tum cer- no   pro- lem De-   i.
and the fourth I saw   was like the Son of God.

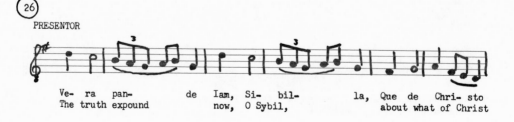

26 PRESENTOR

Ve- ra pan-   de Iam, Si- bil-   la, Que de Chri- sto
The truth expound   now, O Sybil,   about what of Christ

prae- scis si- gna.
did you foresee the sign.

(27)

SYBIL

Iu- di- ci- i si- gnum: Tel- lus su- do- re ma- de- scet.
This was the sign: The earth in sweat was drenched.

E coe- lo rex ad- ve- ni- et per sae- cla fu- tu- rus Sci-
From heaven a king came forth for centuries of future, as it

li- cet in car- ne prae- sens ut iu- di- cet or- bem.
were in the flesh present so that He might judge the earth.

(28)

PRESENTOR (gesturing somewhere offstage)

Iu- de- a in- cre- du- la, Cur ma- nens ad- huc in- ve- re- cun-da?
O Judea incredulous, why do you remain still so shameful?

(Here let them begin the "Benedicamus.")

Lae- ta- bun- di   iu- bi-   le-   mus. Ac- cu- ra- te
With joy   let us be jubilant.   Carefully

ce- le- bre- mus Chri- sti na- ta- li-   ti- a, Sum- ma lae-
let us celebrate Christ's birthday,   the height of

ti- ti- a Cum gra- ti- a.
gladness,   with thanks.

7. The Raising of Lazarus

The Raising of Lazarus

THE ONLY VERSION of the *Lazarus* with musical notation and thus produceable is from the Fleury Playbook (Orléans, Bibliothèque de la Ville MS 201, pp. 233-43), a twelfth-century manuscript. For suggestions as to production and interpretation, see *Production*, pp. 151-69 and 320-23.

In modern *mensural* notation in the *Antiphonale Romanum*, no less, pp. 167*-70*, is a piece entitled *O Filii*. If we assume that there the "O filii" stanza is the refrain, the first stanza would begin "Et mane prima sabbati," which is all the reference the *Lazarus* playscript gives for the opening, probably processional, item. The modern *Antiphonale* presents a normalized transcription, with variations in the melody suppressed and false verbal accentuations thereby created. Medieval practice was to achieve interesting rhythmic variations by adjusting the musical rhythm to verbal accentuations. Restoration of these variations, by eliminating the false accents, results in several alternative measures in the dozen stanzas of the piece. The most frequent variation is in the first two measures, in five stanzas of which is revealed not only the same rhythm as the first two measures of the *Lazarus* melody but also identical intervallics. This coincidence, hardly mere, suggests that the composer of the Fleury *Lazarus* used the musical *incipit* of this mensural liturgical piece as the lift-off for his own superlative composition.

Other medieval pieces with the "Mane prima sabbati" *incipit* but different melodic phrases are in Bibliothèque Nationale MS Latin 1435, fol. 17^v (Sainte-Chapelle), *Antiphonale Romanum*, p. 464, and Udine, Biblioteca Archevescovile MS F25, fols. 96^r-96^v. None of these has the length, rhythmic quality, or opening phrase to compete with the *O Filii* version as the opener for *Lazarus*.

In Item 9, measure 17, the manuscript has an unassignable neume. I have canceled it and also a literary extra in Item 17, where *Heu* is repeated without notation for the repeat. Young (II, 203) does not emend this line, no doubt because he could not take the musical setting into account.

In the second and third measures of Item 31, the notation is not properly aligned with the syllables. I have realigned them as I believe they were intended to be. Elsewhere the musical variants in the fifty stanzas are, I think, intentional, and are followed scrupulously.

The manuscript does not always differentiate the speeches of the two sisters, or those of the Pharisees, Disciples, and even Messengers if more than one. The original assignments are reproduced in Young, II, 200-207.

The Cast

Simon, a Pharisee
Second Pharisee
Third Pharisee
Jesus
Thomas, a Disciple
Peter, a Disciple
Mary Magdalene
Lazarus, her brother
Martha, his sister
Messenger(s)

The Scene: A street. Simon's house. The little house at Bethany. Galilee. Anytime before Easter.

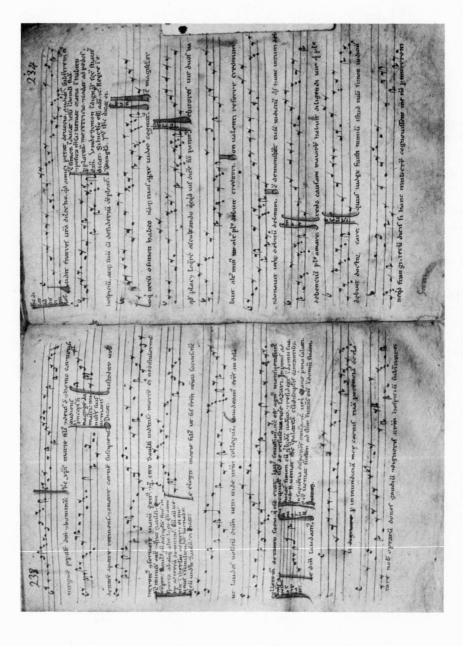

Two pages from the Fleury Playbook (Orléans, Bibliothèque de la Ville MS 201), showing the end of *The Conversion of St. Paul* and the beginning of *The Raising of Lazarus* (p. 233).

The Raising of Lazarus   *Resuscitatio Lazari*

(First let Simon and several Jews, Pharisees, come in, and let
him reside in his house. After this let Jesus come onto the
street with his Disciples, singing "In sapientia disponens
omnia" et cetera, or "Mane prima sabbati.")

1a

CHOIR (at beginning of procession and after each stanza)

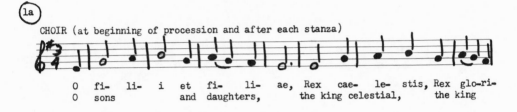

O fi- li- i et fi- li- ae, Rex cae- le- stis, Rex glo-ri-
O sons   and daughters,   the king celestial,   the king

ae, Mor- te sur- re- xit ho- di- e. Al- le- lu- ia!
of glory, from death has risen   today.   Alleluia!

1b

JESUS & DISCIPLES

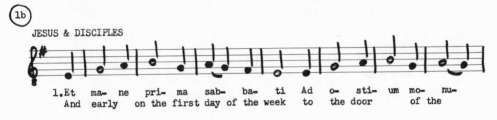

1.Et ma- ne pri- ma sab- ba- ti Ad o- sti- um mo- nu-
And early on the first day of the week to the door   of the

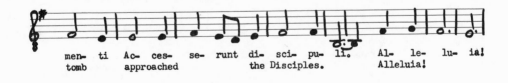

men- ti Ac- ces- se- runt di- sci- pu- li. Al- le- lu- ia!
tomb   approached   the Disciples.   Alleluia!

2. Et Ma- ri- a   Mag- da- le- na,   Et Ia-   co- bi et   Sa-
   And Mary   Magdalene   and Jacobi   and   Salome

lo- me Ve- ne- runt   cor-   pus un-   ge- re.   Al- le- lu- ia!
came   the body   to anoint.   Alleluia!

3. In   al- bis   se- dens An-   ge-   lus Prae-   di- xit mu- li- e- ri-
   In   an alb,   sitting,   the Angel   told   the women:

bus: "In Ga- li-   lae- a   est Do- mi-   nus.   Al- le-   lu- ia! "
     "In Galilee   is   the Lord.   Alleluia!"

4. Et Io-   han- nes A-   po-   sto-   lus Cu-   cur- rit   Pe- tro ci- ti-
   And John   the Apostle   ran   with Peter quickly;

us; Mo- nu- men- to   ve- nit pri- us.   Al- le-   lu-   ia!
to the tomb   he came first.   Alleluia!

5. Di- sci- pu- lis ad- stan- ti- bus, In me- di- o ste- tit
   The Disciples   standing around,   in the midst   stood

Chri- stus, Di- cens, "Pax vo- bis o- mni- bus." Al- le- lu- ia!

6. In hoc .fe- sto san- ctis- si- mo Sit laus et   iu- bi- la- ti-o.
   On this feastday   most holy   be   praise and jubilation.

Be- ne- di- ca- mus Do- mi-, no.   Al- le-   lu- ia!
Let us bless   the Lord.   Alleluia!

(And now let Simon and the Pharisees approach Jesus and

His Disciples, and invite them to his house, saying:)

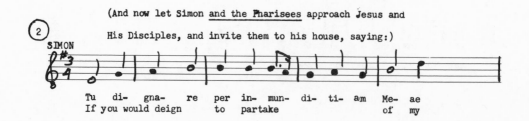

SIMON

Tu di- gna- re per in- mun- di- ti- am Me- ae
If you would deign   to partake   of my

car- nis tu- am pot- en- ti- am De- cla-   ra- re.
table   you would your power   declare.

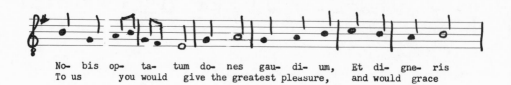

No- bis op- ta- tum do- nes gau- di- um, Et di- gne- ris
To us   you would give the greatest pleasure,   and would grace

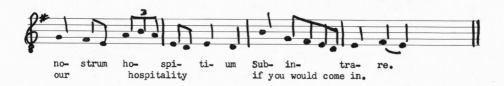

no- strum ho- spi- ti- um Sub in-   tra- re.
our   hospitality   if you would come in.

JESUS

Au- dit, fra- tres, ve- stra di- le- cti- o Quid a- mi- ci
Hear, brethren,   how your pleasure is   by devoted friends

pe- tat de- vo- ti- o. Au- di- a- tur. Sub- in- tre- mus
beseeched. Let this be listened to. Let us accept

ei- us ho- spi- ti- um, At- que su- um iam de- si- de- ri- um
his hospitality, and his invitation now

Com- ple- a- tur.
be responded to.

(Now Simon escorts Jesus into his house. When they are set at table, let
Mary Magdalene, in the dress of a whore, and bearing an alabaster pyx of
ointment, come across the street to Simon's house, and throw herself at
the feet of Jesus, and wash His feet with her tears, drying them with her
long red hair, and anointing His head with ointment. Let Simon, indignant
at her, snobbishly say, not sing:)

④ SIMON (outraged)

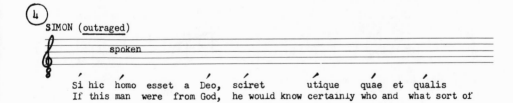

spoken

Si hic homo esset a Deo, sciret utique quae et qualis
If this man were from God, he would know certainly who and what sort of

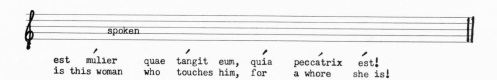

est mulier   quae tangit eum, quia   peccatrix est!
is this woman who touches him, for   a whore she is!

JESUS

Lo- qui te- cum, O Si- mon ha- be- o, Nam- que tu- os
Words   with you, O Simon, I'd have,   for your people

a- per- te vi- de- o   Co- gi- ta-   tus.
clearly   I see   are disturbed (about her).

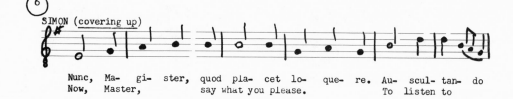

SIMON (covering up)

Nunc, Ma- gi- ster, quod pla- cet lo- que- re. Au- scul- tan- do
Now, Master,   say what you please.   To listen to

quic- quid vis di- ce- re   Sum pa-   ra-   tus.
whatever you wish to say   I am   ready.

(7) JESUS

De- bi- to- res vir du- os ha- bu- it. Al- ter mi- nus,
Debtors　　a certain man　two　　had.　　　One debt was less,

al- ter plus de- bu- it Cre- di- to- ri. Non va- len- ti
the other more.　　　　　　　　　　　　　They not being able

re- fer- re cre- di- tum, Con- do- na- vit u- tri- que
to repay　　the creditor,　he forgave

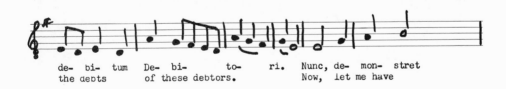

de- bi- tum De- bi- to- ri. Nunc, de- mon- stret
the debts　　of these debtors.　Now, let me have

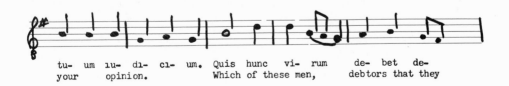

tu- um iu- di- ci- um. Quis hunc vi- rum de- bet de-
your　opinion.　　Which of these men,　debtors that they

ben- ti- um   Plus a-   ma-   re?
were,   more loved him?

8

SIMON

Cre- do cau- sam ma- io- rem ha- bu- it Di- li- gen- di
I suppose that the one who owed more   had   more   cause to

vir qui plus de- bu- it, Do- ctor   ca-   re.
love him,   my dear Doctor.

9

JESUS

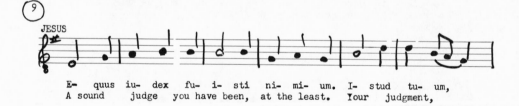

E- quus iu- dex fu- i- sti ni- mi- um. I- stud tu- um,
A sound   judge you have been, at the least. Your judgment,

Si- mon, iu- di- ci- um   Ne- quit   fran- gi. Te- cum
Simon,   cannot be overruled.   To yourself

di- cis si hanc mu- li- e- rem Cog- no- vis- sem,
you say that if this woman I should recognize,

me non per- mit- te- rem Ab hac tan- gi.
I should not have let her touch me.

Ho- spes me- us, in hoc ho- spi- ti- o, Pe- des ac- qua vel
As my host, with all your fine manners, my feet with water or

ca- pud o- le- o Non suf- fu- dit. Pe- des me- os ri-
my head with oil you did not anoint. My feet she

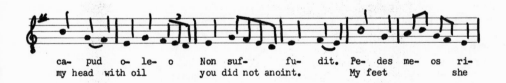

ga- vit la- cri- mis, Ca- put me- um un- guen- tis op- ti- mis
has washed with tears, my head with ointment of the best

Haec per- fu- dit.   Di- le- xi- sti
this(woman)has anointed.   You have pleased me

(To Mary Magdalene)

mul- tum, O fe- mi- na! Tu- i fle- tus tu- a pec-
much,   O womanly one! By your tears   you have

ca- mi- na Di- lu- e- runt. Il- lud e- nim o- ris con-
your sins   washed away.   Verily the words of your

fes- si- o At- que il- la cor- dis com- pun- cti- o
mouth   and   your heart's   compunction

Me- ru- e- runt.
make you respectable.

(After this action, let Mary Magdalene rise and remain. Then let Jesus and the Disciples leave the house, and go out across the street as if to Galilee, where outside the playing area let there have been prepared a place for them to wait. After that, let the Jews [Pharisees and Simon] retire to some other place, as if to Jerusalem, so that there may come to be an adequate place [Bethany] for the two sisters later to be consoled. In fact, let what was the house of Simon, he being now offstage, be transformed to the sisters' house at Bethany, and then let Martha enter. Let Lazarus now begin to be sick, and say thus to Martha:)

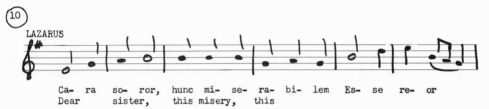

LAZARUS

Ca- ra so- ror, hunc mi- se- ra- bi- lem Es- se re- or
Dear   sister,   this misery,   this

in- me- di- ca- bi- lem Mor- bum   fra- tris.   Ut ger-
incurable disease   will be the death of your brother. If to your

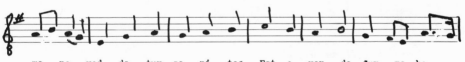

ma- no red- da- tur sa- ni- tas Est o- ran- da sum- ma be-
brother is to be restored health,   prayers must be offered for the

ni- gni- tas No- stri   Pa-   tris. (Mary Magdalene enters.)
blessing   of our   Father.

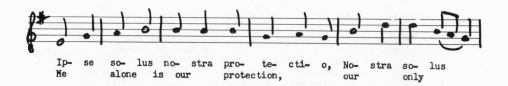

Ip- se so- lus no- stra pro- te- cti- o, No- stra so- lus
He   alone is our   protection,   our   only

est con- so- la- ti- o, Sed nunc ab- est. Ab- est
consolation.   But now He is missing. He is not

qui- dem, sed cor- po- ra- li- ter, Qui u- bi- que pot- en- ti-
here,   bodily,   Though He is potentially able

a- li- ter Prae- sens   ad-   est. (Lazarus is helped to his cot.)
everywhere to be present.

(A Messenger[s] crosses the street in front of the Bethany set.)

(11)

MAGDALENE

Trans- mit- ta- mus e- i iam nun- ci- um Et ro- ge- mus
Let us send   to Him   now a messenger,   and let us implore

ei- us aux- i- li- um, Et da- bi- tur. Si re- sci- scat
Mis help, and it will be given. If He revives

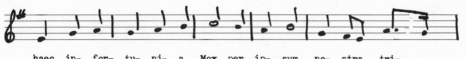

haec in- for- tu- ni- a, Mox per ip- sum no- stra tri-
this unfortunate one, Fast through Him our grief

sti- ti- a Se- da- bi- tur.
will be relieved.

12 MARTHA

Quam- vis e- um nil pror- sus la- te- at, No- strum ta- men
However much He may be hiding, our messenger still

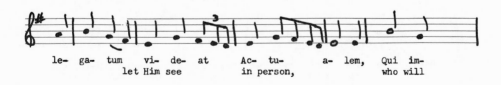

le- ga- tum vi- de- at Ac- tu- a- lem, Qui im-
let Him see in person, who will

plo- ret   ei- us cle- men- ci- am. No- bis su- am
implore   His   mercy.   To us

mon- stret prae- sen- ti- am Cor- po-   ra-   lem.
let Him show His presence   in person.

MARY MAGDALENE

Hinc ad Ie- sum, le- ga- ti,   per- gi- te, Et prae- sen- ti
To   Jesus, O Messenger,   run,   and by these presents

(The sisters give rings to
the Messenger[s].)

prae-sen-tes di-ci-te Hoc man- da- tum: "Nos ro- ga- mus ut nos ex-
tell Him this message: "We pray that you will understand

au- di- at, Et ger- ma- num sa- na- re   ve- ni- at
us,   that our brother may by you be restored to health,

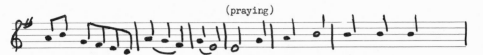

In-   fir-   ma-   tum." Per vos no- scat quan- ta   tri-
he now being very sick."   Through you is known how much

sti- ti- a Sit re- ple- ta   su- a fa- mi- li- a
sadness   is   a part of   one's human destiny,

Pa- ter   bo- nus, Ut vir- tu- te su- ae pot- en- ti- ae
good Father (God),   So that only by virtue of his power

Iam re-   ce- dat Tan- tae tri- sti- ti- ae Tan- tum   o-   nus.
can now be taken   from so much sadness   so great   a burden.

(Jesus and His Disciples enter the street from the opposite side. The
Messenger [s] runs to meet Jesus.)

A- ve, Ie- su, re- dem- ptor o- mni- um! Ad te quod- dam
Hail, Jesu, savior of all! To you a certain

por- ta- mus nun- ci- um Et hoc au- di. A- nu- la- rum
message we bring, and you must hear it. These sad rings

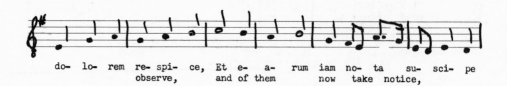

do- lo- rem re- spi- ce, Et e- a- rum iam no- ta su- sci- pe
observe, and of them now take notice,

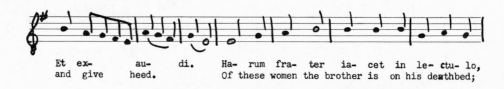

Et ex- au- di. Ha- rum fra- ter ia- cet in le- ctu- lo,
and give heed. Of these women the brother is on his deathbed;

Ma- gno mor- bi con- stri- ctus vin- cu- lo, Sed so-
He against the disease struggles to survive, but he

lu- a- tur. Te prae- sen- tem e- is ex- hi- be- as, At- que
is weakening. You in person should to him appear, and

mor- bum a- bi- re iu- be- as. Hoc ro- ga- tur.
his sickness to go away you should order. This is prayed of you.

15 JESUS (to the Messenger)

I- bo, qui- dem, sed non- dum tem- pus est. Hic ne- qua-quam ad
I shall go, surely, but not yet is the time. This certainly is not

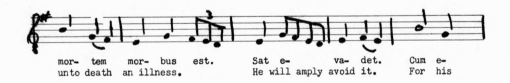

mor- tem mor- bus est. Sat e- va- det. Cum e-
unto death an illness. He will amply avoid it. For his

gro- to da- bo re- me- di- um, Ad- mi- ran- dus stu- por a-
sickness I shall give him a remedy; his admirable spirit against this

stan-   ci- um   Cor in-   va-   det.   (The Messenger leaves
stupor   will stand   up.   for Bethany. Jesus
                                              turns to the Disciples.)

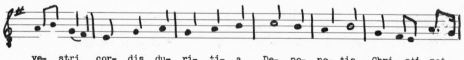

Quod sit e- ger pro- pter vos gau- de- o, Quos tam- di- u
To do this on account of you   I delight,   That for a time

es- se con- do- le- o   Non cre-   den- tes.   Iam- iam
I may comfort those   who do not believe.   At that moment

ve- stri cor- dis du- ri- ti- a   De- po- ne- tis, Chri- sti pot-
you will your hearts' hardness   cast off,   and Christ's

en-   ti- am Ad- mi-   ran-   tes.   (They leave. At Bethany the
power   admire.   Jews [Pharisees, including
                                                Simon] enter the street on
                                                their way to console Martha
                                                and Mary Magdalene in the
                                                Bethany house.)

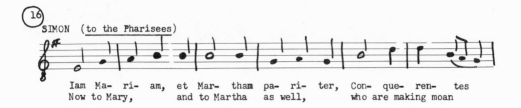

SIMON (to the Pharisees)

Iam Ma- ri- am, et Mar- tham pa- ri- ter, Con- que- ren- tes
Now to Mary, and to Martha as well, who are making moan

la- men- ta- bi- li- ter, A- de- a- mus, Et do- lo- ri
most pitiably, let us go, and for the

fra- trem me- ren- ti- um Iu- xta no- strum pos- se so-
brother's welfare to do what is possible for their

la- ci- um Con- fe- ra- mus.
solace let us try to contribute.

(Now the Jews[Pharisees] present themselves in the house where
Lazarus is dying, and Mary Magdalene and Martha say;)

MARY MAGDALENE

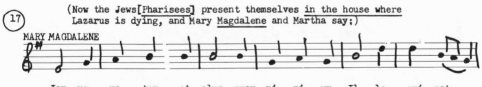

Iam mo- ra- tur, et plus quam ni- mi- um Il- le qui est
Now let death be delayed, as much as possible, for Him who is

so- lus re- fu- gi- um No- strae   spe- i. He- u!
the only refuge,   our only   hope. Alas!

Fru- stra hunc ex- pe- cta- vi- mus. Quod sa- ne- tur
to no purpose   have we hoped.   For how to be healed

non es- se   cer- ni- mus Vel- le   De-   i.
is   not   discernible   without   God.

(18.)

MARTHA

Ec- ce! No- ster ger- ma- nus mo- ri- tur! Iam fra- ter- num
See!   Our   brother   is dying!   Now our brother's

cor- pus dis- sol- vi- túr Le- ge   mor- tis. Mi- se-
body   is yielding   to the rule of death. This

ra- rum hic vi- cem ge- ri- mus; Cum tam gra- vem
miserable happening we bear; with you your

ex- ces- sum cer- ni- mus Di- re sor- tis.
sad fate perceive dreadfully as you leave (us).

(19)

MARY MAGDALENE (to Lazarus)

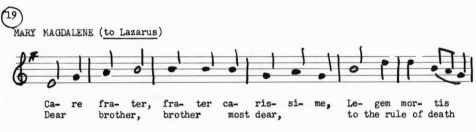

Ca- re fra- ter, fra- ter ca- ris- si- me, Le- gem mor- tis
Dear brother, brother most dear, to the rule of death

iam pas- sus pes- si- me Nos li- qui- sti.
now exposed totally, from us you are fading.

(20)

MARTHA

Pro- pter pri- mi pec- ca- tum ho- mi- nis Ge- ne- ra- lis
Because of the first man's sin, of all sins

tor- men- tum cri- mi- nis Iam sen- si-   sti.
the torment   now you feel.

(21)

SIMON (<u>to the sisters</u>, consoling them)

Non vos ster- nat hoc in- for- tu- ni- um! In- ter tan- tos
Don't be cast down by this misfortune!   In   the worst

ca- sus so- la- ci- um   Est ha-   ben- dum.   Hoc   de
of events some consolation   is to be had.   This

cau- sa vo- bis con- ge- mi-   mus: Sed de- fun- ctum
reasoning   on you let us urge: Yet dead

non es- se cre- di- mus, Sic de-   flen-   dum.
he is not to be thought,   so long as he is mourned.

SECOND PHARISEE

Mo- ri- e- mur et nos si- mi- li- ter. O- mnes gen- tes
Were we dying, we should be the same way. All people

a- dun- cat pa- ri- ter Mor- tis ha- mus. Ta- li
are caught equally on death's hook. by such

le- ge in- tra- mus sae- cu- lum, Ut quan- do- que
means we enter into eternity, and thus eventually

car- nis er- ga- stu- lum Ex- e- a- mus.
the flesh's prison we escape.

THIRD PHARISEE

Pro di- le- cti fra- tris in- te- ri- tu Ne plo- re- tis.
For your beloved brother's demise do not weep.

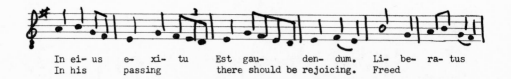

In ei- us   e- xi- tu   Est gau-   den- dum.   Li- be- ra- tus
In his   passing   there should be rejoicing. Freed

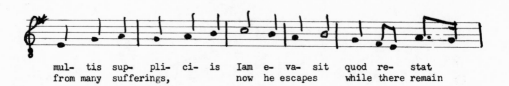

mul- tis sup- pli- ci- is   Iam e- va- sit   quod re-   stat
from many sufferings,   now he escapes   while there remain

a- li- is   Pa- ti-   en-   dum.
others of us still enduring.

MARY MAGDALENE (to Lazarus)

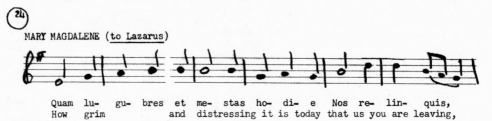

Quam lu- gu- bres et me- stas ho- di- e Nos re- lin- quis,
How grim   and distressing it is today that us you are leaving,

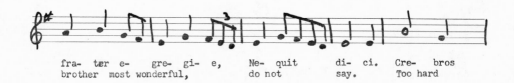

fra- ter e- gre- gi- e,   Ne- quit   di- ci. Cre- bros
brother most wonderful,   do not   say.   Too hard

in   nos   as- sul- tus fa- ci- ent; bo- na no-   stra
that on us would an assault make;   our good

no- bis   sub-   ri- pi- ent I- ni-   mi-   ci.
          would be overcome   by our enemy (death).

(25)

MARTHA

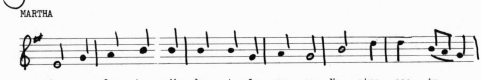

Ca- re   fra- ter, di- le- cte La- za- re, No- stro cae- tu
Dear brother,   beloved   Lazarus,   our relationship

iam fa- cto dis- pa- re   Te de-   fle- mus. Mor- ti que te
now being   altered,   you we mourn.   Death

no- bis sub- ri- pu- it, Nec nos te- cum mo- ri su-
from us snatches you,   and   with you by death

sti- nu- it, In- vi- de- mus.
taken,   we are jealous.

(26)

SIMON

Si iam con- tra as- sul- tus ho- sti- um No- bis fer- re
If now against   the assault of the enemy

de- si- stat cli- pe- um Ve- ster fra- ter, Non vos
no more defense   your brother makes,   he does not

lin- quit si- ne con- si- li- o: I- mo ve- stra fi- et pro-
leave you without advice: to wit, that your protection

te- cti- o Sum- mus Pa- ter.
comes only from the High Father (God).

SECOND PHARISEE

Sa- tis, sci- tis, sic De- o   pla- cu- it, Ip- se ve- strum
It's enough, you know, if to God it is pleasing,   Himself   your

ger- ma- num   vo- lu- it   Sic o-   bi- re.   Vo- lun-
brother   to wish   thus to take away.   By   the

ta- ti su- ae pot- en- ti- ae Pro- hi- be- tur no- strae mi-
will   of His power   are forbidden   our

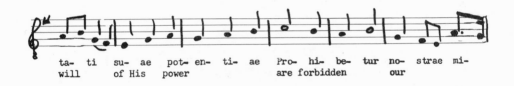

se- ri- ae Con- tra   i-   re.
griefs   from   going against (Him).

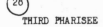

THIRD PHARISEE

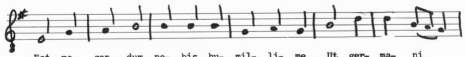

Est ro- gan- dum no- bis hu- mil- li- me, Ut ger- ma- ni
It is asked   of us   to be most humble, so that your brother's

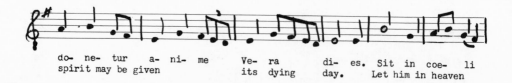

do- ne- tur a- ni- me   Ve- ra   di- es. Sit in coe- li
spirit may be given   its dying   day.   Let him in heaven

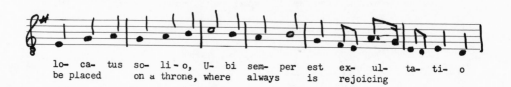

lo- ca- tus so- li- o, U- bi sem- per est ex- ul- ta- ti- o
be placed   on a throne, where always is rejoicing

At- que   qui-   es.
and   peace.

(The Pharisees carry Lazarus off on his cot, and are followed by Mary
Magdalene and Martha. The death-knell tolls, and recedes with the
procession. Then Jesus and the Disciples enter from the opposite side.)

(29)
JESUS (to the Disciples)

In Iu- de- am e- a- mus i- te- rum, Dor- mi- en- tem a
Into Judea   let us go   again,   and the sleeping

so- mpno La- za- rum Ex- ci- te- mus, Et so-
Lazarus from his stupor let us arouse, and his

ro- res e- ius do- lo- ri- bus Iam de- pres- sas
sisters sorrowing, now despairing

et mul- tis fle- ti- bus, Con- for- te- mus.
and very tearful, let us comfort.

(30)
THOMAS

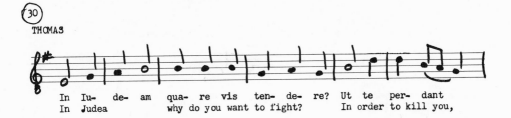

In Iu- de- am qua- re vis ten- de- re? Ut te per- dant
In Judea why do you want to fight? In order to kill you,

sat no- scis, quae- re- re Te Iu- de- os.
as you know, the Jews for you are hunting.

㉛ PETER

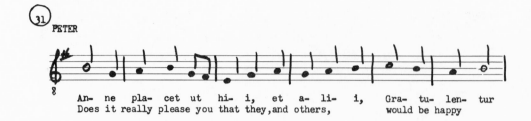

An- ne pla- cet ut hi- i, et a- li- i, Gra- tu- len- tur
Does it really please you that they,and others, would be happy

se ho- mi- ci- di- i Es- se re- os?
if we turned out to be homocides?

㉜ JESUS

Non est ve- strum me re- dar- gue- re. I- mo ve- strum
It is not for me to refute you. Neither do you

est ac- qui- e- sce- re Ver- bis me- is. Vir- tus
have to acquiesce with what I am saying. The power

De- i, que ad- huc te- gi- tur Per Iu- de- os,
of God, which until now has been hidden from the Jews,

ma- ni- fe- sta- bi- tur In Iu- de- os.
is to be manifested in Jewry.

33
THOMAS

In- se- qua- mur e- ius ve- sti- gi- a, Ad- im- ple- ri
Let us follow in His footsteps, so that we can follow

su- a con- si- li- a Per- mit- ta- mus.
His advice.

34
PETER

Fe- sti- ne- mus cum e- o per- ge- re In Iu- de- am,
Let us hurry with Him to rush over to Judea,

et i- bi vi- ve- re De- si- sta- mus.
and there from living let us desist.

(The Messenger sees Jesus approaching, and runs ahead to Bethany house, and says to Martha:)

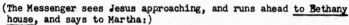

MESSENGER

Ec- ce! Ve- strum ad- ven- tat gau- di- um! Ec- ce! Ve- nit
Look! Your joy approaches! See! Here comes

sal- va- tor gen- ti- um Ex- pe- cta- tus! Iam- iam
the savior of mankind, the expected one! At once

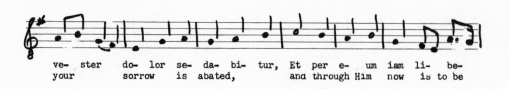

ve- ster do- lor se- da- bi- tur, Et per e- um iam li- be-
your sorrow is abated, and through Him now is to be

ra- bi- tur In- fir- ma- tus.
freed the deadened one.

MARTHA (running to Jesus and throwing herself at His feet)

Quem mors au- sa fu- it in- va- de- re, Si hic es- ses,
Though death the deed has done, if you are here,

nunc sci- rem vi- ve- re Fra- trem me- um. Tu- am
now I'll know that living is my brother.

e- nim vir- tu- tem no- sci- mus, Et te cor- de per- fe- cto
Truly your power we know, and, with heart entire,

cre- di- mus Es- se De- um. Sed et sci- mus
we believe you to be the Lord. But we also know that

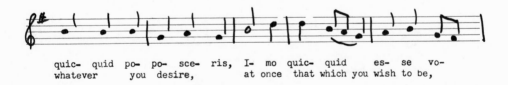

quic- quid po- po- sce- ris, I- mo quic- quid es- se vo-
whatever you desire, at once that which you wish to be,

lu- e- ris, Da- bit De- us. Si sic ve- lis
God will grant it. If this you wish

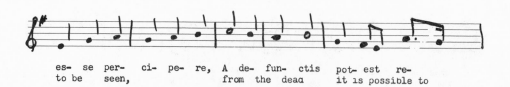

es- se per- ci- pe- re,   A de- fun- ctis   pot- est re-
to be   seen,   from the dead   it is possible to

sur-   ge- re Fra- ter   me-   us.
raise   my brother.

JESUS

Ne de- spe- res fra- trem re- sur- ge- re. Il- lum de- bes et
Do not despair of your brother being raised.   You owe him something, and

pot- es cre- de- re   sur re-   ctu- rum.   Nul- lum
you are able to believe that he may rise again.   Nothing

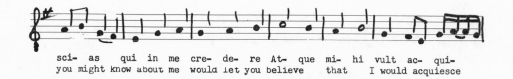

sci- as   qui in me cre- de- re At- que mi- hi vult ac- qui-
you might know about me would let you believe   that   I would acquiesce

e- sce- re Mo- ri- tu- rum.
in his death.

(38)

MARTHA

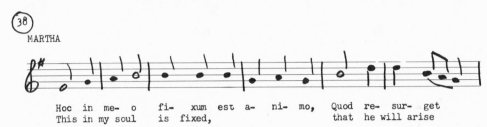

Hoc in me- o fi- xum est a- ni- mo, Quod re- sur- get
This in my soul is fixed, that he will arise

di- e no- vis- si- mo, Di- e il- la, Qua su- pre- mum
at the New Day, that day when the last

fi- et iu- di- ci- um, In qua ca- ro re- sur- get gen- ti- um
judgement is made, at which time will arise all men

Ex fa- vil- la.
from their dust.

E- go ve- stra sum re- sur- re- cti- o. Nul- la pot- est
I am your resurrection. It is not possible to

hos de- spe- ra- ti- o Sub- in- tra- re. Qui- bus
fall into depair. For anyone

cu- ra cum sum- mo stu- di- o Pa- tris me- i se- se ser-
into whose care with deepest concern my Father has sent me

vi- ci- o Pror- sus da- re. Va- de, vo- ca Ma- ri- am
to serve, as a matter of fact. Go, call Mary

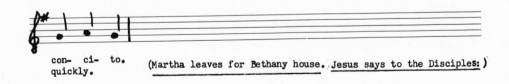

con- ci- to. (Martha leaves for Bethany house. Jesus says to the Disciples:)
quickly.

Ad se- pul- crum post me de- du- ci- to Tu- i
To the sepulcher I lead you to your

fra- tris. Fi- et e- nim ma- ni- fe- stis- si- ma Co- ram
brother. Let now be indeed made manifest

mul- tis vir- tus al- tis- si- ma Me- i Pa- tris.
the highest power of my Father.

(Martha arrives at her house, and whispers to Mary Magdalene:)

(40)

MARTHA

spoken

Ma- gi- ster te vo- cat!
The Master calls for you!

(Without a word Mary Magdalene leaves the house.)

(41)

SIMON (to Martha)

Sunt com- mo- ta Ma- ri- ae vi- sce- ra Cau- sa flen- di
So upset is Mary, because of her mourning,

pe- tit haec mi- se- ra Mo- nu- men- tum. Non de-
that her grief becomes monumental. We should not

be- mus il- lam per- mit- te- re Tan- to fle- tu, tan- tum in-
allow her so much grieving, so likely

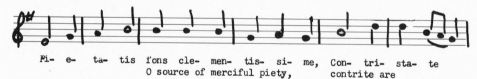

cur- re- re De- tri- men- tum. (All, including Martha,
it is to be harmful to her. follow after Mary Magd.)

(42)

MARY MAGDALENE (at Jesus' feet)

Pi- e- ta- tis fons cle- men- tis- si- me, Con- tri- sta- te
O source of merciful piety, contrite are

no- strae sunt a- ni- mae Fra- tris cau- sa. Te ab-
our souls for our brother's sake. You being

(She rises.)

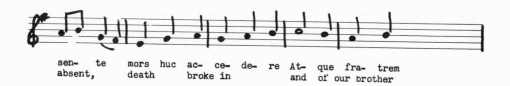

sen- te mors huc ac- ce- de- re At- que fra- trem
absent, death broke in and of our brother

no- strum o- bru- e- re Fu- it au- sa.
robbed us.

Mi- se- re- re no- stri, te pe- ti- mus. A te so- lo
In our wretchedness we beg you. By you only

nos ex- pe- cta- vi- mus Con- for- ta- ri.
can we expect to be comforted.

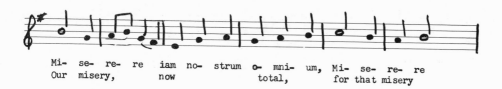

Mi- se- re- re iam no- strum o- mni- um, Mi- se- re- re
Our misery, now total, for that misery

cu- ius   est   pro- pri- um Con- so-   la-   ri.
it would be good to be   consoled.

(43)

JESUS (trembling and crying inwardly, <u>to Mary Magdalene</u>)

Ad se- pul- crum me iam de- du- ci- te, At- que mi- hi
To the sepulcher   now lead me,   and   to me

lo- cum o- sten- di- te   Se- pul-   tu- re. Iam me
the place show   of the entombing.   Now

mo- vet ve- stra mi- se- ri- a, Iam me mo- vent ve- stra su-
your misery   moves me,   now   your sighs move me, and

spi- ri- a, Ve- strae   cu-   rae.
your   sorrows.

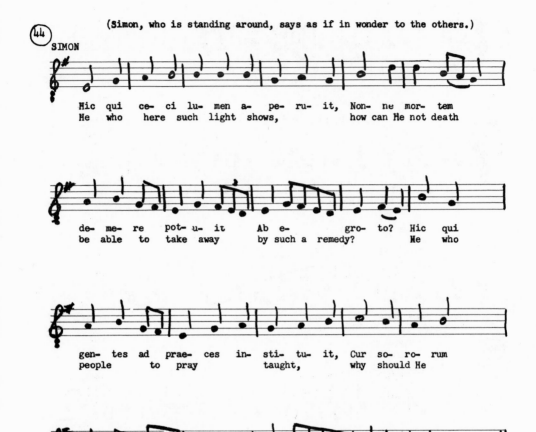

(Simon, who is standing around, says as if in wonder to the others.)

SIMON

Hic qui ce- ci lu- men a- pe- ru- it, Non- ne mor- tem
He who here such light shows, how can He not death

de- me- re pot- u- it Ab e- gro- to? Hic qui
be able to take away by such a remedy? He who

gen- tes ad prae- ces in- sti- tu- it, Cur so- ro- rum
people to pray taught, why should He

ab- es- se vo- lu- it Pi- o vo- to?
wish to be aloof from the pleading of the sisters?

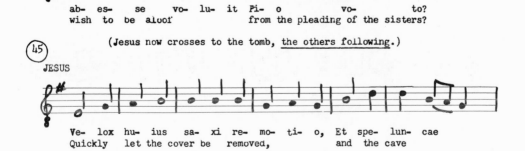

(Jesus now crosses to the tomb, the others following.)

JESUS

Ve- lox hu- ius sa- xi re- mo- ti- o, Et spe- lun- cae
Quickly let the cover be removed, and the cave

fi- at a- per- ti- o Si- ne mo-ra. Qua de-
be opened without delay. Now

(The Disciples go to open the sepulcher.)

be- tis mi- ran- da cer- ne- re, At- que De- i no- men ex-
you may the wonder see, and God's name be

tol- le- re. Haec est ho- ra!
praised. This is the hour!

46

MARTHA (to Jesus)

Per bis du- os di- es iam ia- cu- it. Dat fe- to- rem
For twice two days now he has lain in there. That means that

ca- ro que pu- tru- it Tu- mu- la- ti.
our dear one stinks in the tomb.

(47)

JESUS

Ne de- spe- res! Vi- de- bis glo- ri- am De- i Pa- tris
Do not despair! You will see the glory of God the Father

at- que pot- en- ti- am Su- i na- ti.
and the power of His Son.

(Jesus casts his eyes to heaven and prays:)

De- us, cu- ius vir- tus et fi- li- us Ae- ter- na- lis
O God, whose power and son eternal,

non tem- po- ra- ne- us, cre- dor es- se, Tu- um na- tum
not temporal, I am believed to be, That your son

ut ho- no- ri- fi- ces, At- que me- um no- men glo- ri- fi- ces
you may honor, and my name you may glorify,

Est ne-   ces-   se. (Jesus calls into the tomb.)
is necessary.

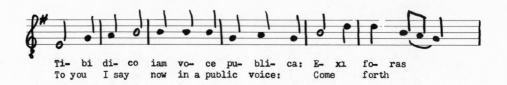

Ti- bi di- co iam vo- ce pu- bli- ca: E- xi fo- ras
To you I say   now in a public voice: Come forth

at- que lae- ti- fi- ca   Cor pa-   ren- tum.   Tu sis
and   gladden   the hearts of your kin.   You may be

do- lor in- si- di- an- ti- bus, At- que cer- tum sis du- bi-
the vexation of our enemies,   and   surely   you should be

tan- ti- bus Ar- gu-   men-   tum.
to the doubting convincing.

(Now Lazarus sits up, and Jesus says to the Disciples:)

Su- sci- ta- tum con- fe- stim sol- vi- te, Et so- lu- tum
The rescued one   speedily   unbind,   and unfettered

a- bi- re si- ni- te.   Quid stu-   pe- tis?
let him go.   Why are you amazed?

(The Disciples obey.)

O- mne De- o es- se pos- si- bi- le rer hoc pa- tet
That all things to God are possible   is through this made

sa- tis cre- di- bi- le Quod vi- de- tis.
sufficiently credible,   as you see.

(Gesturing to the risen Lazarus.)

(Lazarus comes forward and joins Jesus in leading out the "Te Deum.")

(The complete "Te Deum" begins on p. 491.)

8. The Conversion of St. Paul

The Conversion of St. Paul

NO OTHER VERSION of this play exists than the one here transcribed from the Fleury Playbook (Orléans, Bibliothèque de la Ville MS 201, pp. 230-33). After experiencing the beauty of the opening melody, one is lenient toward the theatrical ineptitudes of the play.

The first two measures of Item 7 are, one notices, identical with the first two measures of the Robbers' Items 2, 3, and 5 in *The Image of St. Nicholas.* Furthermore, the third measure of Item 7 of the present play is also found in Items 6-8 of *The Image.* There is no way of determining which borrowed from the other or whether both used a folk melody.

The only indication of the liturgical position of the play is that it ends with the *Te Deum,* and may thus have been associated with the Matins service. The feast of the Conversion of St. Paul is January 25 in the calendar.

The Cast

Saul (St. Paul)
First Knight of Jerusalem
Second Knight of Jerusalem
Two Christian Captives (nonspeaking)
High Priest of Jerusalem
Dominus (The Lord)
Ananias
Judas (nonspeaking)
High Priest of Damascus
Knights of Damascus (nonspeaking)
Barnabus
Other Apostles, for the *Te Deum*

The Scene: Two Jerusalem buildings. Two Damascus buildings. Between them an open space. The Damascus buildings flank a couch for Ananias.

The Conversion of St. Paul   *Conversio Beati Pauli*

(For the playing of "The Conversion of St. Paul" let there be prepared
in a suitable location, as if it were Jerusalem, a certain sedes, and
on it the High Priest of Jerusalem. And let there be prepared another
sedes in the Jerusalem section, and on it a young man in the likeness
of Saul; and let him have with him his armed Knights. On the other side
of the stage area, in front, somewhat distant from those Jerusalem
sedes, let there be prepared, as if it were Damascus, two sedes, on one
of which let there be seated a certain man named Judas, and on the other
the High Priest of the Damascus Synagogue. And between these two sedes
let there be made a couch, on which lies a man in the likeness of Ananias. These things being prepared, let Saul say to his Knights:)

1 SAUL

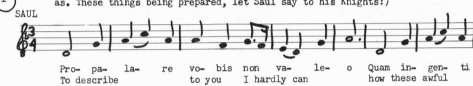

Pro- pa- la- re vo- bis non va- le- o   Quam in- gen- ti
To describe   to you   I hardly can   how these awful

mi- chi sint o- di- o Chri- sti- co- lae, Qui per
Christians are to me hateful,   who   by

fal- la- ci- am To- tam i- stam se- du- cunt pa- tri-
their treacheries   are totally   betraying   the nation.

am. I- te er- go, ne tar- da- ve- ri- tis, Et quo-
Go,   therefore, and do not delay,   and

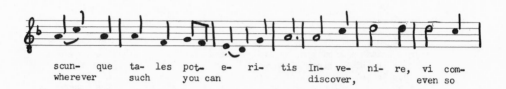

scun-   que   ta- les pot- e- ri- tis In- ve- ni- re, vi com-
where ver   such   you can   discover,   even so

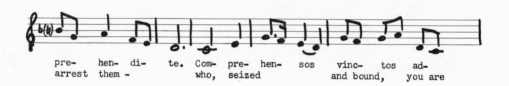

pre-   hen- di-   te. Com- pre- hen- sos   vinc- tos ad-
arrest them -   who, seized   and bound, you are

du-   ci- te.
to bring in.

(Hearing this, let the Knights go, and when they return let them lead
② their two prisoners to their master, saying:)

FIRST KNIGHT

Chri- sti- co- las mul- tos in- ve- ni- mus, Et ex il- lis
Many Christians   have we investigated,   and from those

re- ti- nu- i- mus.
have we detained two.

③ SECOND KNIGHT

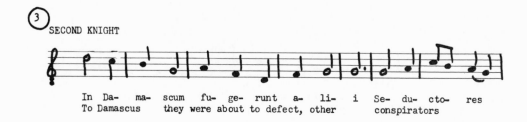

In Da- ma- scum fu- ge- runt a- li- i Se- du- cto- res
To Damascus   they were about to defect, other   conspirators

hu- ius con- sor- ti- i.
to join.

(Now let Saul, as if enraged, rise up, and let him go to the High
Priest of Jerusalem. And when he has come to him, let him say:)

④ SAUL

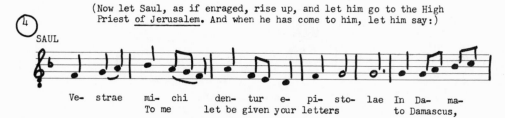

Ve- strae mi- chi den- tur e- pi- sto- lae In Da- ma-
To me   let be given your letters   to Damascus,

scum, u- bi Chri- sti- co- lae Blan- dis ver- bis su- ae fal-
where   Christians,   with bland words   of their

la- ci- ae Gen- tes hu- ius se- du- cunt pa- tri- ae.
plotting,   the people of this nation are seducing.

(Now let the High Priest give him some brief scribble, and let him
say:)

⑤ HIGH PRIEST OF JERUSALEM

Tra- do   vo- bis me- as e- pi- sto- las In Da- ma-scum
I hereby deliver to you   my   letters   to Damascus

con- tra Chri- sti- co-   las. E- va- de-   re ne di-   mi-
against   the Christians.   To escape   do not let

se- ri- tis Chri- sti- co- las   quos in- ve-   ne- ri- tis.
               any Christians   whom you find.

(Let Saul and his Knights leave and cross toward Damascus. Suddenly
there is drum-thunder, and a voice from above says:)

⑥ DOMINUS

Sau- le! Sau- le! Quid me per- se- que-   ris?
Saul!   Saul!   Why   do you persecute me?

Vi- di ma- la que me-   is fe- ce-   ris. Quem di-
I see   the evil which to mine you do.   Why do you

le- xi   cur no- ces po- pu- lo?   Re- cal- ci-   tres
delight   in hurting these people?   Do not kick

ne- qua-   quam sti- mu- lo.
anymore   at all   against my spurring.

(Hearing this, let Saul, as if he had fallen half-dead on the
ground, but not prostrate, say:)

⑦ SAUL

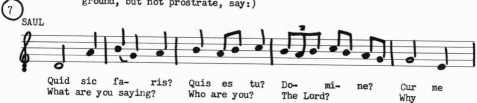

Quid sic fa- ris?   Quis es tu?   Do-   mi- ne?   Cur me
What are you saying?   Who are you?   The Lord?   Why

me- o pri- va- sti lu- mi- ne?   Quan- do tu-   um af- fli-xi
have you deprived me of my sight?   When   have I afflicted

po- pu- lum?   Quis   es?   Et quod ti- bi vo-
your people?   Who   are you? And how   do they

ca-   bu-   lum?
call you?

8 DOMINUS:

Je- sus vo- cor, quem tu   per- se- que-   ris,
Jesus   I am called, whom you   persecute,

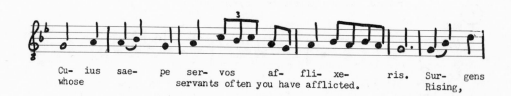

Cu- ius sae-   pe ser- vos af- fli- xe-   ris. Sur-   gens
whose   servants often you have afflicted.   Rising,

ta- men   ur- bem in- gre-   de- re,   Et au- di-   es
nevertheless,   to the city go,   and hear

que de- bes fa- ce-   re.
what you must   do.

(Then let Saul get up, and when his Knights see that he is without
sight let them take him and lead him to Damascus to the house of Judas.
Then let The Lord come to Ananias, and let him say:)

A- na- ni- a, sur- ge quam pro- pe- pe- re, At- que
Ananias, rise up in haste, and

Iu- de do- mum in- gre- de- re. Te ex- pe-ctat
to Judas' house in- go. You are expected

vir, Sau- lus no- mi- ne. Di- ces e- i
by a man, Saul by name. Say to him

que de- bet fa- ce- re.
what he must do.

De hoc Sau- lo au- di- vi plu- ri- ma. Fe- cit tu- is
About this Saul I have heard from many. He does to your

ma- la quam max- xi- ma. Si quem vi- det qui ti- bi ser- vi-
people the most evil possible. If he sees who to you gives service,

at, Sem- per fu- rit ut e- um de- stru- at. Hic prin-
always he frets until that one is destroyed. From his

ceps ha- bet e- pi- sto- las Ut oc- ci- dat o- mnes Chri-
boss he has letters ordering him to kill all

sti- co- las. His de cau- sis hunc Sau- lum ti- me- o.
Christians. For these reasons, then, Saul I fear.

Ad hunc Sau- lum i- re non au- de- o.
To Saul, then, to go I don't dare.

DOMINUS

A- na- ni- a,   sur- ge ve- lo- ci-   ter! Quae- re
Ananias,   rise up   quickly!   Find

Sau- lum fi- du- ci- a- li- ter! Ec-   ce e- nim
Saul,   confidently!   Lo,   even he will

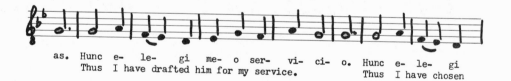

o- rat ut ve- ni- as, Et ut e- um vi- de- re fa- ci-
be praying for you to come,   and for you to make him to see again.

as. Hunc e- le- gi me- o ser- vi- ci- o. Hunc e- le- gi
Thus I have drafted him for my service.   Thus I have chosen

no- stro con- sor- ti- o. Hunc e- le- gi   ut de me
him as our companion.   Thus I have drafted him to

praecet, Et no- men me- um cla- ri- fi- cet.
speak of me,   and my name   to glorify.

(Then, rising, let Ananias go to the house of Judas, and, when he
sees Saul, let him say:)

12 ANANIAS

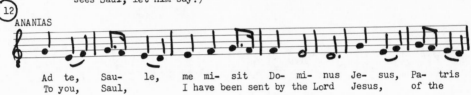

Ad te,   Sau- le,   me mi- sit Do- mi- nus Je- sus, Pa- tris
To you,   Saul,   I have been sent by the Lord Jesus,   of the

ex- cel- si Fi- li- us, Qui in vi- a ti- bi ap- pa- ru-
heavenly Father the Son,   who on the road to you appeared;

it, Ut ve- ni-   rem ad te me   mo- nu- it. Prae- di-
and that I come   to you   he ordered me. You will

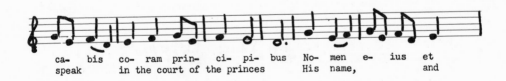

ca- bis co- ram prin- ci- pi- bus No- men e- ius et
speak   in the court of the princes His name,   and

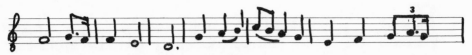

co- ram gen- ti- bus. Ut sis e- ius cae- le- stis
in the court of the people. So that you may be in his heavenly

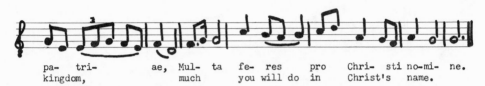

pa- tri- ae, Mul- ta fe- res pro Chri- sti no-mi- ne.
kingdom,   much you will do in Christ's name.

(Then let Saul rise up, and, as if now believing, and speaking out
in a loud voice, let him say:)

13 SAUL

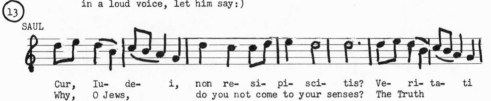

Cur, Iu- de- i, non re- si- pi- sci- tis? Ve- ri- ta- ti
Why, O Jews,   do you not come to your senses? The Truth

cur con- tra- di- ci- tis? Cur ne- ga- tis Ma- ri- am
why do you deny?   Why deny that   Mary

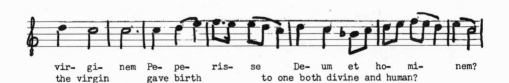

vir- gi- nem Pe- pe- ris- se De- um et ho- mi- nem?
the virgin   gave birth   to one both divine and human?

Je- sus Chri- stus, Ma- ri- ae Fi- li- us, Et De- us est, et
Jesus   Christus,   Mary's   son,   is both God   and

ho- mo car- ne-   us, De- i-   ta- tem   a Pa- tre re- ti-
man   in the flesh,   His divinity   to   the Father owing,

nens, Et a ma-   tre car- nem su- sci- pi- ens.
       and to   the mother His body.

(This overhearing, let the High Priest of Damascus to his armed
Knights say:)

⑭

HIGH PRIEST OF DAMASCUS

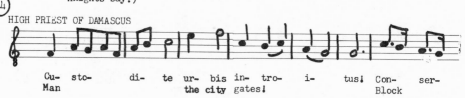

Cu- sto-   di- te ur- bis in- tro-   i-   tus! Con-   ser-
Man   the city gates!   Block

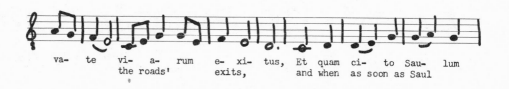

va- te vi- a-   rum   e- xi- tus, Et quam ci- to Sau- lum
     the roads'   exits,   and when as soon as Saul

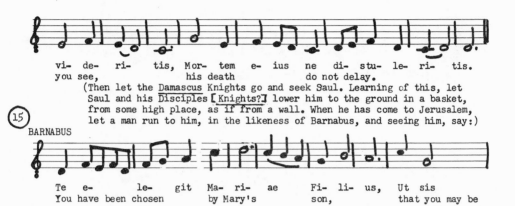

vi- de- ri- tis, Mor- tem e- ius ne di- stu- le- ri- tis.
you see,   his death   do not delay.
(Then let the Damascus Knights go and seek Saul. Learning of this, let
Saul and his Disciples [Knights?] lower him to the ground in a basket,
from some high place, as if from a wall. When he has come to Jerusalem,
let a man run to him, in the likeness of Barnabus, and seeing him, say:)

(15) BARNABUS

Te e- le- git Ma- ri- ae Fi- li- us, Ut sis
You have been chosen   by Mary's   son,   that you may be

fra- trum no- stro- rum so- ci- us. Nunc, ut lau- des
our fraternal   companion.   Now, so that you may

no- bi- scum Do- mi- num, Ve- ni, vi- de no- strum col-
praise with us The Lord,   come   see   our

le- gi- um. Gau- de-   a- mus, fra- tres, in Do- mi- no!
fellowship.   Let us rejoice,   brothers,   in The Lord!

Col- le- te- mur de tan- to so- ci-
Let us be pleased   with such a   member.   Qui nunc e- rat
                                                       He who just now was

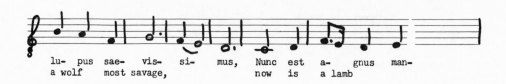

lu- pus sae- vis- si- mus, Nunc est a- gnus man-
a wolf   most savage,   now is a lamb

su- e- tis- si- mus.
of great grace.

(All the Apostles then begin "Te Deum laudamus." So it is ended.)

(The complete "Te Deum" begins on p. 491.)

9. The Wise and Foolish Maidens

The Wise and Foolish Maidens

THE ONLY PLAYSCRIPT on this theme comes from the famous medieval abbey of Saint Martial at Limoges, a musical center and occasional rallying point for French royalty. Eleanor of Aquitaine and her first husband spent the Christmas holidays there in 1137. The manuscript, positively dated as from the last years of the eleventh century, is now in the Bibliothèque Nationale (MS Latin 1139, fols. 53^r-55^v).

Of the forty-four items of dialogue, the speakers of only six are identified in the manuscript, and there is no differentiation among the Wise or Foolish Maidens or between the Merchants. The identification of speakers as in the present transcription has proved logical in production, though one may wonder why the possibilities for distributing the Maidens' speeches usually leave the Fifth Maiden, Wise or Foolish, with no solo. While the speaker of an item often has to be spotted by the substance of the speech, the difficulty is actually very little, most of it with the first six items, which work well for two-by-two danced entrances of the ten Maidens.

Because there are only two original stage directions, and these at the conclusion of the play, I have been sparing of editorializing others. The impressive fact is, moreover, that even in reading the script one is seldom in doubt as to who is speaking to whom. Scribal reticence in this matter may have related also to the high cost of parchment.

The melody of the last item of the play is missing, apparently by oversight, for the verbal scribe ruled the staff and wrote in the verses. I have borrowed the melody of this item from Items 1 and 14, the time signature of the latter item being therefore altered to 3/4 for consistency.

The Cast

First Wise Maiden
Second Wise Maiden
Third Wise Maiden
Fourth Wise Maiden
Fifth Wise Maiden
First Foolish Maiden
Second Foolish Maiden
Third Foolish Maiden
Fourth Foolish Maiden
Fifth Foolish Maiden
Gabriel (the Archangel)
First Oil Merchant
Second Oil Merchant
The Sponsus (the Bridegroom, who is the Christus)
Several Demons (nonspeaking but active)

The Scene: Outside the regal door to the Bridegroom's banquet
room, and adjacent to Hellmouth. Nighttime.

The Wise and Foolish Maidens *Sponsus*

①

FIRST WISE AND FIRST FOOLISH MAIDENS

Ad- est Spon- sus qui est Chri- stus! Vi- gi- la- te, vir-gi- nes!
Arriving is the Bridegroom who is the Christ! Be vigilant, maidens!

(Leading the others in, and turning to them)

②

SECOND WISE & FOOLISH (to audience)

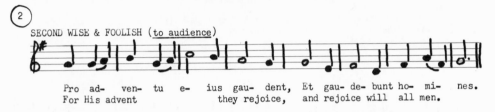

Pro ad- ven- tu e- ius gau- dent, Et gau- de- bunt ho- mi- nes.
For His advent they rejoice, and rejoice will all men.

③

THIRD WISE & FOOLISH (indicating Hellmouth)

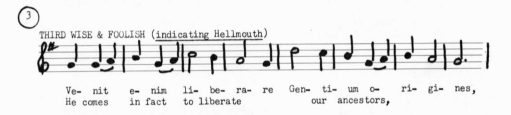

Ve- nit e- nim li- be- ra- re Gen- ti- um o- ri- gi- nes,
He comes in fact to liberate our ancestors,

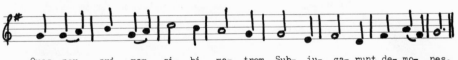

Quas per pri- mam si- bi ma- trem Sub- iu- ga- runt de- mo- nes.
whom because of our first mother (Eve) the devils conquered.

④

FOURTH WISE & FOOLISH (at Hellmouth)

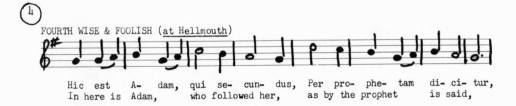

Hic est A- dam, qui se- cun- dus, Per pro- phe- tam di- ci- tur,
In here is Adam, who followed her, as by the prophet is said,

Per quem sce- lus pri- mi A- de A no- bis di- lu- i- tur.
and through whom the sin of the first Adam to us was extended.

⑤

FIFTH WISE & FOOLISH (<u>to a crucifix</u>)

Hic pe- pen- dit ut cae- les- ti pa- tri- ae nos red- de- ret,
Here He hangs so that our heavenly home may be restored to us,

Ac de par- te i- ni- mi- ci Li- be- ros nos tra- he- ret.
and that from our enemies He may set us free.

⑥

ALL MAIDENS

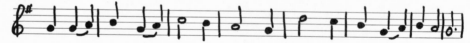

Ve- nit Spon- sus qui no- stro- rum Sce- le- rum pi- a- cu- la,
Comes the Bridegroom who, as the propitiation for our sins

(<u>To audience, but keeping gesture to crucifix</u>)

Mor- te la- vit, at- que cru- cis Sus- tu- lit pa- ti- bu- la.
death suffered, and on the cross bore our burdens.

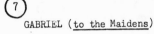

GABRIEL (to the Maidens)

| Oi- | et, | vir- | gi- | nes, | ai- | so | que | vos | di- rum! | Ai- | set |
| Hear, | O | hear, | mai- | dens, | what | we | have | to | tell you! | Take | care |

| pre- | sen | que | vos | com- | man- | da- rum. | A- ten- det | un |
| to o- | bey | what | we | now | com- | mand you. | You a- wait | a |

| es- | pos | Ihe- su | Sal- | vai- | re | a | nom. | Gai- re | noi | dor- |
| bride- | groom | Je- sus | the Sa- | vior | by | name. | Wat- chers | must | not |

| met! | Ai- | sel | l'es- | pos | que | vos | hor a- | ten- det. |
| slum- ber! | Joy | comes | with | Him, | He | whose | hour ap- | proa- ches. |

| Ve- nit | en | ter- | ra | per | los | vo- | stres | pe- | chet. |
| To earth | from | hea -ven | He | came | to | save | you | from your | sins. |

De la vir- gi- ne en Bet- le- em fo   net,   E   flum Ior- da
In Beth- le- hem He was born of a vir- gin,   Wash'd in Jor-dan's

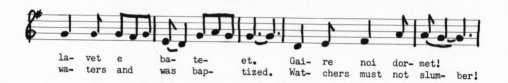

la- vet e   ba- te-   et.   Gai- re   noi dor- met!
wa- ters and   was bap-   tized.   Wat- chers must not slum- ber!

En   fo ba- tut,   ga- bet e   lai- de- ni- et, Sus   e
Then He was   scorned, bea- ten, per- se- cu- ted, Cru- ci-

la   crot ba- tut e clau- fi-   get. En mo- nu-men de- so-
fied for   us up- on the cru- el tree. In sto- ny se- pul- cher

en- tre pau- set.   Gai- re   noi dor- met!   E re-
He   was en- tombed.   Wat- chers must not slum- ber. He was

sors es, la scri- ptu- ra o- di- i. Ga- bri-
raised from death, the Gos- pels tell you. I am the

els soi, eu m'a tra- mes a- i- ci. A- ten- det lo
An- gel Ga- bri- el, sent here to fore- warn you. You will meet the

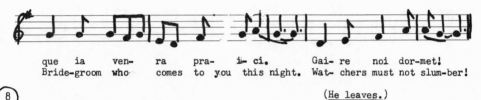

que ia ven- ra pra- i- ci. Gai- re noi dor- met!
Bride- groom who comes to you this night. Wat- chers must not slum- ber!

(He leaves.)

⑧

FIRST FOOLISH (to Wise)

Nos vir- gi- nes que ad vos ve- ni- mus, Ne- gli- gen-
We maidens who to you approach, We have

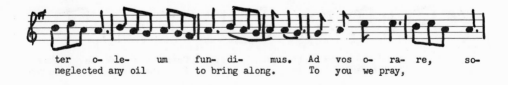

ter o- le- um fun- di- mus. Ad vos o- ra- re, so-
neglected any oil to bring along. To you we pray,

ro- res, cu- pi- mus, Ut ad il- las
sisters, we desire that some of your oil

qui- bus nos cre- di- mus.
we may borrow.

⑨ THREE FOOLISH

Do- len- tas! Chai- ti- vas! Trop i a- vem dor- mit!
Sor- row- ful! Un- hap- py! Ve- ry much too long we slept!

⑩ SECOND FOOLISH

Nos co- mi- tes hu- ius i- ti- ne- ris, Et so- ro-
We are your friends along this way, and sisters

res e- ius- dem ge- ne- ris. Quam- vis ma- le con-
of the same people. Even though you see us in such

ti- git mi- se- ris, Pot- es- tis nos red-de- re su-pe- ris.
misery, You are able to save us from a worse fate.

⑪ FOUR FOOLISH

Do- len- tas! Chai- ti- vas! Trop i a- vem dor- mit!
Sor- row- ful! Un- hap- py! Ve- ry much too long we slept!

⑫ THIRD FOOLISH

Par- ti- mi- ni lu- men lam- pa- di- bus. Pi- e si-
Share with us the light of your lamps. Take pity

tis in- si- pi- en- ti- bus. Pul- se ne nos si-
on our foolishness. Do not push us

mus a fo- ri- bus, Cum vos Spon- sus vo-cet in se-di- bus.
from your doorways, when you the Bridegroom calls in.

(13)

ALL FOOLISH

Do- len- tas! Chai- ti- vas! Trop i a- vem dor- mit!
Sor- row- ful! Un- hap- py! Ve- ry much too long we slept!

(14)

FIRST & SECOND WISE

Nos pre- ca- ri, pre- ca- mur am- pli- us De- si-
We who are so entreated, entreat you even more to leave off

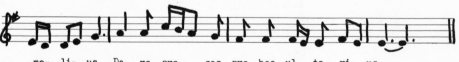

ni- te, so- ro- res, o- ti- us. Vo- bis e- nim nil e- rit
your lazy ways, sisters. For you indeed nothing can be

me- li- us. Da- re pre- ces pro hoc ul- te- ri- us.
be any better, by begging for this further.

(15)

ALL FOOLISH

Do- len- tas! Chai- ti- vas! Trop i a- vem dor- mit!
Sor- row- ful! Un- hap- py! Ve- ry much too long we slept!

THIRD, FOURTH & FIFTH WISE

Ac i- te   nunc, i- te ce-   le- ri-   ter, Ac   ven-
So go away   now, go   with haste,   and   from the

den-   tes ro- ga- te dul-   ci-   ter Ut o- le um ve- stris lam-
merchants   ask for some prettily,   so that oil   for your

pa-   di- bus Dent e- qui-   dem vo- bis   in- er-   ti-   bus.
lamps   they may give   to you   lazy ones.

ALL FOOLISH

Do- len-   tas! Chai- ti- vas! Trop i a-   vem   dor-   mit!
Sor- row- ful! Un- hap- py! Ve- ry much too   long   we slept!

FIRST FOOLISH

Ah, mi- se- re   nos, hic   quid   fa- ci-   mus?
Ah, we in misery,   what can we do about it?

(19)

SECOND FOOLISH

Vi- gi- la- re   num- quid   pot- u- i-   mus?
To watch,   are we really ineligible?

(20)

THIRD FOOLISH

Hunc la- bo- rem,   quem nunc   per- fe- ri-   mus,
This burden,   which now   we endure,

(21)

FOURTH FOOLISH

No-   bis nos- met ip- sae con- tu- li-   mus.
on ourselves   we have put it.

(22)

ALL FOOLISH

Do- len- tas! Chai- ti- vas! Trop i a-   vem   dor-   mit!
Sor- row- ful! Un- hap- py! Ve- ry much too   long   we slept!

(23)

FIRST WISE

De no- str'o- li que- ret nos   a do- ner.
Of our pre- cious oil do not try to bor-row from us.

24 SECOND WISE

No!n au- ret pont. A- let en a- chap- ter.
None, none; no oil for you. Go and buy some oil for your-selves.

25 THIRD WISE

Deus mer- chans que lai ve- et es- ter.
From the mer- chants o- ver there as you can see.

26 FIRST & SECOND FOOLISH

Et det no- bis mer- ca- tor o- ti- us, Qua ha- be-
And may to us the merchants give, unworthy as we are, either for

at mer- ces quas so- ci- us.
profit or out of kindness.

27 THIRD, FOURTH, & FIFTH FOOLISH

O- le- um nunc quae- re- re ve- ni- mus, Ne- gli- gen- ter
Oil now to seek come along, since negligently

quod nos- met fu- di-   mus.
we brought with us none.

(28)

ALL FOOLISH

Do-   len- tas! Chai- ti- vas! Trop i a-   vem   dor-   mit!
Sor-   row- ful! Un-   hap- py! Ve- ry much too   long   we slept!

(29)

ALL FOOLISH

[Vos mar- chaans nos   po-   et co-   se-   ler.] Do- len- tas!
O   you mer-   chants please do help us now with oil. Sor- row- ful!

Chai- ti- vas! Trop i a- vem   dor-   mit!
Un-   hap- py! Ve- ry much too long   we slept!

(30)

FIRST MERCHANT

Dom-   nas gen- tils   no   vos co-   vent es-
Pret-ty young girls, do not stay here. We have no-thing to give, no-thing to

ter.   Ni lo- ia- men   ai- ci   a
sell to you. And it ain't wise for you to stay. Do   not   lin- ger

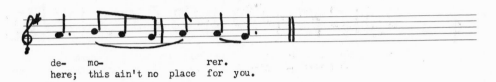

de-   mo-   rer.
here; this ain't no place for you.

(31)

SECOND MERCHANT

Co-   sel que- ret   n'on vos   po-   em do-
What   you want we   can't give, and we can't le-gal-ly sell, le-gal-ly

ner.   Que-   ret lo Deu, chi vos pot co- se-   ler.
of- fer you. It would be bet- **ter** if you asked God to help   you.

(32)

FIRST MERCHANT

A-   let a-   reir   a   vo-   stras sinc se-   ros.
Turn a- round; go on back; find your five **sis-** ters and ask of them.

E   pre- iat las   per Deu   lo   glo- ri-
Beg   of   them for God's sake, God the glo-ri-ous king, glo-ri- ous

os.   De   o- le- o   fa- sen so-   cors a
king a-bove. They then may give to you oil   from their re-serves, oil from

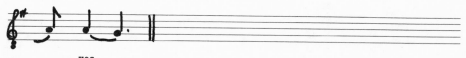

          vos.
their sup- ply.

(33)

SECOND MERCHANT

Fai-   tes o tost que ia ven- ra l'es-   pos.
Bet-ter hur-ry up now, for soon the Bride-groom will be   there.

(34)

FIRST FOOLISH

Ah,   mi- se- re, nos ad   quid ve- ni-   mus?
O   misery,   for what have we come here?

㉟ SECOND FOOLISH

Nil est e- nim il- lut quod quae- ri- mus.
Here is indeed nothing of what we seek.

㊱ THIRD FOOLISH

Fa- ta- tum est et nos vi- de- bi- mus:
We are doomed, and shall see this happen to us:

㊲ FOURTH FOOLISH

Ad nu- pti- as num- quam in- tra- bi- mus.
To the nuptials never shall we enter.

(The Foolish Maidens leave the Merchants.)

㊳ ALL FOOLISH

Do- len- tas! Chai- ti- vas! Trop i a- vem dor- mit!
Sor- row- ful! Un- hap- py! Ve- ry much too long we slept!

(Enter the Bridegroom.)

㊴ FIRST FOOLISH

Au- di, Spon- se, vo- ces plan- gen- ti- um!
Hear, O Bridegroom, our voices wailing!

⟨40⟩ SECOND FOOLISH

A- pe- ri- re   fac no-   bis   o- sti-   um,
Let there be opened   to us   the door to the banquet room.

⟨41⟩ THIRD FOOLISH

Cum so- ci- is [ad dul-   ce   pran- di-   um.
So that with our sisters we may share the beautiful feast.

⟨42⟩ FOURTH FOOLISH

No-   strae cul- pae] prae- be re- me- di-   um!
From our   guilt   grant us   absolution!

⟨43⟩ ALL FOOLISH

Do-   len- tas! Chai- ti- vas! Trop i a- vem   dor-   mit!
Sor- row- ful! Un- hap- py! Ve- ry much too long   we slept!

⟨44⟩ BRIDEGROOM

A- men, di- co. Vos i- gno- sco. Nam ca- re- tis lu- mi- ne,
Amen to that, I say. I know you not. Because you lack   the lamp oil,

Quod qui per- dunt Pro- cul per- gunt Hu- ius au- lae li- mi- ne.
Take yourselves and your lamps   away from this regal door.

A- let,   chai- ti- vas! A- let,   ma- lau- re-   as!
Go, la- zy, wretch- ed ones! Go hence, ma- le- fac-   tors!

A   tot iors mais vos   so pe- nas li-   vre-   as.
In- to e- ver- last- ing sor- row- ing be you de- li-   vered.

En e- fern o- ra se- ret   me- nei- as!
In- to Hell, the mouth of Hell, shall you be led!

(The Demons <u>rush in</u>, seize the Foolish Maidens, and thrust them
into Hellmouth. <u>The Bridegroom beckons to the Wise Maidens, who
follow Him and Ecclesia, the Church, through the regal door.</u>)

10. The Three Daughters

The Three Daughters

AS WITH THE OTHER extant St. Nicholas plays, the only produceable version of *The Three Daughters* is recorded with its music in the twelfth-century Fleury Playbook (Orléans, Bibliothèque de la Ville MS 201, pp. 176-82). Inasmuch as the antiphon at the end of the play is a part of the liturgy for the feast of St. Nicholas, December 6, we may assume that the play was created and performed as a feature of that festal day. There is no indication that the four St. Nicholas plays were staged as a cycle at a single service; in fact, the combined length of the four dramas greatly exceeds that of even the longest single play in the repertory, the *Daniel,* and makes unlikely a cyclic production in the twelfth century.

Today, however, when they are less bound into the liturgy, any combination of the four plays makes a theatrical bill that is unified by the appearances of St. Nicholas and the style of the compositions. Discussion of this style may be found in *Production,* pp. 203-11.

The *O Christe pietas,* which ends *The Three Daughters* and also the Hildesheim version of *The Three Clerks,* does not respond well to a mensural approach. Only the *incipit*s are given in the Fleury manu-script, the remainder to be filled in from a Sarum antiphonary (W. H. Frere, *Antiphonale Sarisburiense* [1901], II, 361-62). The Sarum *incipit* is not identical with its Fleury counterpart, which I now prefer sufficiently to include herein.

The *incipit* for the first four measures of Item 27 is somewhat illiterate. The word *sunt,* interpolated into this repeat of the earlier stanzas, forces subsequent words out of the alignment they had previously had with the melody. The only solution is to call the *sunt* a slip, and omit it, for it has no meaning in the line anyway.

The Cast

Pater
First Daughter
Second Daughter
Third Daughter
St. Nicholas of Myra
First Suitor   ⎫
Second Suitor   ⎬   may be openly played by one actor
Third Suitor   ⎭

   The Scene: Pater's room, stripped of all furnishings but his couch
               and a table with a candlestick.

The Three Daughters   *Tres Filiae*

① PATER

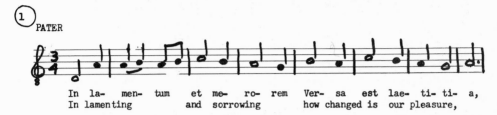

In la- men- tum   et me- ro- rem   Ver- sa   est lae- ti- ti- a,
In lamenting   and sorrowing   how changed is our pleasure,

Quam prae- be-   bat o- lim no- bis Re- rum ha-   bun-
which came   formerly to us   in our abundance

dan-   ci- a.   O   re- rum   i- no- pi-   a!
of things.   O   the lack of things!

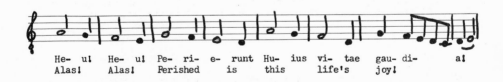

He- u!   He- u! Pe- ri- e- runt Hu- ius vi- tae gau- di-   a!
Alas!   Alas!   Perished   is   this   life's joy!

For- ma, ge- nus, mo- rum splen- dor, Iu- ven- tu- tis glo- ri- a,
Style,   rank,   fashion,   youthful   ambition,

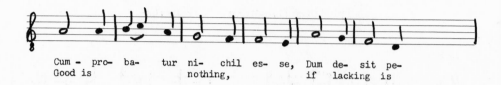

Cum - pro- ba- tur ni- chil es- se, Dum de- sit pe-
Good is   nothing,   if lacking is

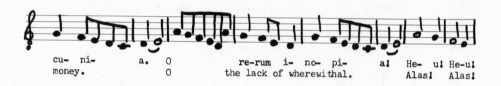

cu- ni-   a.   O   re- rum i- no- pi-   a! He- u! He- u!
money.   O   the lack of wherewithal.   Alas! Alas!

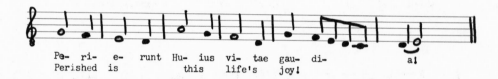

Pe- ri- e- runt Hu- ius vi- tae gau- di-   a!
Perished is   this life's joy!

② THE THREE DAUGHTERS (together)

Fi- nis o- pum dum re- ce- dunt Lu- ctus et su- spi- ri- a.
Finished now is his work, now it gives way to sorrow and sighing.

E- ia! Pa- ter ip- se lu- gens O- pes la- psas prae-di-   a.
Alack! Our father is deploring the loss of his estate.

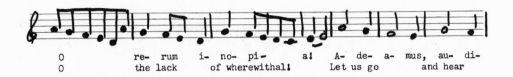

O
O   re- rum i- no- pi-   a! A- de- a- mus, au- di-
             the lack   of wherewithal! Let us go   and hear

a- mus Que ce-   pit con- si- li-   a.
       what is   his advice.

③ PATER (to them)

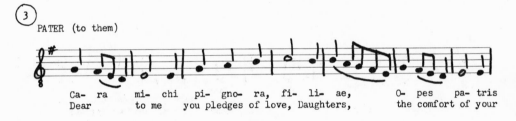

Ca- ra   mi- chi pi- gno- ra, fi- li- ae,   O- pes pa- tris
Dear   to me   you pledges of love, Daughters,   the comfort of your

i- no-   pis   u- ni- cae   Et so-   la- men
father's singular   poverty,   and solace

me- ae mi- se- ri- ae,   Mi- chi   mae- sto   tan- dem con-
of my misfortunes,   To me,   dejected,   in the end

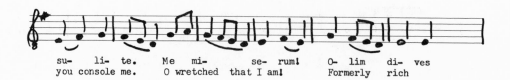

su- li- te.   Me mi-   se- rum!   O- lim di- ves
you console me.   O wretched that I am!   Formerly   rich

et nunc pau- per- ri- mus,   Lu- ce fru- or   et
and now   destitute,   daylight enjoying   but

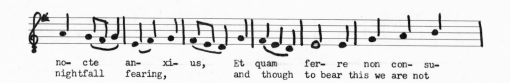

no- cte   an-   xi- us,   Et quam   fer- re non con- su-
nightfall   fearing,   and   though to bear this we are not

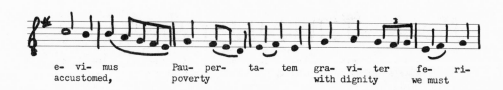

e- vi- mus   Pau- per- ta- tem gra- vi- ter   fe- ri-
accustomed,   poverty   with dignity   we must

mus.   Me mi-   se- rum!   Nec me   me- a tan- tum i-
bear.   O wretched that I am!   Nor to me   is my   poverty

no- pi- a   Quan- tum   ve- stra ve- xat pe-
so much   as   your

nu-   ri- a,   Qua- rum   pri- mum   la- sci- va   cor- po-
destitution.   Sooner or later   prostitution   of your bodies

ra   Lon- ga   mo-   do da- mpnant ie- iu- ni- a.
will be forced by your poverty.

Me   mi-   se-   rum!
O wretched   that I   am!

④ FIRST DAUGHTER

Ca- re   Pa- ter, lu- ge- re de- si- ne,   Nec nos
Dear   Father,   lament   no more,   and do not by

lu- gens lu- gen- dum   pro-   mo- ve,   Et quod ti- bi
deploring your misfortune   increase ours,   and   thus to you

va- le-   o di- ce-   re   Con- si-   li- um, hoc a me
I am bold   to say   what I think.   Take it from me,

re- ci- pe, Ca- re   Pa- ter. U- num   no- bis
         dear   Father.   One way   to us

re- stat au- xi- li- um,   Per de-   de-   cus
remains   available,   Through disgrace

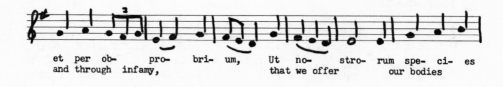

et per ob- pro-   bri- um,   Ut no-   stro- rum spe- ci- es
and through infamy,   that we offer   our bodies

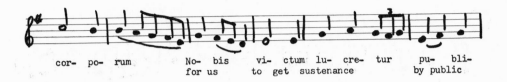

cor- po- rum   No- bis   vi- ctum lu- cre- tur   pu- bli-
for us   to get sustenance   by public

cum,   Ca- re   Pa- ter.   Et me   pri- mam, Pa- ter, si
work,   dear   Father.   And I, as the eldest, Father, if

iu- be- as,   De- de- co- ri sub- mit- tet pi- e-
you agree,   to let my chastity   be disgraced,

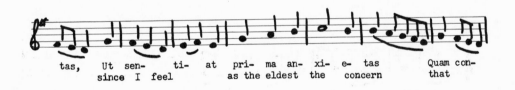

tas, Ut sen- ti- at pri- ma an- xi- e- tas   Quam con-
since I feel   as the eldest the concern   that

tu- lit pri- ma na- ti- vi- tas,   Ca- re   Pa- ter.
belongs   to the firstborn,   dear   Father.

(A bag of gold is tossed through the window by St. Nicholas. It lands
behind the First Daughter, who picks it up.)

PATER

Iam! Iam!   Me- cum gau- de- te, fi- li- ae,   Pau- per-
Now, indeed! With me rejoice,   O Daughters,   from

ta- tis e- la- pso   tem- po- re.   Ec- ce   e- nim
poverty I being spared   for a time.   See,   here is

in au- ri pon- de- re   Quod suf- fi- cit no- strae mi-
enough weight of gold   to   suffice   against our

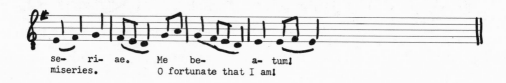

se- ri- ae.   Me be-   a- tum!
miseries.   O fortunate that I am!

DAUGHTERS (together)

Gra- ti- a- rum er- go prae- co- ni- a   Of- fe-
Grateful hymns   therefore   let us offer,

ra- mus, et lau- dum   mu- ne- ra   U- ni   De-   o,
and praise   for the works   of the One   God,

cu- i in sae- cu- la   Laus et   ho- nor,   vir- tus   et
to whom forever be   laud and   honor,   goodness   and

glo- ri- a,   Ca- re   Pa- ter.
glory,   dear   Father.

(The First Suitor enters, and says to Pater:)

⑦ FIRST SUITOR

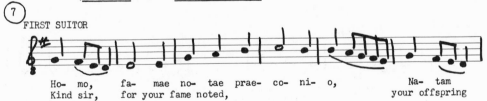

Ho- mo,   fa- mae no- tae prae- co- ni- o,   Na- tam
Kind sir, for your fame noted,   your offspring

tu- am quae- si- tum ve- ni- o,   Quam le- ga- li
seeking,   I am come,   whom into legal

du- cam con- nu- bi- o,   Si   de-   de- ris.
matrimony I'll lead,   if   you please.

(8) PATER (to First Daughter)

Dic, fi- li- a, si tu vis nu- be- re   Hu- ic
Tell me, Daughter,   if you wish to marry   this

iu- ve- ni, ve- nu- sto   cor-   po- re   Et no-   bi- li.
young man,   of charming   mien   and noble.

(9) FIRST DAUGHTER (to Pater)

In te   me- a si- ta con- si- li- a.   Fac ut   lu- bet
With you my   wisdom lies.   Do what you think best

de tu- a   fi- li- a,   Ca-   re   Pa- ter.
for your   daughter,   dear   Father.

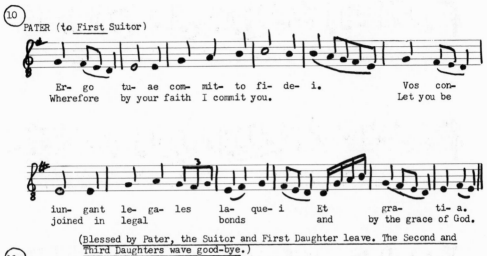

PATER (to First Suitor)

Er- go   tu- ae com— mit— to fi— de— i.   Vos con-
Wherefore   by your faith I commit you.   Let you be

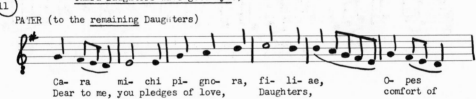

iun— gant le— ga— les   la— que— i   Et   gra—   ti— a.
joined in legal   bonds   and   by the grace of God.

(Blessed by Pater, the Suitor and First Daughter leave. The Second and
Third Daughters wave good-bye.)

PATER (to the remaining Daughters)

Ca— ra   mi— chi pi— gno— ra, fi— li— ae,   O— pes
Dear to me, you pledges of love,   Daughters,   comfort of

pa— tris i— no— pis   u— ni— cae Et so—   la— men
your father's poverty   unique,   and comfort of

me— ae mi— se— ri— ae   Mi— chi mae— sto tan— dem con-
my   sufferings,   to me,   dejected,   finally you are

su- li- te.   Me mi-   se- rum!   O- lim   di- ves
my consolation.   O wrteched that I am!   Formerly   rich

et nunc pau- per- ri-   mus,   Lu- ce   fru- or   et no- cte
and now   we are paupers,   by daylight all right but by night

an- xi- us,   Et quam   fer- re non con- su- e- vi- mus,
fearful,   and though   to bear this we are not accustomed,

Pau- per- ta- tem gra- vi- ter   fe- ri- mus.   Me
poverty   with dignity   we must bear.   O wretched

mi-   se-   rum!
that I am!

12 SECOND DAUGHTER (to Pater)

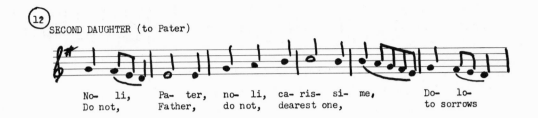

No- li,   Pa- ter,   no- li,   ca- ris- si- me,   Do- lo-
Do not,   Father,   do not,   dearest one,   to sorrows

ri- bus do- lo- res   ad-   de-   re   Nec per   da- mpnum
more sorrow   add,   Nor to   damn

ve- lis in du- ce- re   Pe- ri- cu- lum   in- re- pa-
will you wish to lead us   into peril   irreparable,

ra- bi- le,   Ca- re   Pa- ter. Sci- mus   e- nim
dear   Father. We know   well enough

quod for- ni- can- ti- bus   Ob- stru-   sus sit cae- le- stis
how   by fornications   our way would be blocked to heaven.

ad- di- tus. Pa- ter, er- go ca- ve- re po- sci- mus
Father,   therefore on guard   let us be

Ne nos   ve- lis ad- de- re ta- li- bus,   Ca- re
lest   you should wish to bring us to this extremity,   dear

Pa- ter.   Nec te   ve- lis   et   nos   in- fa- mi- ae
Father.   Nor should you wish   us   to such infamy

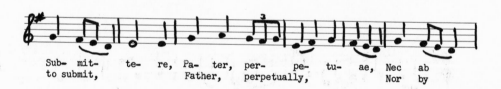

Sub- mit-   te- re, Pa- ter, per-   pe- tu- ae, Nec ab
to submit,   Father, perpetually,   Nor by

i- sta la- bi pau- pe- ri- ae   In ae-   ter- ne
this   present predicament to be immersed in an eternal

la- cum mi- se- ri- ae, Ca- re Pa- ter.
den of suffering, dear Father.

(A second bag of gold is tossed through the window by St. Nicholas.
It lands behind the Second Daughter, who picks it up.)

(13) PATER (to the Daughters)

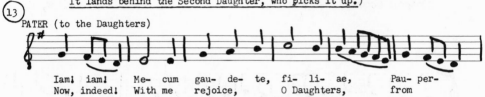

Iam! iam! Me- cum gau- de- te, fi- li- ae, Pau- per-
Now, indeed! With me rejoice, O Daughters, from

ta- tis e- la- pso tem- po- re. Ec- ce e- nim in au- ri
poverty I being spared for a time. See, here is enough weight

pon- de- re Quod suf- fi- cit no- strae mi- se- ri-
of gold to suffice against our miseries.

ae. Me be- a- tum!
O fortunate that I am!

14 DAUGHTERS (together)

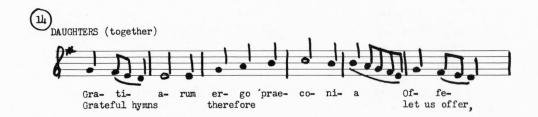

Gra- ti- a- rum er- go ´prae- co- ni a   Of- fe-
Grateful hymns   therefore   let us offer,

ra- mus, et lau- dum   mu- ne- ra   U- ni   De- o, cu- i in
and praise   for the works   of the One God,   to whom

sae- cu- la   Laus et   ho- nor, vir- tus et glo- ri-
forever be   laud and honor, goodness and glory,

a,   Ca- re   Pa-   ter.
dear   re   Father.

15 (The Second Suitor enters, and says to Pater:)
SECOND SUITOR

Ho- mo fa- mae no- tae prae- co- ni- o,   Na- tam tu- am
Kind sir, for your fame noted,   your offspring

quae- si- tum   ve- ni-   o, Quam le-   ga- li du- cam con-
seeking,   I am come,   whom into legal matrimony I'll lead,

nu- bi- o,   Si   de-   de- ris.
                if   you please.

(16)
PATER (to Second Daughter)

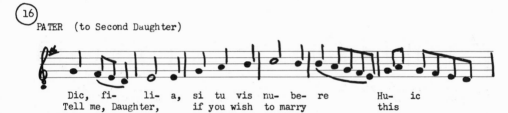

Dic, fi- li- a, si tu vis nu- be- re   Hu- ic
Tell me, Daughter,   if you wish to marry   this

iu- ve- ni, ve- nu- sto cor- po- re   Et no-   bi- li.
young man,   of charming mien   and noble.

(17)
SECOND DAUGHTER (to Pater)

In te   me-   a si- ta con- si- li- a.   Fac ut   lu- bet
With you my   wisdom lies.   Do what you think best

de tu- a fi- li- a, Ca- re Pa- ter.
for your daughter, dear Father.

(18) PATER (to Second Suitor)

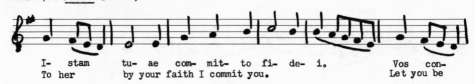

I- stam tu- ae com- mit- to fi- de- i. Vos con-
To her by your faith I commit you. Let you be

iun- gant le- ga- les la- que- i Et gra- ti- a.
joined in legal bonds and by the grace of God.

(Blessed by Pater, the Second Suitor and Second Daughter leave, with the
second bag of gold. The Third Daughter waves good-bye, happy for them,
until she realizes her own plight and her waving fades.)

(19) PATER (to Third Daughter)

Ca- rum mi- chi, pi- gnus, O fi- li- a, Non me me- a
Dear to me, you pledge of love, O Daughter, not

tan- tum i- no- pi- a Quan- tum tu- a ve- xat pe-
all my lack is so vexing as your

nu- ri- a. Tan- tum mi- chi re- stas mi- se- ri-
poverty. So much from me you keep away my misery.

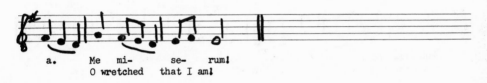

a. Me mi- se- rum!
O wretched that I am!

(20)

THIRD DAUGHTER (to Pater)

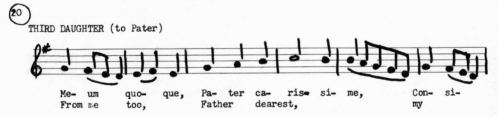

Me- um quo- que, Pa- ter ca- ris- si- me, Con- si-
From me too, Father dearest, my

li- um au- di- re su- sti- ne, At- que fi- nem
advice to hear, be patient, and for the end,

bre- vi- ter col- li- ge.   De- um   ti- me, Pa- ter, et
to be brief,   prepare yourself.   God   you must fear, Father, and

di- li- ge,   Ca- re   Pa- ter. Ni- chil   e- nim De- um ti-
love Him always,   dear   Father.   Nothing is really withheld from

men- ti- bus,   Per scri- ptu- ram de- es- se   no- ta- mus,
those who fear God, as in the Scriptures   we observe,

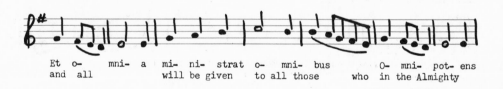

Et o- mni- a mi- ni- strat o- mni- bus   O- mni- pot- ens
and all   will be given   to all those   who in the Almighty

se di- li- gen- ti- bus,   Ca- re   Pa- ter. Ne de-
delight themselves,   dear   Father.   Do not

spe- res pro- pter i- no- pi- am,   Nunc quam   es- se
despair   because of your lack,   since

sci- mus fal-   la- ci- am.   Job re-   spi- ce, Pa- ter,
we know   that is a fallacy.   Think of Job,   Father,

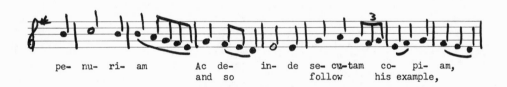

pe- nu- ri- am   Ac de-   in- de se- cu- tam   co- pi- am,
and so   follow   his example,

Ca- re   Pa- ter.
dear   Father.

(A third <u>bag of</u> gold is tossed <u>through the window</u> by St. Nicholas.
Pater prostrates himself at the <u>saint's</u> feet, saying:)

21

PATER

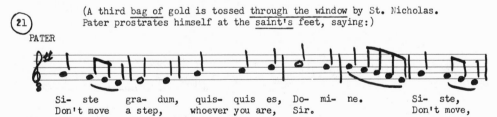

Si- ste   gra- dum,   quis- quis es, Do- mi- ne.   Si- ste,
Don't move   a step,   whoever you are, Sir.   Don't move,

pre- cor, et quis sis   ex- pri- me,   Que de- de-   cus
I beg you, and who you are   explain,   you who from the depths

tol- lens in- fa- mi- ae,   O- nus   quo- que le- vas i-
are raising me from infamy,   the burden also of lack you are lifting.

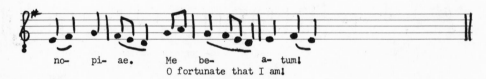

no- pi- ae.   Me be-   a- tum!
O fortunate that I am!

(22)
ST. NICHOLAS to Pater)

Ni- cho-   la- um me vo- cant no- mi- ne.   Lau- da
Nicholas   they call me   by name.   Praise be

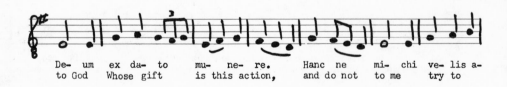

De- um ex da- to   mu-   ne- re.   Hanc ne   mi- chi ve- lis a-
to God Whose gift   is this action,   and do not   to me   try to

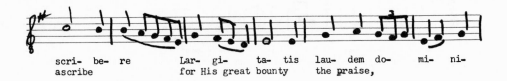

scri- be- re   Lar- gi- ta- tis   lau- dem do-   mi- ni-
ascribe   for His great bounty   the praise,

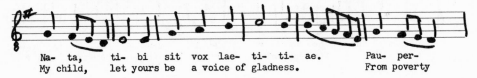

ce,   Quae-   so,   Fra- ter.
         I pray you,   Brother.

(St. Nicholas leaves.)

(23) PATER (after seeing St. Nicholas out, and turning to the Third Daughter)

Na- ta,   ti- bi sit vox lae- ti- ti- ae.   Pau- per-
My child, let yours be a voice of gladness.   From poverty

ta- tis e- la- pso   tem- po- re.   Ec-   ce   e- nim
     I am saved   for a while.   See,   here is a plenty

in au- ri pon- de- re   Quod suf-   fi- cit no- strae mi-
of gold   to   suffice   against our

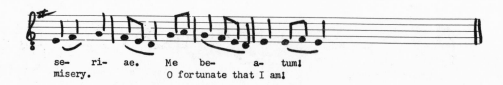

se- ri- ae.   Me be-   a- tum!
misery.   O fortunate that I am!

(24)

THIRD DAUGHTER (to Pater)

Gra- ti- a- rum er- go prae- co- ni- a   Of- fe- ra- mus,
Grateful hymns   therefore   let us offer,

et lau- dum   mu- ne- ra   U- ni   De- o, cu- i   in   sae- cu-
and praise   for the works   of the One God,   to Whom forever be

la   Laus et   ho- nor, vir- tus et   glo- ri- a,
       laud and   honor,   goodness and   glory,

Ca- re   Pa- ter.
dear   Father.

(The Third Suitor enters, and says to Pater:)

25 THIRD SUITOR

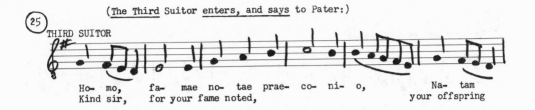

Ho- mo, fa- mae no- tae prae- co- ni- o, Na- tam
Kind sir, for your fame noted, your offspring

tu- am quae- si- tum ve- ni- o, Quam le- ga- li
seeking, I am come, whom into legal

du- cam con- nu- bi- o, Si de- de- ris.
matrimony I'll lead, if you please.

26 PATER (to his Daughter)

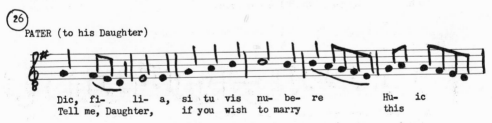

Dic, fi- li- a, si tu vis nu- be- re Hu- ic
Tell me, Daughter, if you wish to marry this

iu- ve- ni, ve- nu- sto cor- po- re Et no- bi- li.
young man, of charming mien and noble.

(27) THIRD DAUGHTER (to Pater)

In te me- a si- ta con- si- li- a.   Fac ut   lu- bet
With you my   wisdom lies.   Do what you think best

de tu- a   fi- li- a,   Ca-   re   Pa- ter.
for your   daughter,   dear   Father.

(28) PATER (to Third Suitor)

I- stam   tu- ae com- mit- to fi- de- i.   Vos con-
To her   by your faith I commit you.   Let you be

iun- gant le- ga- les   la- que- i Et   gra-   ti- a.
joined   in legal   bonds   and   by the grace of God.

(Blessed by Pater, and given the third bag of gold, the Third Suitor and
Third Daughter take Pater's arms. St. Nicholas intones the beginning of
the processional epilogue, and the four characters lead out the Choir.)

(29) ST. NICHOLAS   free rhythm

O   Chri- sti pí-   e-   tas,
O   Christ's   love,

ALL (<u>including</u> Choir)

o- mni pro- se- quen- da lau- de,
let all forever praise Him,

qui su- i fa- mu- li Ni- cho- la- i me- ri- ta lon- ge
Whose servant Nicholas' merit far

la- te- que de- cla- rat, nam ex tum- ba
and wide He declares, and even from the tomb

e- ius o- le- um ma- nat, cunc- tos- que
his energy flows, and the lazy and

lan- gui- dos sa- nat.
languid restores.

11. The Three Clerks

The Three Clerks

THIS SLIGHT PLAY seems to be a companion piece to *The Three Daughters*. The Clerks follow the Daughters—ladies first—in the Fleury Playbook (Orléans, Bibliothèque de la Ville MS 201, pp. 183-87). This association suggests an original companionship at Fleury.

Both being St. Nicholas plays, they were surely performed during the feast of St. Nicholas, December 6. The *Daughters* is attached to the Vespers service on that feast day, the *Clerks* to the Matins service by virtue of its closing with the *Te Deum*. Because the two plays were scheduled for the principal morning and evening services, one may even wonder if they were not designed to be performed on the same day rather than in successive Decembers. While two other St. Nicholas plays from Fleury are also to be associated with the same feast day, they are not as closely related to each other or to the *Clerks* and the *Daughters* as the latter are. There is thus less reason to posit the performance of more than these two on a single feast day.

Because Fleury was a leading educational and cultural center in the twelfth century, the feast day of the patron saint of scholars would certainly there receive extraordinary attention and celebration. There may be more than the chanciness of survival in the fact that, while related versions of three St. Nicholas plays exist elsewhere, only Fleury has four plays about the saint. Each of the three that exist elsewhere, moreover, is clearly superior in its Fleury version.

For medieval illustrations and other suggestions as to the style of the original production of *The Three Clerks*, see *Production*, pp. 213-19 and 337-40.

In Items 8 and 16, where halves of the double melody are repeated, I have substituted the other half.

The Cast

First Clerk
Second Clerk
Third Clerk
Innkeeper
The Old Woman
St. Nicholas

The Scene: A road, onto which gives the door to an inn. The public
room of the inn. Nightfall.

The Three Clerks   *Tres Clerici*

FIRST CLERK

Nos quos cau- sa   di- scen- di   li- te- ras
Becuase we are   travelling   in foreign lands

A- pud   gen- tes   trans- mi- sit   ex- te- ras,
among   strangers,

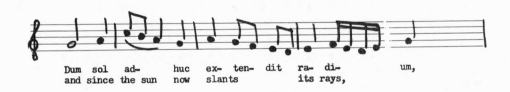

Dum sol ad-   huc   ex- ten- dit ra- di-   um,
and since the sun   now   slants   its rays,

Per- qui- ra- mus   no- bis ho-   spi- ti- um.
Let us search   for a lodging.

SECOND CLERK

Iam sol e- quos   te- net in   li- to- re,
Now the sun his steeds   reins in at   the shore-line,

Quos ad   prae-sens   mer- get sub e- quo- re.
and   presently   plunges them   into the sea.

Nec est no-   ta no- bis haec pa- tri-   a.
Nor is there any information for us   about this country.

Er- go quae- ri   de- bent ho-   spi- ti- a.
Therefore we must inquire   about lodging.

(Second Clerk rings the bell of the inn. The Innkeeper appears.)

(3) THIRD CLERK (gesturing toward the Innkeeper)

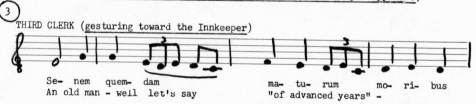

Se- nem quem- dam   ma- tu- rum   mo- ri- bus
An old man - well let's say   "of advanced years" -

Hic ha- be- mus   co- ram lu-   mi- ni- bus.
have we   in front of us in the light.

For- san, no-   stris com- pul- sus   prae- ci-   bus,
Perchance,   if by our pleading he were moved,

E- rit ho- spes   no- bis ho- spi- ti- bus.
he would host   us   for lodging.

④ ALL THREE CLERKS (to the Innkeeper)

Ho- spes, ca- re,   quae- ren- do   stu- di- a,
Mine host, dear Sir,   seeking   an education,

Huc re- li- cta   ve- ni- mus   pa- tri- a.
and far from our homes,   we come here.

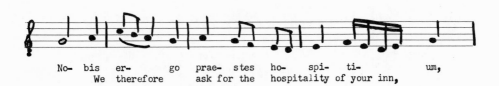

No- bis er-   go   prae- stes ho- spi- ti-   um,
We   therefore   ask for the   hospitality of your inn,

Dum du- ra- bit   hoc no- ctis   spa- ti- um.
Now that is drawing nigh   this night's   space of time.

⑤
INNKEEPER (<u>gruffly</u>)

Ho- spi- te- tur   vos fa- ctor   o- mni- um,
Let hospitality   to you be offered by somebody else,

Nam non da- bo   vo- bis ho-   spi- ti- um.
So I won't give   you   no hospitality.

Nam nec me-   a in hoc u- ti- li-   tas.
'Cause it wouldn't to me have any use at all.

(<u>The Old Woman, the Innkeeper's wife, appears from within.</u>)

Nec est ad hoc   nunc op- por- tu- ni- tas.
There's nothing about it   of any use to me.

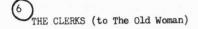

6

THE CLERKS (to The Old Woman)

Per te, ca- ra,   sit im- pe-   tra- bi- le
Through you, sweetheart,   let it be possible to supply

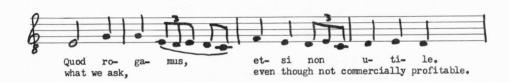

Quod ro- ga- mus,   et- si non u- ti- le.
what we ask,   even though not commercially profitable.

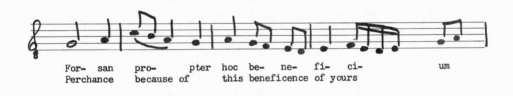

For- san pro- pter hoc be- ne- fi- ci-   um
Perchance because of this beneficence of yours

Vo- bis De- us   do- na- bit pu- e- rum.
to you God   will give a son.

7

THE OLD WOMAN (drawing the Innkeeper aside)

Non his da- re,   con- iux, ho- spi- ti- um,
Not to give them husband, lodging,

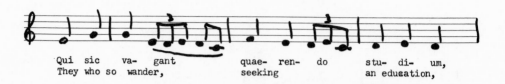

Qui sic va- gant   quae- ren- do   stu- di- um,
They who so wander,   seeking   an education,

So— la sal—   tem com— pel— lat ka— ri—   tas.
Their wandering at least   compels   charity.

Nec est da- p mnum,   nec est u-   ti- li- tas.
It won't hurt us any,   even though it's not profitable.

⑧
INNKEEPER

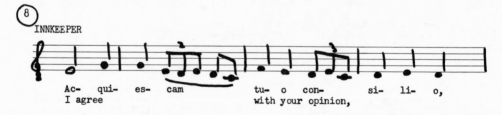

Ac— qui— es— cam   tu— o con—   si— li— o,
I agree   with your opinion,

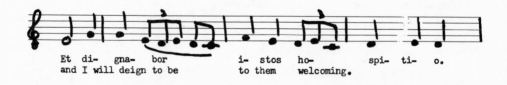

Et di— gna— bor   i— stos ho—   spi— ti— o.
and I will deign to be   to them   welcoming.

Ac- ce- da- tis, Sco- la- res, i- gi-   tur.
Come along, then,   Students,   let's go in.

Quod ro- ga- stis   vo- bis con-   ce- di-   tur.
What you ask for   to you   is conceded.

(The Clerks are shown to their offstage cubicle. When they are
asleep, the Innkeeper returns with the Old Woman.)

INNKEEPER

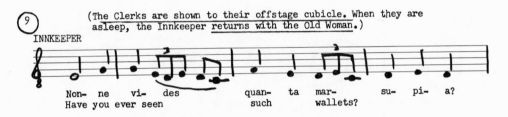

Non- ne vi- des   quan- ta mar-   su- pi- a?
Have you ever seen   such   wallets?

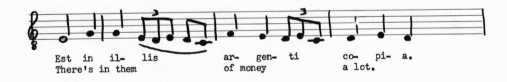

Est in il- lis   ar- gen- ti   co- pi- a.
There's in them   of money   a lot.

sic

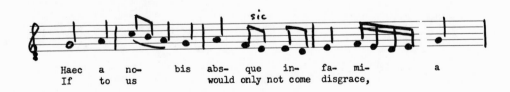

Haec a no- bis abs- que in- fa- mi-   a
If to us   would only not come disgrace,

Pos- si- de- ri   pos- set pe-   cu- ni-   a.
we might have us   a lot of cash.

⑩ THE OLD WOMAN

Pau- per- ta- tis   o- nus su- stu- li- mus,
Poverty's   burden   we have borne,

Mi ma- ri- te,   quam- di- u   vi- xi- mus.
my husband,   as long as   we've lived.

Hos si mor-   ti do- na- re vo- lu-   mus,
If   to death   we wanted to give these,

Pau- per- ta- tem   vi- ta- re pos- su- mus.
poverty   we'd be able to banish.

E- va- gi- nes   er- go iam   gla- di- um!
Unsheath,   therefore, now   your blade!

Nam- que pot- es   mor- te ia- cen- ti- um,
and thus be able   to death to throw them,

Es- se di- ves quam di- u vi- xe-   ris.
while you would be rich as long as   you lived.

At- que sci- et   ne- mo quod fe- ce- ris.
And   know about it would nobody, what you did.

(She and the Innkeeper stalk out to kill the Clerks. St. Nicholas
comes to the inn, rings the bell, and as the wicked couple appears
he changes his posture to that of a tired pilgrim, a "peregrinus."

⑪

NICHOLAS

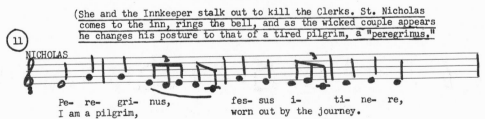

Pe- re- gri- nus,   fes- sus i- ti- ne- re,
I am a pilgrim,   worn out by the journey.

Ul- tra mo- do   non pos- sum   ten- de- re.
Further on my way   I cannot   go.

Hu- ius er-   go per no- ctis spa- ti-   um
    Therefore   for a night's   space

Mi- chi prae- stes,   prae- cor, ho- spi- ti- um.
for me   I request,   I beg you   for lodging.

⑫ INNKEEPER (aside to the Old Woman)

An di- gna- bor   i- stum ho- spi- ti- o,
Should I deign to give   this one lodging too,

Ca- ra con- iux,   tu- o con- si- li- o?
dear   wife,   in your opinion?

(13)
THE OLD WOMAN

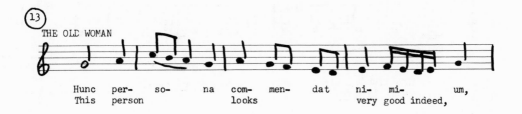

Hunc per- so- na com- men- dat ni- mi- um,
This person looks very good indeed,

Et est di- gnum ut des ho- spi- ti- um.
and is worthy for you to give him lodging.

(14)
INNKEEPER

Pe- re- gri- ne, ac- ce- de pro- pi- us.
Pilgrim, come on in.

Vir vi- de- ris ni- mis e- gre- gi- us.
A man you appear to be, very distinguished.

Si vis, da- bo ti- bi co- me- de- re.
If you wish, I'll get you something to eat too.

Quid- quam vo- les   tem- pta- bo quae- re-   re.
Whatever   you like   I'll try   to find.

(St. Nicholas sits at table as Innkeeper and the Old Woman
bring in food.)

(15) NICHOLAS

Ni- hil ex his   pos- sum co-   me- de- re.
None   of these things   can I   eat.

Car- nem vel- lem   re- cen- tem   e- de- re.
The flesh of a sheep,   freshly slaughtered,   I'll eat.

(16) INNKEEPER

Da- bo ti-   bi car- nem quam ha- be-   o,
I'll give you   what meat   I have,

Nam- que car- ne   re- cen- te ca- re-   o.
but   meat   freshly slaughtered I'm out of.

Nunc di- xi- sti pla- ne men- da- ci- um.
Now you have told a plain lie.

Car- nem ha- bes re- cen- tem ni- mi- um.
Meat you have, very fresh indeed.

Et hanc ha- bes ma- gna ne- qui- ti- a,
And you have done an enormously vile thing,

Quam ma- cta- ri fe- cit pe- cu- ni- a.
to murder for money.

Mi- se- re- re no- stri, te pe- ti- mus,
Be merciful to us, we pray you,

19

THE OLD WOMAN (on her knees)

Nam te san- ctum   De- i co-   gno- vi- mus.
now that you, a saint   of God,   we recognize.

20

INNKEEPER and THE OLD WOMAN

No- strum sce-   lus ab- ho- mi- na- bi-   le
        Surely   our abominable deed

Non est ta- men   in- con- do- na- bi- le.
is not,   nevertheless,   unpardonable.

21

NICHOLAS

Mor- tu- o- rum   af- fer- te   cor- po- ra,
The bodies of the dead   bring forth,

Et con- tri- ta   sint ve- stra   pe- cto- ra.
and contrite   let   your   hearts be.

Hi re- sur- gent per De- i gra- ti- am,
Let these rise up through God's grace,

Et vos flen- do quae- ra- tis ve- ni- am.
and may you, bewailing, seek forgiveness.

(22) NICHOLAS (praying)

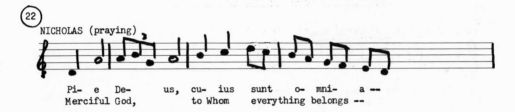

Pi- e De- us, cu- ius sunt o- mni- a --
Merciful God, to Whom everything belongs --

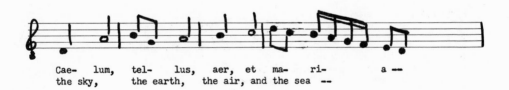

Cae- lum, tel- lus, aer, et ma- ri- a --
the sky, the earth, the air, and the sea --

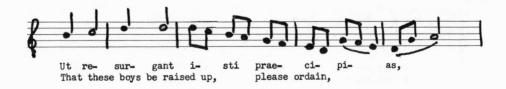

Ut re- sur- gant i- sti prae- ci- pi- as,
That these boys be raised up, please ordain,

Et   hos ad   Te   cla- man- tes   au-
and may those who to You cry

di-   as.
be heard.

(The Three Clerks appear on stage, as good as new.)

23

NICHOLAS (beginning the "Te Deum")   free rhythm

Te De- um lau- da-   mus;
You God   we praise;

24

FIRST CLERK

te Dó- mi- num con- fi- té-   mur.
You the Lord   let us acknowledge.

25

SECOND CLERK

Te ae- tér- num Pa-   trem
You the everlasting Father

㉖ THIRD CLERK

o- mnis ter- ra ve- ne- ra- tur.
by all the earth is worshipped.

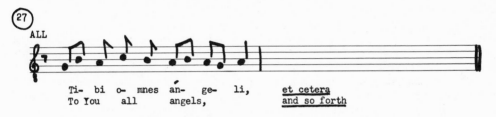

㉗ ALL

Ti- bi o- mnes an- ge- li, et cetera
To You all angels, and so forth

(The complete "Te Deum" begins on p. 491.)

12. The Image of St. Nicholas

12. The Judge of St. Nicholas

The Image of St. Nicholas

LIKE THE MIRACLE PLAY *The Son of Getron,* but unlike the *Daughters* and the *Clerks,* this St. Nicholas play has a heading of some length in which the plot is related. This is not, I think, a prologue and should therefore not be offered to the audience before the play begins.

As with the *Clerks,* the Fleury *Image* has a rival version by Hilary, student under Abelard, and one regrets that the manuscript of that version lacks the musical settings and is hence unproduceable.

The produceable version is in the Fleury Playbook (Orléans, Bibliothèque de la Ville MS 201, pp. 188-96). Considerable attention to the quality of this play is given in *Production,* pp. 221-28 and 341-43. Since that publication, our production of *The Image* in 1973 disclosed that the opening and closing moments of the play can profit from more detailing of action than the manuscript rubrics supply.

The first item, the Jew's, is addressed to an image of St. Nicholas which is hanging upstage. While the Jew's moves result in his approaching the icon from many angles, the point should be made that the Jew is mistaking the image for the real St. Nicholas and that the icon is the "obcaecans idolum" of the Jew's final words to the audience.

When the Jew wakens for the last scene he may, as the manuscript states, "find" that the chest is again full of treasure, a discovery he could make from his couch. In our production he awakened and slowly rose to his feet. He noticed the chest, with its lid replaced. He rushed to it, threw off the lid, checked that the contents were there, and then turned to the audience, repeatedly urging them to rejoice with him. As a surprise not mentioned in the playscript but suggested by manuscript arrangements in the *Daughters* and the *Clerks,* St. Nicholas appeared when his name was mentioned and was in position to intone the beginning of the recessional, *Statuit ei Domine,* a few moments later.

As usual, only the *incipit* of the recessional is given in the playscript, the action at that point being returned to the liturgy and its available service books. The version here printed at the end of the play is transcribed from the modern *Graduale Romanum,* pp. [32] - [33].

The Cast

The Jew (Hilary calls him Barbarus)
First Robber
Second Robber
Third Robber
St. Nicholas

    The Scene: The Jew's sumptuous quarters. A street. The Robbers'
               hideout.

The Image of St. Nicholas   *Iconia Sancti Nicolai*

(Another miracle of St. Nicholas and of a certain Jew who secretly at home
daily venerates an image of the Saint. Moreover, the Jew has become rich, and
when he travels to look after his affairs he leaves his house unlocked in the
custody of St. Nicholas' image. While he is gone, Robbers make off with the
Jew's treasure. Afterwards St. Nicholas restores this to him, the Saint
ordering all of it to be returned.)

JEW (to the image of St. Nicholas)

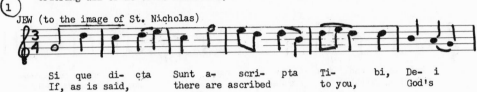

Si que di- cta   Sunt a- scri- pta Ti-   bi, De- i
If, as is said,   there are ascribed to you, God's

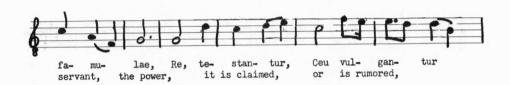

fa- mu-   lae, Re, te- stan- tur,   Ceu vul- gan-   tur
servant,   the power, it is claimed,   or is rumored,

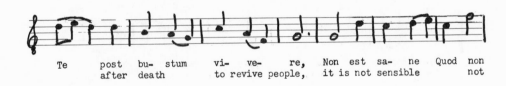

Te post bu- stum vi- ve-   re, Non est sa- ne Quod non
after death   to revive people, it is not sensible   not

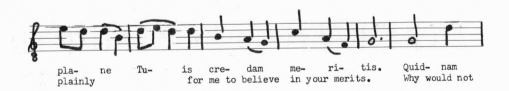

pla-   ne Tu- is cre- dam me- ri- tis. Quid- nam
plainly   for me to believe in your merits. Why would not

mi- ri Quod non vi- ri De te dant Chri- sti- co- lae?
the admiration of all Christians to you be given?

Qui ca- ren- tes sen- su, men- tes A- stru- unt com-
Who, even without sense, wouldn't gain something

po- ne- re? Quo qui lu- ce Ca- rent du- ce Vi- sum,
in the spirit? Those who the light of sight have lost are led,

di- cunt, su- me- re. Tu- que mor- ti Da- tos
they say, to see again. And you to those gone to death

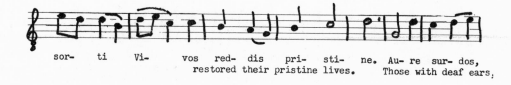

sor- ti Vi- vos red- dis pri- sti- ne. Au- re sur- dos,
restored their pristine lives. Those with deaf ears,

Vo- ce mu- tos, At- que clau- dos gres- si- bus,
     mute voices,   and   halting   gait,

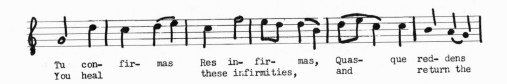

Tu con- fir- mas Res in- fir- mas, Quas- que red- dens
You heal   these infirmities,   and   return the

vi- ri- bus. Quem sic bo- num Me pa- tro- num De- le-
afflicted to health.   Such a good   patron saint   I am

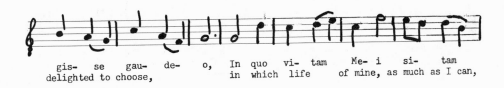

gis- se gau- de- o, In quo vi- tam Me- i si- tam
delighted to choose,   in which life   of mine, as much as I can,

Et si- sten- dam fla- gi- to. Er- go re- rum Te me-
     to be established   I entreat you.   Therefore of my goods

a- rum Ser- va- to- rem sta- tu- o. Tu que bo- nus,
the guardian   I set you up. You who are good,

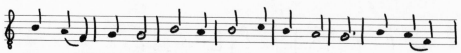

prae- sens do- mus, Ex- cu- ba dum a- be- ro.   Ad quam,
being present in the house, have the watch   while I am away. To which end,

se- ram Nun- quam fe- ram. Te cu- sto- de cre- di- to.
no key   will   I use.   In your watchfulness I trust.

Non est mul- ti Tan- ta ful- ti Ge- sto- rum pot- en- ti- a.
There are not many   who are so   sustained by   the strength of achievement.

Hu- ic si prae- sit, Ne quid de- sit Te- cto cum sub-
So in this presence, nothing   need be   hidden   of my

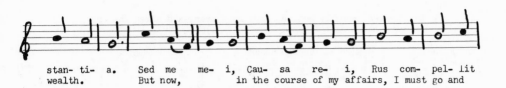

stan- ti- a.   Sed me   me- i, Cau- sa   re- i,   Rus com- pel- lit
wealth.   But now,   in the course of my affairs, I must go and

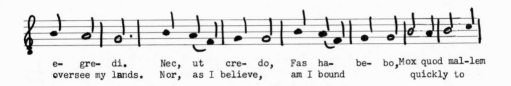

e- gre- di.   Nec, ut   cre- do,   Fas ha-   be- bo, Mox quod mal-lem
oversee my lands.   Nor, as I believe,   am I bound   quickly to

re- gre- di. Iam que   va- le, Nec quid ma- le   Nos tra-
return.   And now   goodbye,   and don't let harm come to us

ctent ma- le- fi-   ci. Vi- gil   cu-   ra, Ne ia- ctu-   ra   Do- mus
      by evil doers.   Watch   carefully   lest   to my house

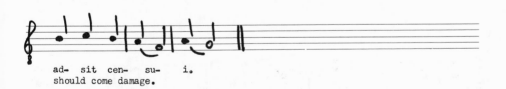

ad- sit cen- su-   i.
should come damage.

(Jew leaves. Shortly let the Robbers appear, and after the Jew has gone let them talk among themselves.)

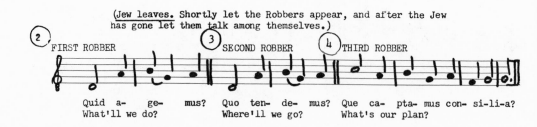

FIRST ROBBER   SECOND ROBBER   THIRD ROBBER

Quid a- ge- mus?   Quo ten- de- mus?   Que ca- pta- mus con- si-li-a?
What'll we do?   Where'll we go?   What's our plan?

THREE ROBBERS (together)

O- por- te- ret Ut im- ple- ret No- stra quis-quam mar- su- pi- a.
We got to   fill   our   sacks   with something.

FIRST ROBBER

Au- di- te, so- ci- i, me- a con- si- li- a: Vir hic est
Hear,   pals,   my   suggestion: This here man is

Iu- de- us, cu- ius pe- cu- ni- a. Si vul- tis, iam e-rit
a Jew,   with lots of money.   If you want to, now

no- stra pe- nu- ri- a Re- le- va- ta.
our   hard times   could be fixed up.

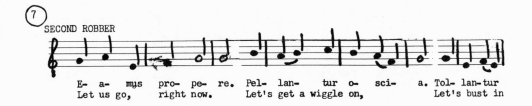

SECOND ROBBER

E- a- mus pro- pe- re. Pel- lan- tur o- sci- a. Tol- lan-tur
Let us go, right now. Let's get a wiggle on, Let's bust in

ia- nu- ae, fran- gan- tur ho- sti- a. Iu- de- i for-si-tan
the door, beat up the victim. Of the Jew perhaps

(They try the door; it is not locked. They enter easily.)

hu- ius in- cu- ri- a, Iam es- se pot-e- rit no- stra pe-
this carelessness now may to our

cu- ni- a Aug- men- ta- ta.
income add something.

(They look around.)

THIRD ROBBER (noticing the image)

O me- i co- mi- tes, i- te su- a- vi- us, Vos- que pro-
Hey, old pals, go kind of slow, and

spi- ci- te nunc di- li- gen- ti- us. Vir ta- lis cau-ti-us
take a good look around right now.   This guy (the image) warily

ser- vat   quam a- li- us Rem de qua me- tu- it,
watches,   which is something   to be feared,

et vi- gi- lan- ti- us Est ser- va- ta.
and he is a watchful   guard.

(Then let them come to the place where they must rob, and let there be
a complete treasure chest, which they gather around.)

⑨
FIRST ROBBER

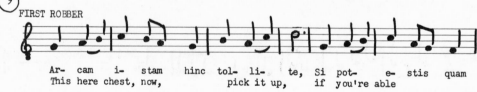

Ar- cam i- stam hinc tol- li- te, Si pot- e- stis quam
This here chest, now,   pick it up,   if you're able

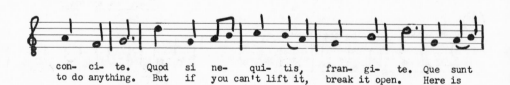

con- ci- te. Quod si ne- qui- tis, fran- gi- te. Que sunt
to do anything. But if you can't lift it, break it open. Here is

in e- a ca- pi- te.
the lid of it.

(Let them take hold of the chest but not be able to lift it.)

(10) SECOND ROBBER

Nos o- por- tet hinc ar- cham fran- ge- re. Quam ne- qui- mus
We'll have to break this chest open. We can't even

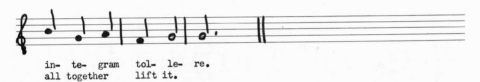

in- te- gram tol- le- re.
all together lift it.

(Then the Third Robber, coming and finding the lock not fastened, says:)

(11) THIRD ROBBER

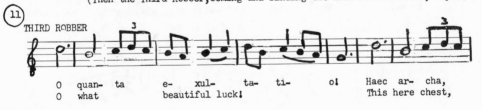

O quan- ta e- xul- ta- ti- o! Haec ar- cha,
O what beautiful luck! This here chest,

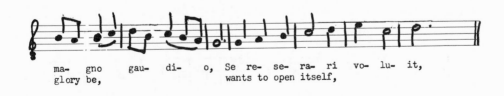

ma- gno gau- di- o, Se re- se- ra- ri vo- lu- it,
glory be, wants to open itself,

⑫ THREE ROBBERS (together)

Et   se   no- bis   a-   pe- ru- it!
and   give itself to us!

(Putting what was in the chest into their sacks, the Robbers leave.
And then the Jew, returning and noticing the robbery, says:)

⑬ JEW

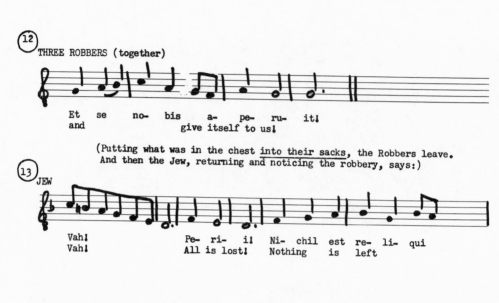

Vah!   Pe- ri- i! Ni- chil est re- li- qui
Vah!   All is lost! Nothing   is   left

mi-   chil Cur es- se ce-   pi?   Cur, ma- ter, Cur, sae- ve,
to me!   Why   am I   so cheated? Why, Momma,   why, cruelly,

pa- ter, fo- re me tri- bu- i- sti? He-   u!
Poppa,   did you bring me into the world? Alas!

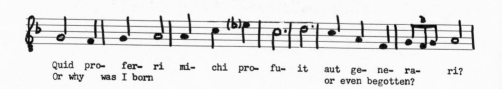

Quid pro- fer- ri mi- chi pro- fu- it aut ge- ne- ra-   ri?
Or why   was I born   or even begotten?

Cur na- tu- ra pa- rens, con- si- ste- re me sta- tu-
Why, by lusty nature parented, did you decide to have me?

e- bas? Que lu- ctus mi- chi, que ge- mi- tus hos
What grief to me, what sorrows

pro- spi- ci- e- bas! Quod que- rar in tan- tam mi- chi
you looked forward to! What

cri- men ob- es- se ru- i- nam? Qui mo- do di- ves
offense sought in me such ruin? I who was rather rich,

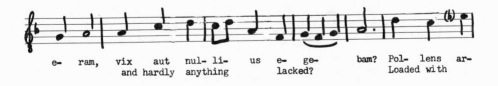

e- ram, vix aut nul- li- us e- ge- bam? Pol- lens ar-
and hardly anything lacked? Loaded with

gen- to, pre- ci- o- sis ve- sti- bus, au- ro. Sum mi-
money,   expensive   clothes,   gold.   I am

ser,   Id- que me- i mo- les   est pau- pe- ri- e- i.
miserable, and all that to me is left   is   poverty.

Nam la- tet   ex ha- bi- tu me post mo- do quo   fru- ar
Now nothing remains   of what   tu me   formerly   I used

u- su. Quod le- vi- us fer-   rem, si fer-   re
to enjoy. How light-hearted   I was,   to leave

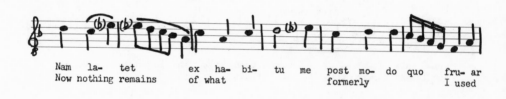

pri- us di- di-   cis- sem. Sed, ni de- ci- pi- or, e- go
the chest unlocked.   But, not to fool myself,   I

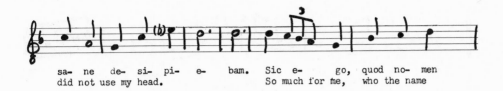

sa- ne de- si- pi- e- bam. Sic e- go, quod no- men
did not use my head.   So much for me, who the name

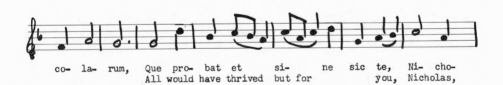

Ni- cho- la- i ma-   ne co-   le- bam. Quid-   ni
of Nicholas   daily   worshipped.   Why shouldn't

no- xa?   Fi- des no- cu- it mi- chi Chri- sti-
I feel hurt? The faith of the Christians has hurt me.

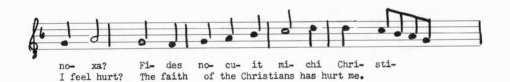

co- la- rum, Que pro- bat et   si-   ne sic te, Ni- cho-
All would have thrived but for   you, Nicholas,

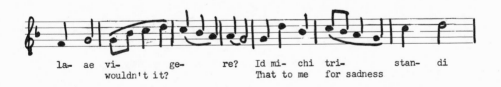

la- ae vi-   ge-   re? Id mi- chi tri-   stan-   di
     wouldn't it?   That to me for sadness

cau- sam de- dit et la- cri- man- di. Nec
a reason gives, and weeping. Nor

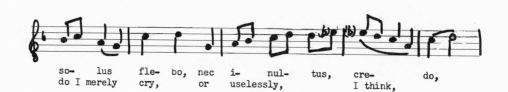

so- lus fle- bo, nec i- nul- tus, cre- do,
do I merely cry, or uselessly, I think,

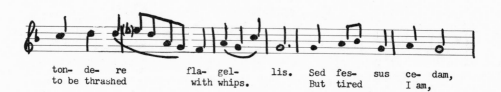

do- le- bo. Tu me- ri- tis sub- da- re pro- bris
lament. You (the image) deserve for your disgraceful act

ton- de- re fla- gel- lis. Sed fes- sus ce- dam,
to be thrashed with whips. But tired I am,

no- ctis ti- bi tem- po- ra cre- dam. Quod ni- si
and for the space of a night I'll let you off. But unless

ma- ne   me- a   re- pa-   res ti- bi cre- di- ta
in hand   you restore everything, believe you me,

cau- sa, Pri-   mo fla-   gel-   la- bo   te,
          first   I'll whip   you,

post-   que   fla-   gel- la cre-   ma- bo!
and after that   the whip   I'll burn!

(He collapses on his couch.)

(14)   (On another *sedes* the Three Robbers are dividing the loot furtively.)
NICHOLAS (surprising them)

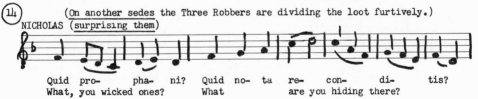

Quid pro-   pha- ni? Quid no- ta re- con-   di-   tis?
What, you wicked ones?   What   are you hiding there?

Quid de-   men-   tes, ut ve- stra di- vi- di-   tis?
What, you fools,   are you dividing up?

In- te- ri- i- stis! Quid, per- di- ti,
You should be wiped out! Why, you lost souls,

ge- ri- tis ho- mi- num? Vos vo- bis
do you treat a man this way? For yourselves

ab- du- xit fra- us dae- mo- num. Oc-
your theft has created a devil. You

cu- bu- i- stis! Vos an tran- sit o- mni- um
should drop dead! You probably should endure every

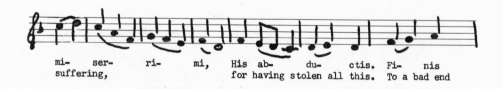

mi- ser- ri- mi, His ab- du- ctis. Fi- nis
suffering, for having stolen all this. To a bad end

tae- ter- ri- mi, Quem me ru-
don't you deserve to come?

i- stis? Non me la- tent, in- pu- den- tis- si- mi,
It does not escape me, you impudent rascals,

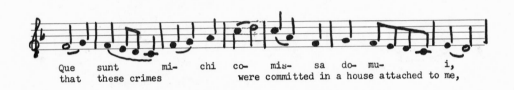

Que sunt mi- chi co- mis- sa do- mu- i,
that these crimes were committed in a house attached to me,

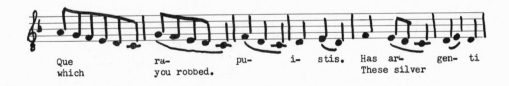

Que ra- pu- i- stis. Has ar- gen- ti
which you robbed. These silver

mar- chas, his ve- sti- bus, Hanc au- ri
coins, these clothes, this gold

mas- sam in- si- gni- bus Con- ti-
in a bag   are evidences   that incriminate you.

nu- i- stis. Mi- chi au- tem sunt pro- bra tur- pi-
To me   also   these are sinful acts,

um Mi- chi qui- dem et cau- sa ver-
and   you   are worthy of being whipped,

be- rum, Que per- pe- tra- stis.
you who   did them.

Quod si no- ctis hu- ius prae- sen- ti- a
But if   by this night all these things

fe- sti- nate re- fer- tis o- mni- a,
speedily you take back,

Id de- vi- ta- tis. Ne de-
this punishment you may avoid. But don't

pren- si ma- ne a po- pu- lo, Me in- di- can- te,
gesture with the hand to people, pointing me out,

di- gnas pa- ti- bu- lo. Poe-
or you will deserve to be hanged. The punishment

nas sol- va- tis.
you will work out. (The Saint leaves.)

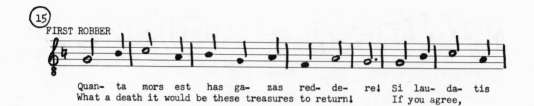

Quan- ta mors est has ga- zas red- de- re! Si lau- da- tis
What a death it would be these treasures to return!   If you agree,

vo- lo di- vi- de- re.
I'd like to divide them up.

In i- sto ne- go- ti- o, e- ge- mus con- si- li- o.
In   this   business,   let's put our heads together.

Nun- quam lae- tus fu- e-   ro Si haec sic red- di- de-ro.
Never   will I be happy again   if this stuff I return.

Est me- li-   us haec no- bis red- de- re Quam sic
It is better   for us these things to return   than so

vi- tam pen- den- do per- de- re.
our life, by hanging, to lose.

18 THREE ROBBERS (together)

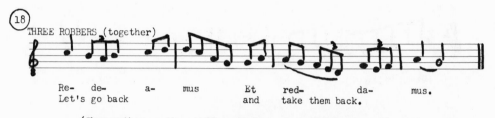

Re- de- a- mus Et red- da- mus.
Let's go back and take them back.

(They gather up the stuff in their sacks, cross over to the Jew's house, and fill the chest to overflowing. Then they leave, with comic sadness. Waking, the Jew finds that his treasure is there, and exclaims to the audience:)

19 JEW

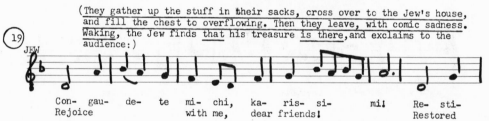

Con- gau- de- te mi- chi, ka- ris- si- mi! Re- sti-
Rejoice with me, dear friends! Restored

tu- tis cunc- tis que per- di- di! Gau-
is everything that was lost! Let us

de- a- mus! Que me- a di- sper- sit in-
rejoice! What was lost by my

cu- ri-   a,   Ni- cho- la- i re- sum- psi   gra- ti- a.
carelessness,   Nicholas   has restored   by his grace.

Gau-   de-   a-   mus!   Con- lau- de-   mus
Let us rejoice!   Let us all praise

hunc De- i fa- mu-   lum. Ab- iu- re-   mus ob-
this God's   servant.   Let us abjure

cae- cans i- do- lum. Gau-   de-   a-
blind   idols.   Let us rejoice!

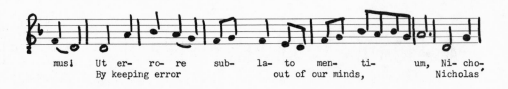

mus! Ut er- ro- re   sub- la- to men- ti-   um, Ni- cho-
By keeping error   out of our minds,   Nicholas'

la- i me- re- a- mur con- sor- ti- um. Gau-
patronage we may deserve.

free rhythm

de- a- mus! Sta- tu- it e- i Do- mi- nus
Let us rejoice! Established has the Lord

te- sta- men- tum pa- cis, et prin- ci- pem fe- cit
a covenant of peace, and His prince has He appointed,

e- um, ut sit il- li sa- cer- do- ti- i di- gni- tas
so that His priests may be revered

in ae- ter- num. Me- men- to, Do- mi-ne,
forever. I remember, O Lord,

Da- vid, et o- mnis man-su- e- tu- di- nis e- ius.
I David do,   all   His great mercies.

Glo- ri- a Pa- tri et Fi- li- o, et Spi- ri- tu- i San- cto.
Glory   be to the Father and to the Son, and to the Holy Spirit.

Si- cut e- rat in prin- ci- pi- o, et nunc, et sem- per, et
As it   was   in the beginning,   is now, and ever shall be,

in sae- cu- la sae- cu- lo- rum. A- men.
world without end.   Amen.

(The miracle is finished.)

13. The Son of Getron

The Son of Getron

IN THE FLEURY MANUSCRIPT (Orléans, Bibliothèque de la Ville MS 201, pp. 196-205) *Getron* is the fourth in the sequence of St. Nicholas plays, and the most ambitious. As I noticed in *Production,* p. 234, no other play of the sixteen herein presented characterizes so largely by melodic motif. The cast of characters is large, with eleven solo roles and groups of Schoolboys and Paupers (choirboys) and of King's Knights. This compares with five in *The Image,* six in the *Clerks,* and presumably six in the *Daughters,* but is not in the proportions of the *Daniel* and the *Herod.*

The manuscript source of the concluding item, the *Copiosae Karitatis,* I have transcribed from a service book of the twelfth century, now in Bibliothèque Nationale MS Latin 12044, fol. 224ᵛ. The Fleury manuscript gives only the *incipit* at the end of the *Getron.*

Suggestions for production of the play may be found in *Production,* pp. 229-39 and 344-45.

The Boy's theme is also the major theme of *The Three Daughters.* In the fifth measure of this melody there is a five-note cluster that may be realized as either four eighth-notes and a quarter, or a quarter and four eighths. There being no absolute compunction in terms of rhythmic mode to prefer one pattern to the other, I have used one figure in the *Daughters,* the other in *Getron.*

There is, moreover, a melodic similarity between the first ten measures of Item 17 and Item 11 of *The Image.* We have already observed (p. 243)) the correspondence of other items of *The Image* with those of *The Conversion of St. Paul.* The direction of these several indebtednesses may be imponderable.

The addition of the word *servus* to the last line of Item 22, as cogently recommended by the literary editors of the play, requires a matching measure of notation, which I have borrowed from a parallel melodic passage in Items 19, 24, and 26.

The Cast

King Marmorinus
Prime Minister
Second Minister
Third Minister
Other Knights of the Court (nonspeaking)
Getron
Euphrosina
The Boy, Adeodatus
St. Nicholas (nonspeaking)
Citizen
Schoolboys and Paupers (nonspeaking)

The Scene: The court of King Marmorinus. A street leading to the
gates of Excoranda. The church of St. Nicholas.

The play takes place over the space of a year, ending on
December 6, the feast of St. Nicholas.

The Son of Getron   *Filius Getronis*

(At the showing of how St. Nicholas rescued the Son of Getron from the
hands of Marmorinus, King of the Agarenes, let there be set up in an
adequate place King Marmorinus on a high platform, along with his armed
knights, Ministers, as if seated in his court on his throne. In another
place let there be prepared Excoranda, Getron's city, and on the set
Getron; his wife, Euphrosina; her Consolers; and Adeodatus, the son of
Getron and Euphrosina. Let there also be in the eastern part of the city
of Excoranda the church of St. Nicholas, in which the Boy is to be kidnapped. All this being ready, let the Ministers of King Marmorinus enter
his court, and let them either speak in unison or just the first of them.)

(1)

PRIME MINISTER

Sal- ve, Prin- ceps! Sal- ve, Rex o- pti- me! Que sit
Hail, O Chief! Hail, O King the best! That there be

tu- ae vo- lun- tas a- ni- mae Ser- vis tu- is
done the will of your soul, to your servants

ne tar- des di- ce- re. Su- mus que vis pa- ra- ti
do not delay to say what. We are strong enough your orders

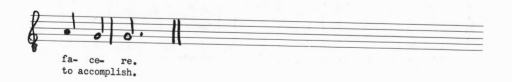

fa- ce- re.
to accomplish.

KING

I- te er- go ne tar- da- ve- ri- tis, Et quas- cun- que
Go, then, and without delay, and whatever

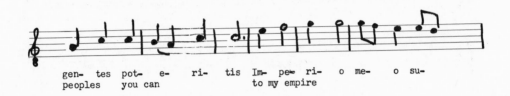

gen- tes pot- e- ri- tis Im- pe- ri- o me- o su-
peoples you can to my empire

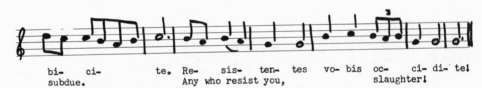

bi- ci- te. Re- sis- ten- tes vo- bis oc- ci- di- te!
subdue. Any who resist you, slaughter!

(Meanwhile let Getron and Euphrosina, with a group of Schoolboys and
and their Son leading, go to the set of the church of St. Nicholas,
as if to a solemn celebration. And let the King's armed Ministers
see the procession coming and the Son in the front fearless. Then,
the King's Ministers having kidnapped the Boy, let them return with
him to the court of the King, and let all or the Second of them say:)

SECOND MINISTER

Quod ius- si- sti, Rex bo- ne, fe- ci- mus. Gen- tes
What you have commanded, good King, we have done. Many peoples

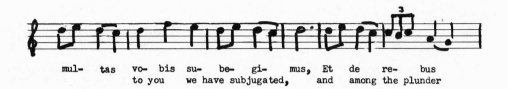

mul- tas vo- bis su- be- gi- mus, Et de re- bus
to you we have subjugated, and among the plunder

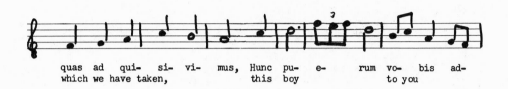

quas ad qui- si- vi- mus, Hunc pu- e- rum vo- bis ad-
which we have taken, this boy to you

du- ci- mus!
we lead.

THIRD MINISTER

Pu- er i- ste, vul- tu lau- da- bi- lis, Sen- su
This boy, good-looking, sensible,

pru- dens, ge- ne- re no- bi- lis, Be- ne de- bet
prudent, of noble birth, very well should,

no- stra iu- di- ci- o,   Sub- ia- ce-   re ve- stro ser- vi- ci- o.
in our opinion,   fit   into your service.

KING

Ap- pol- lo- ni qui re-   git o- mni- a Sem- per   sit laus,
To Apollo,   who reigns over all,   always   be praise,

vo- bis- que gra- ti-   a,   Qui fe- ci- stis mi-   chi tot
and be to you gracious,   who has made   for me so many

pa- tri-   as Sub- iu- ga- tas et tri- bu-   ta- ri- as.
countries   subjects   and tributaries.

(to the Boy)

Pu- er bo- ne, no- bis e- dis- se- re De qua   ter- ra,
My good boy,   to us   tell   from what land,

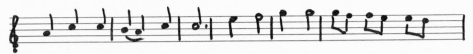

de quo sis ge- ne- re, Cu- ius ri- tu gens tu- ae
from what family you are,   and of what religion are the people of your

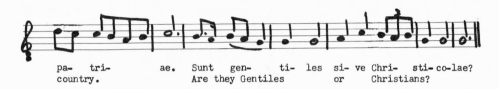

pa- tri-   ae.   Sunt gen-   ti- les si- ve Chri- sti- co- lae?
country.   Are they Gentiles   or   Christians?

⑥

BOY

Ex- co- ran- de prin- ci- pans po- pu- lo.
From Excoranda,   a populous capital.

Pa- ter me- us, Ge- tron vo- ca- bu- lo, De- um
My father -   Getron he is called -   loves God,

co- lit, cu- ius sunt ma- ri- a   Qui fe-   cit nos
and His people are many,   He who made   us

et vos et   o- mni- a.
and you and   everything.

(7)

KING

De- us me- us A- pol-   lo. De- us est Qui me fe- cit.
My god   is Apollo.   He is the God who   made me.

Ve- rax et bo-   nus est. Re- git ter- ras, re- gnat in
Faithful and good   he is. He rules the earth, he reigns in

ae- the-   re. Il- li   so- li de- be- mus cre- de- re.
the heavens.   In him alone   must we   believe.

(8)

BOY

De- us tu- us men- dax et ma- lus est.   Stul- tus,
This god of yours is a liar and evil.   He is stupid,

cae- cus, sur- dus et mu- tus est. Ta- lem de- um
blind, deaf, and dumb. Such a god

non de- bes co- le- re Qui non pot- est se ip-sum
you should not worship, who is not even able himself

re- ge- re.
to control.

⑨

KING

No- li, pu- er, ta- li- a di- ce- re. De- um me- um
Do not, boy, such things say. This god of mine

no- li de- spi- ce- re. Nam si e- um i- ra- tum
you must not despise. For if his wrath

fe- ce-   ris, E- va-   de- re ne-qua-quam   pot- e- ris.
you should incur,   to escape   you would never, ever be able.

(Meanwhile, back at Excoranda, let Euphrosina, having heard of the
kidnapping of her son, go to the church of St. Nicholas, and when she
does not find him there, let her say in a lamentable voice:)

EUPHROSINA

He- u!   He- u!   He- u!   mi- chi   mi-   se- re! Quid
Alas!   Alas!   Alas!   to me   what grief!   What

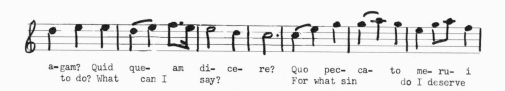

a-gam? Quid   que-   am di- ce-   re?   Quo pec- ca-   to me-ru- i
to do? What   can I   say?   For what sin   do I deserve

per-   de- re   Na- tum   me- um,   et ul- tra
to lose   my son,   and no longer

vi- ve-   re?   Cur me pa- ter in- fe- lix ge-   nu- it?
to live?   Why did my father, unhappy,   beget me?

Cur me ma- ter in- fe- lix a- blu- it? Cur me nu- trix la-cta-re
Why did my mother, unhappy, bathe me? Why did my nurse have to

de- bu- it? Mor- tem mi- chi qua- re non prae- bu- it?
suckle me? Why is not death to me permitted?

(11)

CONSOLERS (entering)

Quid te iu- vat haec de- so- la- ti- o? No- li fle- re
What can help you in this desolation? Do not weep

pro- tu- o fi- li- o. Sum- mi Pa- tris e- xo- ra Fi- li- um
for your son. With the heavenly Father will prevail the Son,

Qui con- fe- rat e- i con- si- li- um.
who will offer Him a suggestion.

(12)

EUPHROSINA (as if not caring for their consolations)

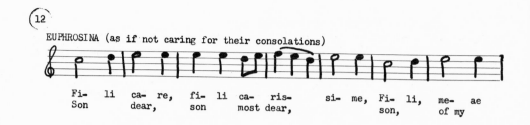

Fi- li ca- re,   fi- li ca- ris-   si- me,   Fi- li,   me- ae
Son   dear,   son   most dear,   son,   of my

ma- gna pars a- ni- mae,   Nunc es no- bis   cau- sa   tri-
spirit the largest part,   now you are to us   a cause of

sti- ti- ae,   Qui- bus e- ras   cau- sa lae-   ti- ti- ae!
sadness,   to whom   you were   a cause   of joy!

(13)

CONSOLERS

Ne de- spe- res de De- i gra-   ti- a,   Cu- ius   ma-   gna

mi- se- ri- cor- di- a   I- stum ti- bi do- na-   vit
mercy   to you   gave

pu- e- rum. Ti- bi red- det aut hunc aut a- li- um.
this boy. To you He will return either this or another one.

14

EUPHROSINA

An- xi- a- tus est in me spi- ri- tus. Cur mo- ra- tur
Troubled is within me my spirit. Why is delayed

me- us in- te- ri- tus? Cum te, fi- li, non pos- sum
my ruin? Without you, my son, I cannot

cer- ne- re. Mal- lem mo- ri quam di- u vi- ve- re.
see. I choose to die today rather than to live.

15

CONSOLERS

Lu- ctus, do- lor, et de- spe- ra- ti- o Ti- bi no- cent,
Sorrow, grief, and desperation to you are hurting,

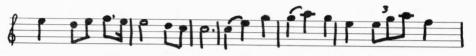

nec pro- sunt fi- li- o. Sed pro e- o de tu-   is
nor do they help your son.   But, for   his sake, of your

o-   pi- bus Da cle- ri- cis at- que pau-   pe- ri- bus.
means,   give to the schoolboys and   paupers.

Ni- cho- la- i ro- ga cle-   men-   ti- am, Ut ex- o- ret
To Nicholas   pray   for clemency,   that he may ask

mi- se- ri- cor- di- am Sum- mi Pa- tris pro tu-   o
for the mercifulness   of the heavenly Father for your

fi-   li- o. Nec fal- le- tur tu- a pe-   ti- ti- o.
son.   Nor can fail   your   petition.

(16)
EUPHROSINA

Ni- cho- la- e, pa- ter san- ctis- si- me, Ni- cho-
O Nicholas,   father most sanctified,   O Nicholas,

la- e, De- o ca- ris- si- me, Si vis ut te
     to God most dear,   if you wish me to

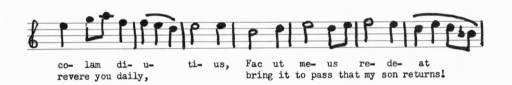

co- lam di- u- ti- us, Fac ut me- us re- de- at
revere you daily,   bring it to pass that my son returns!

fi- li- us! Qui sal- va- sti mul- tos in pe- la- go, Et tres
You who have saved many   at sea,   and three

vi- ros a mor- tis vin- cu- lo, Pre- ces me- i
young men from death   have won,   I pray   that my

pre- can- tis au- di- as, Et ex il- lo me cer- tam
prayer   you hear,   and of   such a miracle make me certain.

(Enter Getron.)

(to Getron)

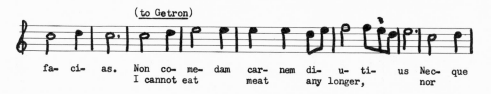

fa- ci- as. Non co- me- dam car- nem di- u- ti- us Nec- que
            I cannot eat   meat   any longer,   nor

vi- no fru- ar ul- te- ri- us, Nul- lo mo- do
wine   drink anymore.   In no way

lae- ta- bor am- pli- us, Do- nec me- us re- di-
can I enjoy life further,   unless my son   returns.

bit fi- li- us.

⑰

GETRON

Ca- ra so- ror, lu- ge- re de- si- ne. Tu- ae ti- bi
Dear girl, lament no more. To you

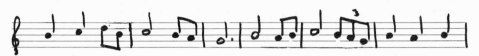

nil pro- sunt la- chri- mae. Sed o- re- tur pro no- stro
nothing will come from your tears. Instead, let for our

fi- li- o Sum- mi Pa- tris pro- pi- ti- a- ti- o.
son be prayed the heavenly Father's propitiation.

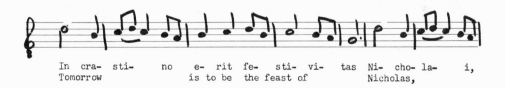

In cra- sti- no e- rit fe- sti- vi- tas Ni- cho- la- i,
Tomorrow is to be the feast of Nicholas,

quem Chri- sti- a- ni- tas To- ta de- bet de- vo- te
whom all Christianity should devoutly

co- le-   re, Ve- ne- ra- ri   et   be- ne- di- ce- re.
revere,   should venerate and   bless.

Au- di, er-   go,   me- a con- si- li-   a: A- de-
Hear,   therefore,   my   advice: Let us

a-   mus e- ius sol- lem- pni- a. Con- lau- de- mus
go   to his   high Mass.   Let us all praise

e-   ius ma- gna- li-   a. De- pre- ce- mur e-   ius suf-
his   mighty works.   Let us pray   for his assistance.

fra- gi- a. De- i for-   san est   in- spi- ra- ti-   o
From God possibly   an inspiration

Que me mo-   net pro no- stro fi- li- o.   Est o-
will show me something about our   son.   It is to be

ran- da   cum De- i   gra- ti-   a Ni- cho- la- i
beseeched,   with God's   grace,   Nicholas'

ma-   gna cle- men- ti- a.
great   clemency.

(Let them then rise up, and go to the church of St. Nicholas, and when
they are entered therein let Euphrosina lift her hands to heaven, and say:)

(18)

EUPHROSINA

Sum- me Re- gum, Rex o- mni-   um, Rex u- ni- cus et
Heavenly ruler,   king of all,   the one king   and

spes mor- ta- li- um, No-   strum no-   bis fac re- di
our hope against mortality,   to us   make to be returned

fi- li- um, Vi- tae no- strae so- lum so- la- ci- um!
our son,   of our lives   the only   solace!

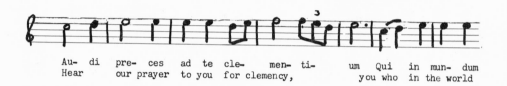

Au- di pre- ces ad te cle- men- ti- um Qui in mun- dum
Hear   our prayer to you for clemency,   you who in the world

mi- si- sti fi- li- um. Qui **nos** ci- ves coe- lo- rum
sent   our son,   who   us a city   of heaven

fa-   ce- ret Et in- fer- ni   clau- stris e- ri- pe- ret!
could make,   and Hell's   gates   break open!

De- us Pa- ter, cu- ius pot- en- ti- a Bo- na bo- nis
God the   father,   whose   power   all good to the good

mi- ni- strat o- mni- a,   Pec- ca- tri- cem me no- li
brings,   I am sinful   but do not

sper-   ne- re, Sed me me- um na- tum fac   cer- ne- re!
spurn me,   but   my   son   make me   to see!

Ni- cho- la- e,   quem san- ctum di-   ci- mus, Si sunt ve- ra
O Nicholas,   whose saintliness we call upon,   if it be   true

que de te cre-   di- mus, Tu- a no- bis et no-   stro
what of you we believe,   for us   and for our

fi- li- o Er- ga De- um pro- sit o- ra- ti- o!
son   to God make your   prayer!

(Let her [them] go out of the church, and let her go to her own house, and
let her set a table, and on the table bread and wine, as a collation for
the schoolboys and paupers. They being called and beginning to partake,
on the Marmorinus set let him say to his Ministers:)

KING

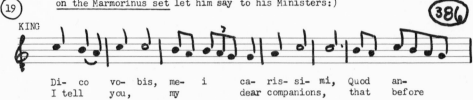

Di- co vo- bis, me- i ca- ris- si- mi, Quod an-
I tell you, my dear companions, that before

te hanc di- em non ha- bu- i Fa- mem tan- tam quan- tam nunc
today I have not had a hunger so great as now

ha- be- o. Fa- mem i- stam fer- re non va- le- o.
I have. Such hunger I cannot stand.

Vos i- gi- tur quo ve- sci de- be- am Pre- pa- ra- te,
Therefore some food I must have prepared,

ne mor- tem su- be- am. Quid tar- da- tis? I- te, ve-
before I die of hunger. What are you waiting for? Go,

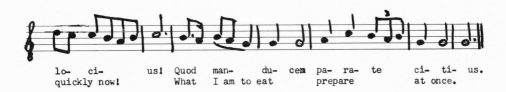

lo- ci-   us! Quod man- du- cem pa- ra- te   ci- ti- us.
quickly now!   What I am to eat   prepare   at once.

 (20)   (Let the Ministers bring on food, and let them say to the King:)

PRIME MINISTER

Ad prae- ce- ptum tu- um par- a- vi- mus Ci- bos tu-   os,
At your request   we have prepared you your food,

et   huc ad- tu-   li-   mus.
and   to it bid you.

(21)

SECOND MINISTER

Nunc, si ve-   lis, pot- e- ris   pro- pe- re   Qua gra-
Now, if you please,   you can   speedily   that

va-   ris fa-   mem ex- tin- gue- re.
bothersome   hunger   extinguish.

(22)
(Let water be poured <u>in a basin</u>, and let the King wash his hands,
and then, beginning to eat, let him say:)

KING

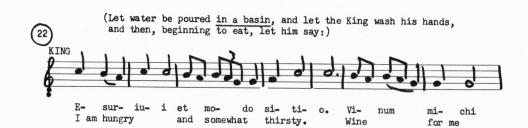

E- sur- iu- i et mo- do si- ti- o.   Vi- num   mi- chi
I am hungry   and somewhat thirsty.   Wine   for me

da- ri prae- ci- pi- o,   Quod af- fe- rat mi- chi   quam
I request be brought,   and that it be brought to me   at

ci- ti-   us Ser- vus me- us Ge- tro- nis   fi- li- us.
once   by my servant,   Getron's   son.

(23)
(Let the Boy, hearing this, sigh deeply, and say to himself:)

BOY

He- u! He- u! He- u! mi- chi mi-   se- ro! Vi- tae me- ae
Alas!   Alas!   Alas!   to me   misery!   My life's

fi- nem de- si- de-   ro.   Vi- vus e-   nim quam- di- u
end   I wish for.   Living   only for a few days.

fu-   e- ro, Li- be- ra- ri ne-   qua-   quam   pot- e- ro.
To be rescued   never, ever   can I be.

24

KING (to the Boy)

Pro qua cau- sa su- spi-   ras ta- li- ter? Su- spi-
For what   reason   do you sigh   like that?   Sighing

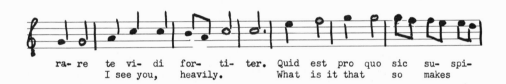

ra- re te vi- di for- ti- ter. Quid est pro quo sic su- spi-
I see you,   heavily.   What is it that   so   makes

ra- ve-   ris? Quid te   no- cet, aut un- de quae- re-ris?
you sigh?   What   pains you,   or   what do you seek?

25

BOY

Re- cor-   da- tus me- ae mi- se- ri- ae   Me- i
Mindful   of my misery,   of my

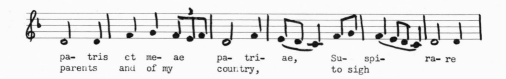

pa- tris et me- ae   pa- tri- ae,   Su- spi-   ra- re
parents   and of my   country,   to sigh

ce- pi et ge- me- re,   Et in-   tra   me ta- li-
I choose and to groan,   and to myself   such things

a   di-   ce- re: An- nus   u- nus ex- ple- tur ho- di-
to say as: One year ago today   it has been

e   Post- quam   ser- vus fa- ctus mi-   se-   ri- ae, Pot-
since   I was made a servant of misery,

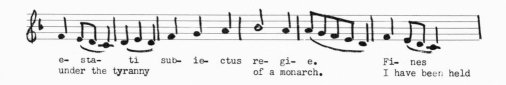

e- sta-   ti sub- ie- ctus re- gi- e.   Fi- nes
under the tyranny   of a monarch.   I have been held

hu- ius in- tra- vi   pa- tri-   ae.
in this   alien country.

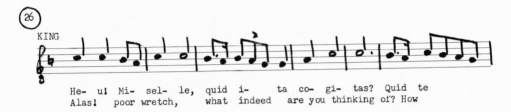

KING

He- u! Mi- sel- le, quid i- ta co- gi- tas? Quid te
Alas! poor wretch, what indeed are you thinking of? How

iu- vat cor- dis an- xi- e- tas? Ne- mo pot- est te mi- chi
does a troubled heart help you?   Nobody can   you from me

tol- le-   re Quam- di- u te non ve- lim   per- de- re.
separate   as long as   I do not wish to part with you.

(Meanwhile let some one in the likeness of Nicholas appear in the King's
court. Let him pick up the Boy by the hair of his head and carry him,
clutching the covered wine goblet, to the gates of Excoranda. And let
Nicholas then retire, as if not wishing to be observed. Then let a Citizen
approach and say to the Boy:)

CITIZEN

Pu- er, quis est, et quo vis per- ge- re? Cu- ius ti- bi
Boy, who are you, and where do you wish to go? Who to you

de- dit lar- gi- ti- o Cy- phum i- stum cum re- cen- ta- ri- o?
gave this present of a goblet with a lid?

BOY

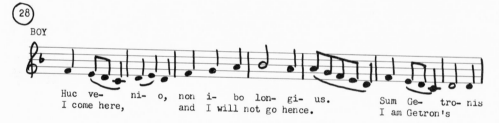

Huc ve- ni- o, non i- bo lon- gi- us. Sum Ge- tro- nis
I come here, and I will not go hence. I am Getron's

u- ni- cus fi- li- us. Ni- cho- la- o sit laus et
only son. To Nicholas be praise and

glo- ri- a, Cu- ius hic me re- du- xit gra- ti- a.
glory, by whose grace I am here returned.

(The Citizen runs to Getron and says:)

CITIZEN

Gau- de, Ge- tron; nec fle- as am- pli- us! Ex- tra fo- res
Rejoice, Getron; do not weep anymore! Outside the gates

stat tu- us fi- li- us. Ni- cho- la- i lau- det ma- gna li-
stands your son. Praise be to Nicholas' greatness,

a, Cu- ius e- um re- du- xit gra- ti- a.
whose grace led back the boy.

(And let Euphrosina also hear from the same sort of messenger, and let
her run to her son outside the gates, whom she showers with many
kisses, and let her say:)

EUPHROSINA

De- o no- stro sit laus et glo- ri- a, Cu- ius
To our God be praise and glory, whose

ma- gna mi- se- ri- cor- di- a, Lu- ctus no- stros
great mercy, our sorrow

ver- tens in gau- di- um, No- strum no- bis re-
changing into joy,   to us   has

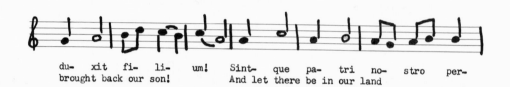

du- xit fi- li- um! Sint- que pa- tri no- stro per-
brought back our son! And let there be in our land

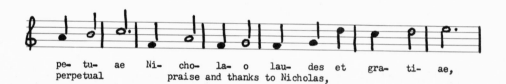

pe- tu- ae Ni- cho- la- o lau- des et gra- ti- ae,
perpetual   praise and thanks to Nicholas,

Cu- ius er- ga De- um o- ra- ti- o nos
by means of whose prayer God

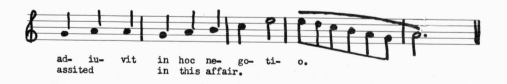

ad- iu- vit in hoc ne- go- ti- o.
assited   in this affair.

(31)

(Led by Euphrosina and the Boy, the company leaves, singing:)

ALL

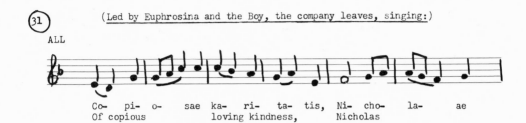

Co- pi- o- sae ka- ri- ta- tis, Ni- cho- la- ae
Of copious   loving kindness,   Nicholas

pon- ti- fex, Qui cum De- o glo- ri- a- ris in
the high priest, who with God you are glorified in

coe- li pa- la- ti- o, Con- de- scen- de, sup- pli- ca- mus,
the heavenly palace,   look down,   we beg you,

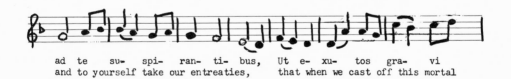

ad te su- spi- ran- ti- bus, Ut e- xu- tos gra- vi
and to yourself take our entreaties,   that when we cast off this mortal

car- ne per- tra- has ad su- per- os.
coil   you will lead us on to the world above.

14. The Play of Daniel

The Play of Daniel

THIS EDITION of the Beauvais *Daniel,* transcribed from British Museum MS Egerton 2615, fols. 95^r-108^r, is offered as an unadapted transcription of the original, with no additions to the cast or text, no expressed instrumentation, and no effort to mensuralize in other than the medievally customary triple rhythms. For suggestions as to the production and interpretation of this edition of the play, and for a critique of the Pro Musica adaptation, see *Production,* pp. 245-55.

The play may have some evolutionary connection to the Daniel prophecy in *The Procession of the Prophets.* For an interesting but inconclusive discussion of this matter, see Young, II, 304-6. Nor is there more than surmise as to when in the liturgical calendar for the Christmas season the play may have been performed. The boisterous quality of the *Daniel* does not positively associate it with the Feast of Fools. Other plays with a similar exuberance have quite other bearings in the liturgical calendar. More likely does it seem to me that a play of such dimensions and spectacle as the *Daniel* was created as a lavish entertainment for royalty or nobility who were spending the Christmas season at Beauvais.

Items assigned by the manuscript to a group of characters may often have been distributed among its individual members. Sometimes this distribution can be identified by the contrasting vocal ranges of sections of an item, as for example the Legates' Item No. 33. Elsewhere, as in the Satraps' Item 27, there are clear opportunities for solo verses and choral refrains. I have distinguished the separate roles of the three angels of the playscript by naming them First, Second, and Herald.

A feature of the play is its frequent use of the *conductus,* a medieval liturgical form that involves singing in procession. The medieval formula for moving a group of worshipping clerics from one church area to another was, as is cited in *Production,* pp. 37 and 42, bells—lights—procession. The *conductus,* as its name suggests, was a lyric song used by the Choir to escort or conduct the celebrant of an office either to or from the chancel during the service—an accompaniment to a processional action, a song by the conductors of the leader. What seems to have been exploited in the *conductus* was its dance rhythm. One cannot therefore imagine a Choir, or subgroups of it, simply shambling through such items as Nos. 6, 12, 17, 26, 27, 28, and 33. The image of a dancing girl with handbells, portrayed vividly in a Limoges Troper of the tenth century, might appropriately illustrate a *conductus* in action. (See frontispiece.)

Item 12 has been transposed a fourth lower, to G; Item 13 a fifth higher, to C, for the Queen.

It is suggested that Item 48 be repeated after Item 49, as a *conductus* to escort Habakkuk to Daniel.

The last item of the play, No. 58, is the first stanza of a hymn by Fulbert of Chartres, composed in the tenth century long before the *Daniel* play was conceived anywhere. The words to all four stanzas are in Young, II, 433, but require some adjustment of the melody. The same first stanza appears in a twelfth-century Magi play from Limoges (see Young, II, 35), and the hymn was apparently still popular then. For remarks about it see J. Chailley, *Histoire Musicale du Moyen Age* (1950), p. 84.

The Cast

Belshazzar's Princes (men)
Belshazzar's Satraps (women or boys)
King Belshazzar
Two Magi
Belshazzar's Queen
Daniel
Belshazzar's General (nonspeaking)
King Darius
Darius' Courtiers (men)
Darius' Musicians (nonspeaking)
Two Counselors to Darius (tenor, baritone)
Two Legates (messengers) (tenor, baritone)
First Angel (nonspeaking)
Second Angel (man)
Habukkuk
Herald Angel

> The Scene: The throne room of King Belshazzar, and later of King
> Darius. At one side, Daniel's house. At the other, a
> country footpath. Late November, near Advent. Christ-
> mastide.

The Play of Daniel   *Danielis Ludus*

① PRINCES

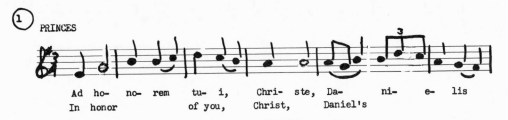

Ad ho- no- rem tu- i, Chri- ste, Da- ni- e- lis
In honor   of you, Christ, Daniel's

lu-   dus i- ste. In Bel- va- co est in- ven- tus,
play   this is. In Beauvais   it was composed,

Et   in- ve- nit   hunc   iu- ven-   tus.
and   was made   in our   youth.

(Then let King Belshazzar enter, and let his Princes sing this
sequence, as a conductus, leading him in:)

② PRINCES

A- stra te- nen- ti Cun- cti- pot- en- ti Tur- ba vi- ri- lis
The star- holder,   almighty one,   this crowd of men

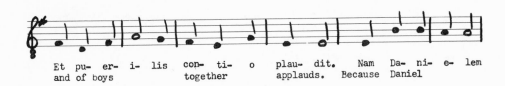

Et pu- er- i- lis con- ti- o   plau- dit. Nam Da- ni- e- lem
and of boys   together   applauds. Because Daniel

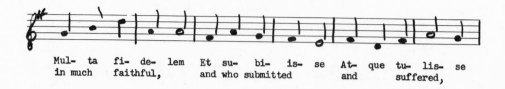

Mul- ta fi- de- lem   Et su-   bi- is- se   At- que tu- lis- se
in much   faithful,   and who submitted   and   suffered,

Fir- mi- ter au- dit.
alertly   (the crowd) listens.

(Then let King Belshazzar ascend his throne, and let the Satraps,
applauding him, sing:)

③ SATRAPS

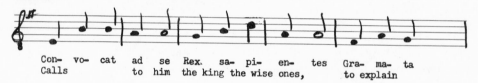

Con- vo- cat ad se Rex. sa- pi- en- tes Gra- ma- ta
Calls   to him the king the wise ones,   to explain

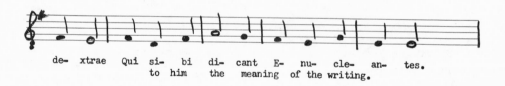

de- xtrae Qui si- bi di- cant E- nu- cle- an- tes.
           to him   the   meaning of the writing.

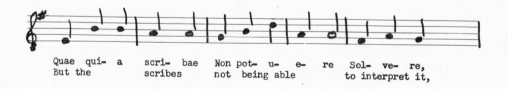

Quae qui- a   scri- bae Non pot- u- e- re Sol- ve- re,
But the   scribes   not being able   to interpret it,

re- gi I- li- co mu- ti Con- ti- cu- e- re.
before the king there they kept silent.

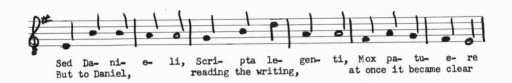

Sed Da- ni- e- li, Scri- pta le- gen- ti, Mox pa- tu- e- re
But to Daniel, reading the writing, at once it became clear

Quae pri- us il- lis Clau- sa fu- e- re.
what earlier to the others had been obscure.

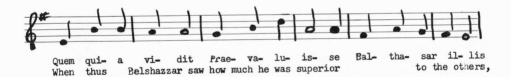

Quem qui- a vi- dit Prae- va- lu- is- se Bal- tha- sar il- lis
When thus Belshazzar saw how much he was superior to the others,

Fer- tur in au- la Prae- po- su- is- se. Cau- sa re- per- ta,
he had him in the royal hall placed above them. A case invented,

Non sa- tis a- pta, De- sti- nat il- lum O- re le- o- num
not very   apt,   was decided against him, and by the mouths of lions

Di- la- ce- ran- dum.   Sed, De- us, il- los An- te ma-
he was to be torn to pieces.   But then, O God, these evil ones against

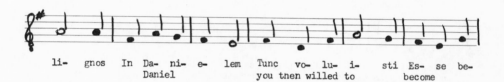

li- gnos In Da- ni- e- lem Tunc vo- lu- i-   sti Es- se be-
        Daniel   you then willed to   become

ni- gnos. Huic quo- que pa- nis, Ne sit i- na- nis,
friendly. To him some   bread,   lest he faint,

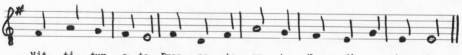

Mit- ti- tur a te Prae- pe- te va- te Pran- di- a dan- te.
was sent by   by you by a winged   prophet, food   bringing.

④

SATRAPS (a salutation)

Rex, in ae- ter- num   vi-   ve!
O King,   forever   live!

⑤
(And let the King speak boldly to them:)

BELSHAZZAR

Vos   qui pa- re- tis me- is vo- ci- bus, Af- fer- te va-   sa
You   who obey   my   words,   bring   the vessels

me- is u- si- bus, Quae tem- plo pa- ter me- us ab- stu-
of my   rites,   which from the temple my father   took

lit, Iu- de- am gra- vi- ter cum per- cu- lit.
when Judea   he grievously   smote.

(Let the Satraps, bringing vessels, sing this sequence - <u>a conductus</u> -
⑥   in praise of the King:)

SATRAPS

Iu- bi- le- mus re- gi no- stro ma- gno ac pot- en- ti!
Let us rejoice   in our king,   great   and powerful!

Re- so- ne- mus lau- de di- gna vo- ce com- pe- ten- ti!
Let us sing out with praises fitting, with voices full!

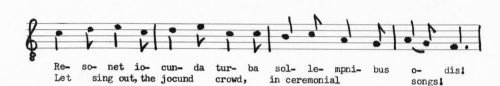

Re- so- net io- cun- da tur- ba sol- le- mpni- bus o- dis!
Let sing out, the jocund crowd, in ceremonial   songs!

Cy- tha- ri- zent, plau- dant ma- nus, mil- le so- nent mo-dis!
Let them play the kitharas, clap their hands, a thousand verses sing!

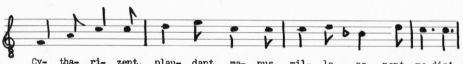

Pa- ter e- ius de- stru- ens Iu- de- o- rum tem- pla Ma- gna
His father in destroying the Jews' temple a great deed

fe- cit, et hic re- gnat e- ius per e- xem- pla.
did, and this one reigns by his example.

Pa- ter e- ius spo- li- a- vit re- gnum Iu- de- o- rum.
His father despoiled the kingdom of the Jews.

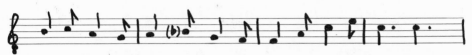

Hic e- xal- tat su- a fe- sta de- co- re va- so- rum.
This one exalts him by his feasts with the decorous vessels.

Haec sunt va- sa re- gi- a qui- bus spo- li- a- tur
These are the regal vessels which were taken as spoils of war

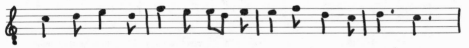

Ihe- ru- sa- lem, et re- ga- lis Ba- by- lon di- ta- tur.
from Jerusalem, and the Babylonian royalty enrich.

Prae- sen- te- mus Bal- tha- sar i- sta re- gi no- stro,
Let us present these to Balshazzar our king,

Qui sic su- os   per- or- na-   vit pur- pu- ra et o- stro.
Who   so his own   arrays   in purple robes.

I- ste   pot-   ens,   i- ste   for- tis, i- ste glo- ri- o-sus,
This one powerful,   this one   brave,   this one glorious,

I-   ste pro- bus, cu- ri- a- lis, de- cens et for- mo- sus.
this one righteous, courtly,   handsome, and graceful.

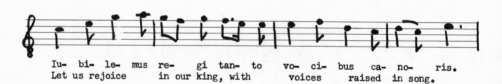

Iu- bi- le- mus re-   gi tan- to   vo- ci- bus ca- no-   ris.
Let us rejoice   in our king, with   voices   raised in song.

Re- so- ne-   mus o-   mnes u-   na lau- di- bus   so- no- ris.
Let us sing out, all of us as one,   in praises   harmonious.

Ri- dens plau- dit Ba- by- lon, Ihe- ru- sa- lem plo- rat.
Laughing   Babylon applauds;   Jerusalem   weeps.

Haec or- ba- tur, haec tri- um- phans Bal- tha- sar a- do- rat.
She was raped, while triumphant Belshazzar is worshipped.

O- mnes er- go e- xul- te- mus tan- tae pot- e- sta- ti,
Let all therefore exult at such power,

Of- fe- ren- tes re- gis va- sa su- ae ma- ie- sta- ti.
offering to the king these vessels betokening his majesty.

⑦ (Then let the Princes say:)

PRINCES

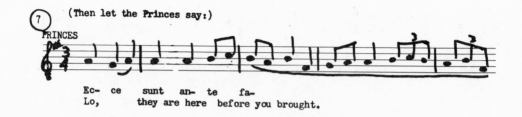

Ec- ce   sunt an- te fa-
Lo,   they are here before you brought.

ci-   em   tu- am.

(Meanwhile let there appear before the King a right hand, writing on
the wall, "Mene,Tekel,Peres." When the King sees this, let him cry
⑧ out in fright:)

BELSHAZZAR

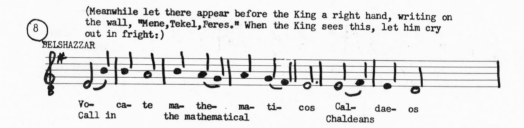

Vo-   ca- te ma- the- ma- ti- cos Cal- dae- os
Call in   the mathematical   Chaldeans

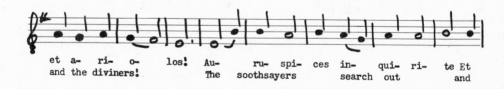

et a- ri- o-   los! Au-   ru- spi- ces in-   qui- ri-   te Et
and the diviners!   The soothsayers   search out   and

ma- gos in- tro- du-   ci- te!
the wise men bring   forth!

(9) (Now let the Magi be led in, who say to the King:)

MAGI

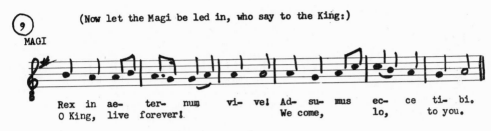

Rex in ae- ter- num vi- vel Ad- su- mus ec- ce ti- bi.
O King, live forever! We come, lo, to you.

(And the King answers:)

(10) BELSHAZZAR

Qui scri- ptu- ram hanc le- ge- rit Et sen- sum a- pe- ru-
Who this writing reads and its meaning discloses

e- rit, Sub il- li- us pot- en- ti- a Sub- de- tur Ba- by-
over others shall have power in Babylon,

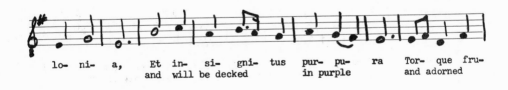

lo- ni- a, Et in- si- gni- tus pur- pu- ra Tor- que fru-
and will be decked in purple and adorned

e- tur au- re- a.
with a golden collar.

(11) (And the Magi, not knowing how to interpret it, say to the King:)

MAGI

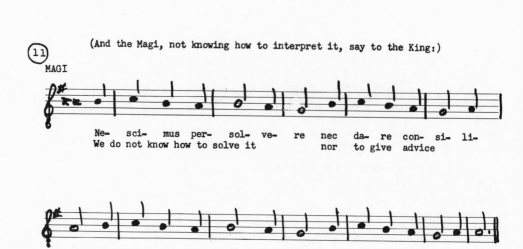

Ne- sci- mus per- sol- ve- re nec da- re con- si- li-
We do not know how to solve it   nor   to give advice

um, Quae sit su- per- scri- pti- o, nec ma- nus in- di- ti- um.
as to what is the interpretation,   or the writing's import.

(12) (The Satraps sing a conductus to bring the Queen to Belshazzar.)

SATRAPS

Cum do- cto-rum   Et ma-   go-rum O- mnis ad-   sit
With the learned doctors and the Magi   all   the council is here.

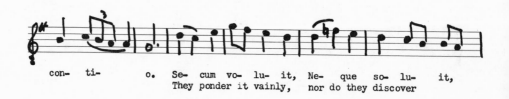

con- ti-   o. Se- cum vo- lu- it, Ne- que so- lu-   it,
They ponder it vainly,   nor do they discover

Quae sit   ma- nus vi- si-   o. Ec- ce   pru- dens,
What is   the writing's meaning.   Behold   the prudent one,

Styr- pe   clu- ens,   Di-   ves cum   pot- en- ti-   a.
the royalty elect,   rich   in   influence.

In   ve- sti-   tu   De- au- ra- to,   Con- iunx   ad-   est
Dressed   in gold,   the queenly wife is here.

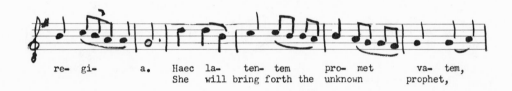

re- gi-   a.   Haec la- ten- tem   pro- met   va- tem,
                    She   will bring forth the unknown   prophet,

Per   cu- ius   in- di- ci-   um Rex de- scri- bi Su- um
Through whose   insight   the King will have it described

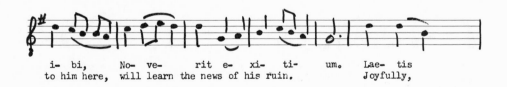

i- bi,   No- ve-   rit e- xi- ti-   um.   Lae- tis
to him here, will learn the news of his ruin.   Joyfully,

er- go   Haec vi-   ra- go   Co- mi- te-   tur
therefore, this heroine   comes forth.

plau- si-   bus.   Cor- dis, o-   ris Que   so- no- ris
                     With strings, with voices that sound together

Per- so- ne- tur vo- ci-   bus.
let us make music.

(Then the Queen, at the throne, venerates the King, saying:)

(13) QUEEN

Rex, in ae- ter- num   vi- ve! Ut scri- ben- tis
O King, live   forever!   So that of these writings

no-   scas in- ge- ni- um, Rex Bal- tha-   sar, au- di con-
you   may know the meaning, King Belshazzar,   hear   my

si- li- um. Cum Iu- dae- ae ca- pti- vis po- pu- lis Pro-
counsel. With the Jewish captive people

phe- ti- ae do- ctum o- ra- cu- lis. Da- ni- e- lem
an oracular prophet was led here. Daniel

a su- a pa- tri- a Ca- pti- va- vit pa- tris vi- cto- ri-
from his country was made captive by our victorious

a. Hic sub tu- o vi- vens im- pe- ri- o, Ut man- de- tur,
He under your rule now living, he can be ordered,

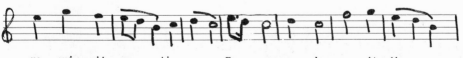

re- qui- rit ra- ti- o. Er- go man- da ne sit di-
reason requires. Therefore order him without

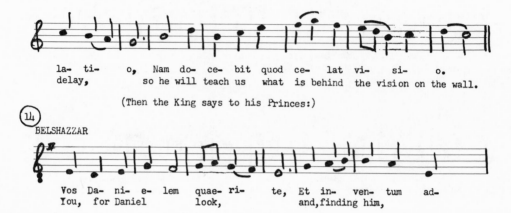

la- ti-   o, Nam do- ce- bit quod ce- lat vi- si-   o.
delay,   so he will teach us what is behind the vision on the wall.

(Then the King says to his Princes:)

⑭

BELSHAZZAR

Vos Da- ni- e- lem quae- ri- te, Et in- ven- tum ad-
You, for Daniel   look,   and, finding him,

du- ci- te.
bring him here.

(Then the Princes, finding Daniel, say to him:)

⑮ PRINCES

Vir pro- phe- ta De-   i, Da- ni- el, vien
Man- prophet   of God,   Daniel,   come

al the Roi! Ve- ni de- si- de- rat par- ler
to the King! Come, he desires   to speak

a   toi.   Pa- vet et tur-   ba-   tur, Da- ni- el,
to   you.   He is fearful and disturbed,   Daniel,

vien   al   Roi!   Vel- let   quod   nos la-   tet
come   to the King! He wishes   what   from us is hidden

sa-   voir   par   toi.   Te di- ta- bit   do-   nis,
to learn   from   you.   To you he will give   gifts,

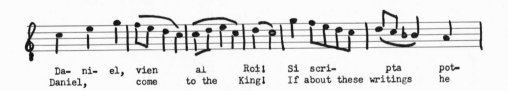

Da- ni- el, vien   al   Roi!   Si scri-   pta   pot-
Daniel,   come   to the   King!   If about these writings   he

e-   rit sa-   voir   par   toi.
may   learn   from   you.

(16)
DANIEL (to the Princes)

Mul- tum mi- or cu- ius con-   si-   li- o Me re-
Much   do I wonder by whose advice   I am

qui-   rat re- ga- lis ius- si- o. I- bo ta- men
summoned   by the royal   command.   I shall go, nevertheless,

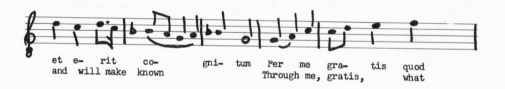

et e- rit co-   gni- tum Per me gra- tis quod
and will make known   Through me, gratis,   what

est ab- scon- di-   tum.
is obscure.

(As the Princes lead Daniel toward the King, they sing a conductus:)

(17)
PRINCES

Hic ve- rus De- i fa- mu- lus, Quem lau- dat o- mnis
This is a true   servant of God,   who is praised by all

po- pu- lus,   Cu- ius   fa- ma   pru- den-   ti- ae
people,   whose   reputation for wisdom

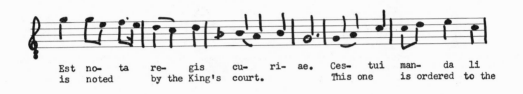

Est no- ta   re- gis   cu-   ri- ae.   Ces- tui man-   da li
is   noted   by the King's court.   This one is ordered to the

Roi   par   nos.
King by   us.

(18) DANIEL

Pau- per et   e- xu-   lans en- vois al Roi par   vos.
A pauper and an exile,   I am sent to the King by you.

(19) PRINCES

In iu- ven-   tu- tis glo- ri- a, Ple- nus   cae- le- sti
In his youthful   glory,   Full of   heavenly

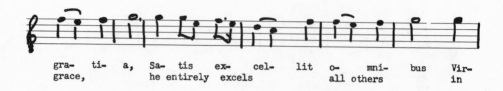

gra- ti- a,   Sa- tis ex- cel-   lit   o- mni-   bus   Vir-
grace,   he entirely excels   all others   in

tu- te, vi- ta,   mo- ri-   bus. Ces- tui man-   da
virtue,   life,   conduct.   This one is ordered

li   Roi   par   nos.
to the King by   us.

(20) DANIEL

Pau- per   et   e- xu-   lans en- vois al Roi par   vos.
A pauper   and an exile,   I am sent to the King by you.

(21) PRINCES

Hic est   cu-   ius au- xi- li- o Sol- ve- tur   il- la
He it is   whose   help   is to explain   that

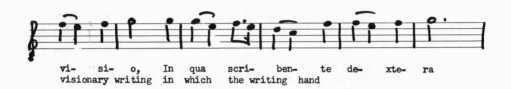

vi- si- o, In qua scri- ben- te de- xte- ra
visionary writing in which the writing hand

Mo- ta sunt re- gis vi- sce- ra. Ces- tui man- da
shook the King's vitals. This one is ordered

li Roi par nos.
to the King by us.

(22)

DANIEL

Pau- per et e- xu- lans en- vois al Roi par vos.
A pauper and en exile, I am sent to the King by you.

(Daniel coming before the King, says:)

Rex, in ae- ter- num vi- ve!
O King, forever live!

BELSHAZZAR (to Daniel)

Tu- ne Da- ni- el no- mi- ne di- ce- ris Huc ad-
Are you not Daniel   by name   called,   the one who

du- ctus cum Iu- dae- ae mi- se- ris? Di- cunt te ha- be- re
was led here with the Jewish miserable ones? They say you have

De- i spi- ri- tum, Et prae- sci- re quod- li- bet ab-
God's   spirit,   and can foresee   whatever is

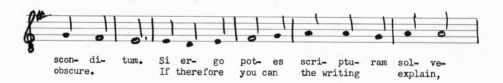

scon- di- tum. Si er- go pot- es scri- ptu- ram sol- ve-
obscure.   If therefore you can the writing   explain,

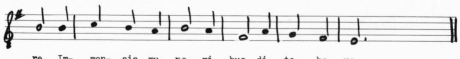

re, Im- men- sis mu- ne- ri- bus di- ta- be- re.
immense   gifts   will be bestowed on you.

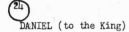

DANIEL (to the King)

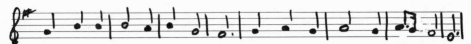

Rex, tu- a no- lo mu- ne- ra; Gra- tis sol- ve- tur li- te- ra.
O King, I do not want your gifts; gratis I'll explain the handwriting.

Est au-tem haec so- lu- ti- o: In- stat ti- bi con- fu- si- o.
This is, however, the explanation: Coming at you is confusion.

Pa- ter tu- us prae o- mni- bus Pot- ens o- lim pot- en- ti- bus,
Your father before all others was powerful once,

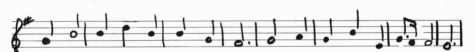

Tur- gens ni- mis su- per- bi- a De- ie- ctus est a glo- ri-
Swollen excessively with pride, he was thrown down from glory.

a. Nam cum De- o non am- bu- lans, Sed se- se De- um
For with God he did not walk, but himself God

si- mu- lans,   Va- sa tem- plo di- ri- pu- it, Quae su- o
simulated,   the vessels in the temple he stole   which to his own

u- su ha- bu- it. Sed post mul- tas in- sa- ni- as Tan- dem
use   he had.   But af ter many such insanities   finally

per- dens di- vi- ti- as For- ma nu- da- tus ho- mi- nis,
losing   his wealth,   and of his humanity stripped,

Pa- stum gu- sta- vit gra- mi- nis. Tu quo- que e- ius fi- li-
on grassy food he ate.   You also,   his   son,

us, Non ip- so mi- nus im- pi- us, Dum pa- tris a- ctus
are not   less   sinful,   since your father's acts

se- que- ris, Va- sis e- is- dem u- te- ris.   Quod qui- a
you follow,   these same vessels   using.   Since this

De- o di- spli- cet, In- stat tem- pus quo vin- di- cet,
to God   is displeasing,   the time is now   when He vindicates Himself,

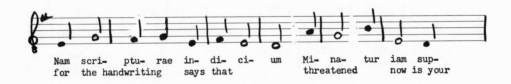

Nam scri- ptu- rae in- di- ci- um Mi- na- tur iam sup-
for the handwriting   says that   threatened   now is your

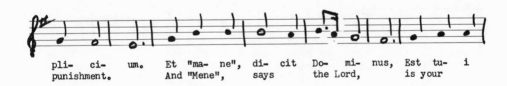

pli- ci- um. Et "ma- ne", di- cit Do- mi- nus, Est tu- i
punishment.   And "Mene",   says   the Lord,   is your

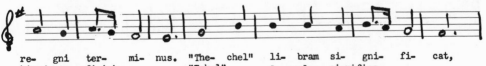

re- gni ter- mi- nus. "The- chel" li- bram si- gni- fi- cat,
kingdom's finish.   "Tekel"   a scales signifies,

Quae te mi- no- rem in- di- cat. "Phares," hoc est di-
which means that you are getting weaker. "Peres," this is a

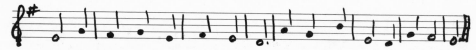

vi- si- o, Re- gnum trans- por- tat a- li- o.
division, and means that your kingdom will be given to others.

BELSHAZZAR

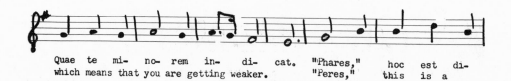

Qui sic sol- vit la- ten- ti- a Or- ne- tur ve- ste re- gi- a.
He who so explains the hidden meaning, let him be dressed in regal robes.

(Daniel being seated beside the King, and festooned in regal decorations,
    the King calls to his general of the army:)

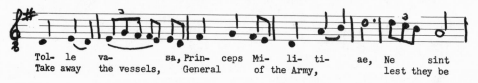

Tol- le va- sa, Prin- ceps Mi- li- ti- ae, Ne sint
Take away the vessels, General of the Army, lest they be

mi- chi cau- sa mi- se- ri- ae.
to me a cause of misery.

(Then, leaving the court, the Satraps take with them the vessels,
and the Queen leaves with them. The Satraps sing the conductus
of the Queen:)

SATRAPS

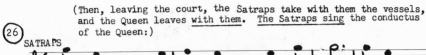

Sol- vi- tur in li- bro Sa- lo- mo- nis: Di- gna laus et
It is written in the book of Solomon: Worthy and fitting

con- gru- a ma- tro- nis. Pre- ci- um est e- ius si quam
is praise to our matrons. Precious is she as much as

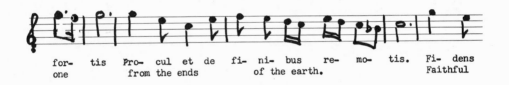

for- tis Pro- cul et de fi- ni- bus re- mo- tis. Fi- dens
one from the ends of the earth. Faithful

est in e- a cor ma- ri- ti Spo- li- is di- vi- ti- bus
is he in his heart, the husband, though he have great riches.

pot- i- ti. Mu- li- er haec il- li com- pa- re- tur
His wife is to be compared to

Cu- ius rex sub- si- di- um me- re-   tur. E- ius nam fa-
the one whom her king   supports.   For her

cun- di- a ver- bo-   rum Ar- gu- it pru- den- ti- am
eloquence   in speech   competes with the wisdom of

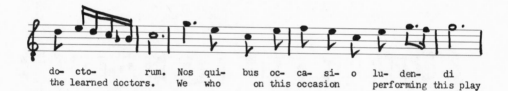

do- cto-   rum. Nos qui- bus oc- ca- si- o lu- den- di
the learned doctors. We who   on this occasion   performing this play

Hac di- e con- ce- di- tur sol- le-   mpni. De- mus hic prae-
today   agree.   Let us proceed with

co- ni- a de- vo- ti, Ve- ni- ant et con- ci- nent
this celebration devoted to her, coming along and singing.

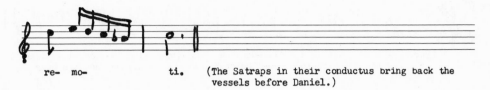

re- mo-   ti.   (The Satraps in their conductus bring back the
                      vessels before Daniel.)

(27) SATRAPS

Re- gis va- sa re- fe- ren- tes Quem Iu- dae- ae tre- munt gen- tes,
The royal vessels return   whose owner the Jews fear,

Da- ni- e- li ap- plau- den- tes, Gau- de- a- mus!
to Daniel   giving praise,   Let us rejoice!

Lau- des si- bi de- bi- tas Re- fe- ra- mus! Re- gis cla- dem
Praises   to him owing   let us offer!   The King's fall

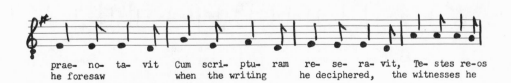

prae- no- ta- vit Cum scri- ptu- ram re- se- ra- vit, Te- stes re-os
he foresaw   when the writing   he deciphered,   the witnesses he

Hunc ho- no- rant   et Cal- de-   i   Et gen- ti- les et Iu- dae- i.
honored   both by the Chaldeans and the gentiles and the Jews.

Er- go iu- bi- lan- tes e-   i, Gau- de- a- mus! Lau- des si- bi
Therefore praising him,   let us rejoice!   Praises to him

de- bi- tas Re- fe- ra-   mus!
owing   let us offer!

(And so on. Suddenly let King Darius appear with his Courtiers, and
let there come ahead of him the Kitharists and Courtiers, singing
and playing **a conductus**, thus:)

COURTIERS

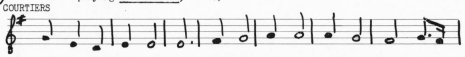

Ec- ce rex Da- ri-   us! Ve- nit cum prin- ci- pi- bus, No-
Here comes King Darius!   He comes with his courtiers,

bi- lis no- bi- li- bus. E- ius et cu- ri-   a   Re- so-
the noble with his nobles. He   and his court   make a

com- pro- ba- vit, Et Su- san- nam li- be- ra- vit. Gau- de- a- mus!
proved were false, and Susannah he set free. Let us rejoice!

Lau- des si- bi de- bi- tas Re- fe- ra- mus! Ba- by- lon hunc
Praises to him owing let us offer! Babylon then

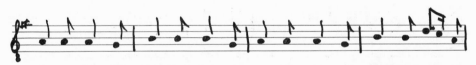

e- xu- la- vit Cum Iu- dae- os ca- pti- va- vit, Bal- tha- sar quem
exiled him when the Jews she captured, but Belshazzar him

ho- no- ra- vit. Gau- de- a- mus! Lau- des si- bi de- bi- tas
honored. Let us rejoice! Praises to him owing

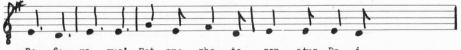

Re- fe- ra- mus! Est pro- phe- ta san- ctus De- i
let us offer! He is a holy prophet of God

nat lae- ti- ti- a, Ad- sunt et tri- pu- di- a. Hic est mi-
joyful sound,   and there is also dancing.   He is

ran- dus, Cun- ctis ve- ne- ran- dus. Il- li im- pe- ri- a
wonderful, by all   admired.   To him empires

sunt tri- bu- ta- ri- a. Re- gem ho- no- rant o- mnes et
are tributary.   The King   all   honor   and

a- do- rant. Il- lum Ba- by- lo- ni- a Me- tu- it et
adore.   Him   Babylon   fears,   and so

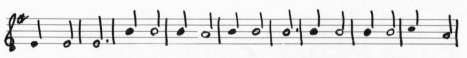

pa- tri- a. Cum ar- ma- to a- gmi- ne Ru- ens et cum tur- bi-
does the country. With armed   troops   he ruins, and like a whirl-

ne   Ster- nit co- hor- tes, con- fre- git et for- tes. Il- lum
wind he deploys his cohorts,   and shatters   the strong. He

ho- ne- stas Co- lit et no- bi- li- tas.   Hic est Ba-   by-
by honorable men and noble is revered.   This is   the

lo- ni- us No- bi- lis rex, Da- ri- us.   Il- li   cum tri- pu- di-
Babylonian   noble   king, Darius.   With him in dancing

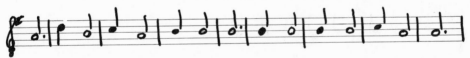

o Gau- de- at haec con- ti- o,   Lau- det et cum gau- di-   o
let rejoice   this assembly,   let him be praised with joy for

E-   ius fa- cta for- ti-   a, Tam ad- mi- ra- bi- li-   a.
his   actions   powerful,   so   admirable he is.

Si- mul o- mnes gra- tu- le- mur.   Re- so- nent   et tym- pa- na.
All together let us be thankful.   Sing   out,   and beat the drums.

Cy- tha- ri- ste tan- gant cor- das. Mu- si- co-   rum
Let the kitharists   pluck   their strings.   Let the musical

(Harp arpeggia here)

or- ga- na Re- so- nent ad e- ius prae- co- ni-   a!
instruments   resound   in   his   praise!

(Before the King Darius mounts his throne, let two soldiers, running ahead,
throw out Belshazzar, as if killing him. Then, King Darius being seated
in his majesty, let the Courtiers exclaim:)

(29) COURTIERS

Rex, in ae- ter- num   vi- ve!
O King,   live   forever!

(Then let two Counselors, kneeling to the King, covertly tell him
to have Daniel called up, and let some [Legates] be ordered to bring
him[Daniel] in. Meanwhile let these two Counselors, anticipating
Daniel's arrival, say this to the Court:)

(30)

COUNSELORS

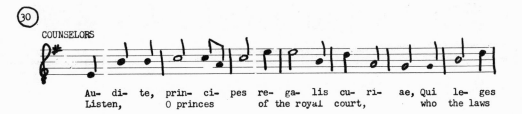

Au- di- te, prin- ci- pes re- ga- lis cu- ri- ae, Qui le- ges
Listen, O princes of the royal court, who the laws

re- gi- tis to- ti- us pa- tri- ae. Est qui- dam sa- pi- ens
make for the whole country. He is someone wise

in Ba- by- lo- ni- a, Se- cre- ta re- se- rans de- o- rum
in Babylon, secrets he discloses by the gods'

gra- ti- a. E- ius con- si- li- um re- gi com- pla- cu- it,
grace. His advice to a king is pleasing,

Nam pri- us Bal- tha- sar scri- ptum a- pe- ru- it.
For he first to Belshazzar the handwriting interpreted.

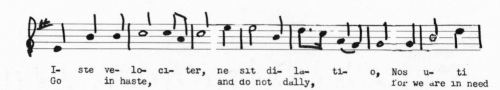

I- ste ve- lo- ci- ter, ne sit di- la-   ti-   o, Nos u- ti
Go   in haste,   and do not dally,   for we are in need

vo- lu- mus e- ius con- si- li- o.   Fi- at, si ve- ne-
         of his   advice.   He will be made, if he comes,

rit, con- si- li- a- ri- us Re- gis, et fu- e- rit
counselor   to the King, and will be

in re- gno ter- ti- us.
in the kingdom Number Three.

(The Legates, finding Daniel, say to him on behalf of the King:)

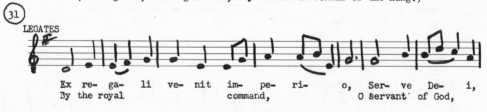

LEGATES

Ex re- ga- li ve- nit im- pe- ri-   o, Ser- ve De-   i,
By the royal   command,   O servant of God,

no- stra le- ga- ti- o. Tu- a re- gi lau- da- tur
comes this our legation. To the King has been praised

pro- bi- tas, Te com- men- dat mi- ro cal- li- di- tas.
your uprightness. Commended is your amazing astuteness.

Per te so- lum cum no- bis pa- tu- it Si- gnum de- xtrae
Through you only to us made clear the handwriting

quod o- mnes la- tu- it. Te rex vo- cat ad su- am
which to others was obscure. You the King calls to his

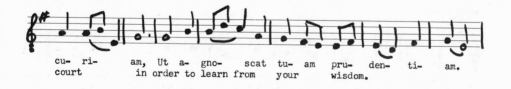

cu- ri- am, Ut a- gno- scat tu- am pru- den- ti- am.
court in order to learn from your wisdom.

E- ris, su- pra ut di- cit Da- ri-   us, Principalis   lis
You will be,   so says   Darius,   his principal

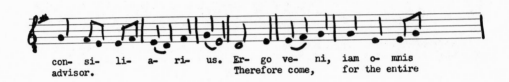

con- si- li- a- ri- us. Er- go ve- ni, iam o- mnis
advisor.   Therefore come,   for the entire

cu- ri-   a Prae- pa- ra-   tur ad tu- a gau- di- a.
court   is being prepared   to welcome you with joy.

(32) DANIEL

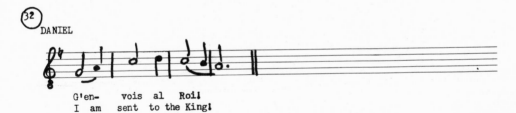

G'en-   vois al Roi!
I am   sent to the King!

(The Legates sing a conductus to lead Daniel to the King.)

(33) LEGATES

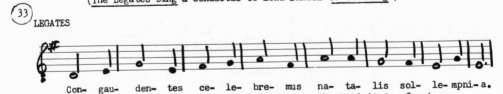

Con- gau- den- tes ce- le- bre- mus na- ta- lis sol- le- mpni- a.
Rejoicing together   let us celebrate   the Nativity's feast.

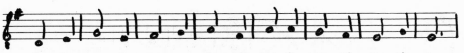

Iam de mor- te nos re- de- mit De- i sa- pi- en- ti- a.
Now from death we are redeemed by God's wisdom.

Ho- mo na- tus est in car- ne, qui cre- a- vit o- mni- a.
He made (Christ) to be born a man in the flesh, who (God) created all things.

Na- sci- tu- rum quem prae- di- xit pro- phe- tae fa-
His birth was foretold in the prophet's

cun- di- a. Da- ni- e- lis iam ces- sa- vit un- cti-
eloquence. Through Daniel now is stopped the anointing's

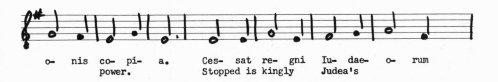

o- nis co- pi- a. Ces- sat re- gni Iu- dae- o- rum
power. Stopped is kingly Judea's

con- tu- max po- ten- ti- a.　In hoc na- ta- li-
obstinate　　　power.　　　　In this Nativity

ti- o, Da- ni- el, cum gau- di- o Te lau- dat haec
　　　Daniel,　　　with joy　　you　the assembly

con- ti- o.　Tu Su- san- nam li- be- ra- sti de mor- ta- li
praises.　　You Susannah　　had exonerated　from a mortal

cri- mi- ne, Cum te De- us in- spi- ra- vit su- o san- cto
crime,　　　when　God　inspired you　　with his holy

fla- mi- ne.　Te- stes fal- sos com- pro- ba- sti re- os
flame.　　　The false testifiers　you proved them to be,　the

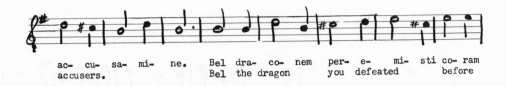

ac- cu- sa- mi- ne.   Bel dra- co- nem per- e-   mi- sti co- ram
accusers.   Bel the dragon   you defeated   before

ple- bis a- gmi-   ne.   Et te De- us ob- ser- va- vit le-
crowds of people.   And   God looked after you   in

o- num vo- ra- gi-   ne.   Er- go sit laus De- i ver- bo,
the lions' den.   Therefore be praise to God's word,

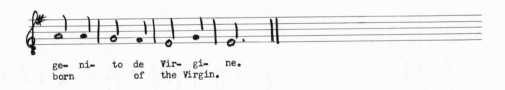

ge- ni- to de Vir- gi- ne.
born   of the Virgin.

(34) DANIEL (to Darius)

Rex in ae- ter- num vi- ve!
O King, live   forever!

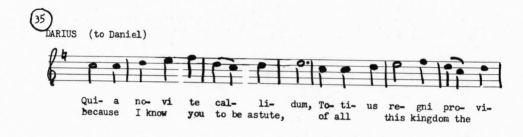

(35) DARIUS (to Daniel)

Qui- a no- vi- te cal- li- dum, To- ti- us re- gni pro- vi-
because I know you to be astute, of all this kingdom the

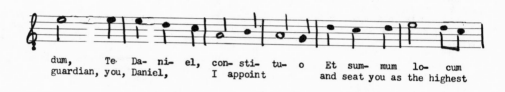

dum, Te Da- ni- el, con- sti- tu- o Et sum- mum lo- cum
guardian, you, Daniel, I appoint and seat you as the highest

tri- bu- o.
tribune.

(36) DANIEL (to Darius)

Rex, mi- chi si cre- di- de- ris, Fer me nil ma- li
O King, if in me you believe, through me no wrong

fe- ce- ris.
will you do.

(Then let the King make Daniel sit beside him. And let the other
Counselors, jealous of Daniel because he is in more favor with the
King, and plotting with others to have Daniel killed, say to the King:)

37 COUNSELORS

Rex in ae- ter- num   vi- vel   De- cre-   ve- runt   in
O King,   live forever!   They decreed   in

tu- a cu- ri- a Prin- ci- pan- di qui- bus   est glo- ri-
your   court -   the princes did,   to whom   is glory -

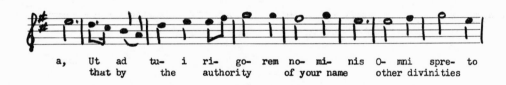

a, Ut ad   tu- i ri- go- rem no- mi- nis O- mni spre- to
    that by   the   authority of your name other divinities

vi- go- re ni- mi- nis, Per tri- gin- ta di- e-   rum
of authority should be spurned, for a thirty-   day

spa-   ti- um A- do- re- ris ut de- us o- mni- um,   O
period   to adore you   as god of all,   O

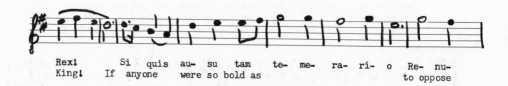

Rex!   Si quis au- su tam te- me- ra- ri- o Re- nu-
King!   If anyone   were so bold as   to oppose

e- rit tu- o con- si- li- o, Ut prae- ter te co-
     your   command,   in order to put ahead of you

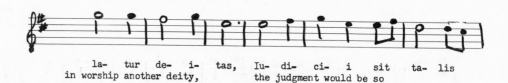

la- tur de- i- tas, Iu- di- ci- i sit ta- lis
in worship another deity,   the judgment would be so

fir- mi- tas, In le- o- num tra- da- tur fo- ve- am,
severe   that into the lions' den he would be thrown.

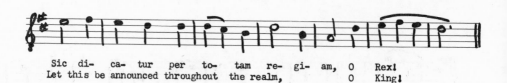

Sic di- ca- tur per to- tam re- gi- am, O   Rex!
Let this be announced throughout the realm,   O   King!

E- go man- do Et re- man- do Ne sit spre- tum Hoc de-
I   order and command   that respected be this

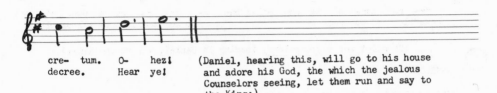

cre- tum. O- hez!   (Daniel, hearing this, will go to his house
decree.   Hear ye!   and adore his God, the which the jealous
                       Counselors seeing, let them run and say to
                       the King:)

COUNSELORS

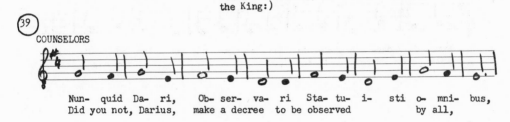

Nun- quid Da- ri,   Ob- ser- va- ri Sta- tu- i- sti o- mni- bus,
Did you not, Darius, make a decree to be observed   by all,

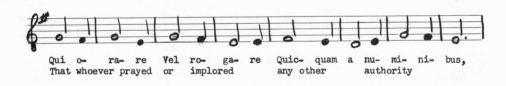

Qui o- ra- re Vel ro- ga- re Quic- quam a nu- mi- ni- bus,
That whoever prayed or implored   any other   authority

Ni te de- um Il- lum re- um Da- re- mus le- o- ni- bus?
and not you as god, the culprit we should give to the lions?

Hoc e- di- ctum Sic in- di- ctum Fu-it a prin- ci- pi- bus.
This edict   thus   was proclaimed   by your princes.

(And let the King, not knowing wherefore they said this, reply:)

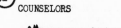 DARIUS

Ve- re ius- si me o- mni- bus A- do- ra- ri a gen- ti- bus.
Verily   I do order me   to be adored   by all peoples.

(Then let those Counselors, leading in Daniel, say to the King:)

COUNSELORS

Hunc Iu- dae- um Su- um De- um Da- ni- e- lem vi- di- mus
This Jew, Daniel, his God   we saw

A- do- ran- tem Et pre- can- tem, Tu- is spre- tis le- gi- bus.
adoring   and imploring,   in defiance of your laws.

(But let the King, wishing to exonerate Daniel, say:)
DARIUS

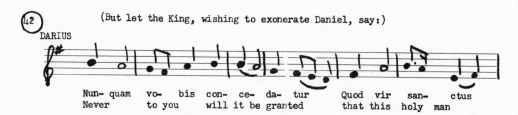

Nun- quam vo- bis con- ce- da- tur Quod vir san- ctus
Never   to you will it be granted   that this holy man

sic per- da- tur.
be so condemned.

(Then let the Courtiers, hearing this, show him [Darius] the book, saying:)

43 COURTIERS

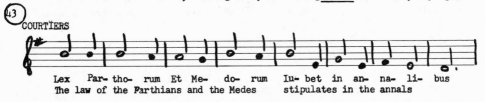

Lex Par- tho- rum Et Me- do- rum Iu- bet in an- na- li- bus
The law of the Parthians and the Medes stipulates in the annals

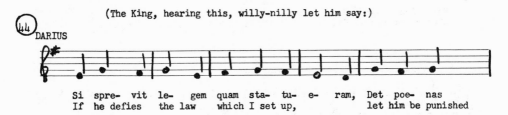

Ut qui spre- vit Quae de- cre- vit Rex, de- tur le- o- ni- bus.
that whoever defies what is decreed by the King, will be given to the lions.

(The King, hearing this, willy-nilly let him say:)

44 DARIUS

Si spre- vit le- gem quam sta- tu- e- ram, Det poe- nas
If he defies the law which I set up, let him be punished

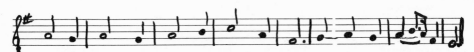

i- pse quas de- cre- ve- ram.
as I decreed.

(Then let the Courtiers seize Daniel, and let him, looking
at the King, say:)

DANIEL

He- u, he- u, he- u! Quo ca- su sor- tis ve- nit
Alas, alas, alas! By what fate am I thus come

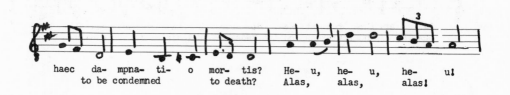

haec da- mpna- ti- o mor- tis? He- u, he- u, he- u!
to be condemned to death? Alas, alas, alas!

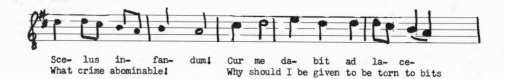

Sce- lus in- fan- dum! Cur me da- bit ad la- ce-
What crime abominable! Why should I be given to be torn to bits

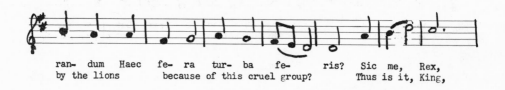

ran- dum Haec fe- ra tur- ba fe- ris? Sic me, Rex,
by the lions because of this cruel group? Thus is it, King,

per- de- re quae- ris? He- u! Qua mor- te mo- ri Me
to kill me you seek? Alas! By what death for me to die

co- gis? Par- ce fu- ro- ri!
do you plan? Spare me your fury!

(And let the King, not having the power to free him, say to him:)

46 DARIUS

De- us quem co- lis tam fi- de- li- ter Te li- be- ra- bit
The God whom you worship so faithfully will liberate you

mi- ra- bi- li- ter.
miraculously.

(Then let them throw Daniel in the den. At once
let an Angel, holding a sword, hold off the
the lions so that they do not touch him [Daniel],
and let Daniel as he enters the den say:)

47 DANIEL

Hu- ius re- i non sum re- us. Mi- se- re- re me— i,
Of this charge I am not guilty. Have mercy on me,

De- us! E- le- y- son! Mit- te, De- us, huc pa- tro- num
O God! Eleyson! Send down, O God, a patron

Qui re- fre- net vim le- o- num. E- le- y- son!
Who will restrain   the vim of the lions. Eleyson!

(Meanwhile let a Second Angel summon Habakkuk to take the food he was
carrying to his reapers, <u>and give it</u> to Daniel in the lions' den,
saying:)

48 SECOND ANGEL

A- ba- cuc, tu se- nex pi- e, Ad la- cum Ba- by- lo- ni-ae,
Habakkuk,   you old   holy one, to the den   of Babylon,

Da- ni- e- li fer pran- di- um. Man- dat ti- bi Rex
to Daniel,   take that food.   So orders you   the King

O- mni- um.
of all.

49 HABAKKUK

No- vit De- i co- gni- ti- o Quod Ba- by- lo- nem
God knows   that this Babylon

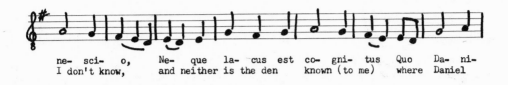

ne- sci- o, Ne- que la- cus est co- gni- tus Quo Da- ni-
I don't know, and neither is the den known (to me) where Daniel

el est po- si- tus.
is situated.

(50) (Then let the Second Angel, snatching him up by the hair of his head,
take him to the den, and let Habakkuk, offering the food to Daniel, say:)

HABAKKUK

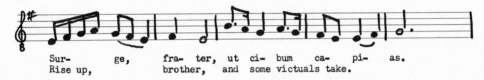

Sur- ge, fra- ter, ut ci- bum ca- pi- as.
Rise up, brother, and some victuals take.

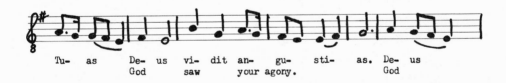

Tu- as De- us vi- dit an- gu- sti- as. De- us
God saw your agony. God

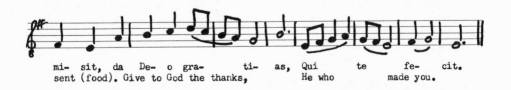

mi- sit, da De- o gra- ti- as, Qui te fe- cit.
sent (food). Give to God the thanks, He who made you.

(And let Daniel, accepting the food, say:)

DANIEL

Re-   cor- da- tus   es   me- i,   Do- mi- ne! Ac- ci- pi- am in
You have remembered me,   O Lord!   I take (this food) in

tu-   o   no- mi- ne.   Al- le-   lu- ia!
your   name.   Alleluia!

(This having been accomplished, let the Second Angel take Habakkuk back
to his place. Then let the King, descending from his throne, come to
the den, saying tearfully:)

DARIUS

Te- ne pu- tas, Da- ni- el, sal- va- bit, ut e- ri- pi-
Didn't you think,   Daniel,   that you would be saved, that you would be

a- ris A ne- ce pro-   po- si-   ta,   quem tu co- lis
plucked from the intended death   by Him whom you worship

et- ve- ne-   ra- ris?
and venerate?

53 DANIEL

Rex in ae- ter- num vi- ve!   An- ge- li- cum so- li- ta
O King,   live forever!   An angelic   patron

mi- sit pi- e- ta- te pa- tro- num, Quo De- us   ad
He has sent with His usual mercy,   by whom God   in

tem-   pus con- pe- scu- it o- ra le- o- num.
time   held in check   the mouths of the lions.

(Then the King joyfully will exclaim:)

54 DARIUS

Da- ni- e- lem e- du- ci- te, Et e- mu- los im- mit- ti- te!
Daniel   release,   and the jealous ones toss in!

(When the Counselors have been defrocked and are being led to the den,
they will cry out, as a conductus:)

55 COUNSELORS

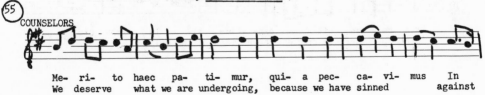

Me- ri- to haec pa- ti- mur, qui- a pec- ca- vi- mus   In
We deserve   what we are undergoing, because we have sinned   against

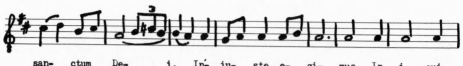

san- ctum   De-   i.   In- iu- ste e- gi- mus, In- i- qui-
a holy one   of God.   Unjustly   we acted,   an iniquity

ta-   tem fe- ci-   mus.
we perpetrated.

(They being thrown into the den are at once consumed by the lions.
And the King seeing this, let him say:)

56 DARIUS

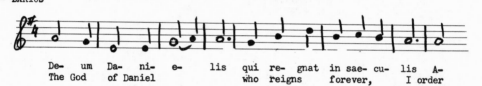

De- um Da- ni- e-   lis   qui re- gnat in sae- cu- lis A-
The God   of Daniel   who reigns   forever,   I order

do- ra- ri iu- be- o a cun- ctis   po- pu- lis.
to be adored   by all   peoples.

(Daniel, being received again in his first rank, will prophesy:)

57 DANIEL

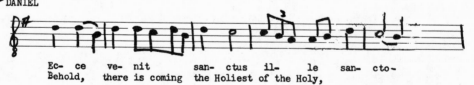

Ec- ce ve- nit   san- ctus il- le san- cto-
Behold,   there is coming the Holiest of the Holy,

rum san- ctis- si- mus, Quem Rex i- ste iu- bet
Whom the King (Darius) himself orders

co- li po- tens et for- tis- si- mus. Ces- sant
worshipped, He (God) being potent and strongest. Cease do

pha- na, ces- set re- gnum, ces- sa- bit et
the temples, cease does the kingdom, and also will cease

un- cti- o. In- stat re- gni Iu- dae- o- rum
the anointing. At once the rule over the Jews

fi- nis et op- pres- si- o.
is ended and their enslavement.

(Then a <u>Herald</u>   Angel, unexpectedly, will exclaim:)

58 HERALD ANGEL

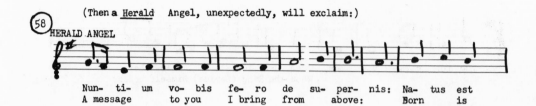

Nun- ti- um vo- bis fe- ro   de su- per- nis: Na- tus est
A message   to you   I bring from   above: Born   is

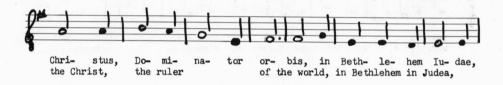

Chri- stus, Do- mi- na- tor   or- bis, in Beth- le- hem Iu- dae,
the Christ,   the ruler   of the world, in Bethlehem in Judea,

Sic e- nim pro- phe- ta di- xe- rat an- te!
as indeed   the prophet   said   of old!

(These being heard, let the cantors begin "Te Deum laudamus." The "Daniel"
is finished.)

(<u>The complete "Te Deum" begins on p. 491.</u>)

15. The Play
of the Annunciation

The Play of the Annunciation

THE CONCLUSION OF *The Annunciation* is complicated by the circumstances of the processional ceremony in which the play is floated. The manuscripts of the Cividale and the Paduan versions are classified as Processionals (see Young II, 247-50 for ascription details). At Cividale, Mary did not continue her final *Magnificat* speech into a procession, but instead the Choir was to break into the *Te Deum laudamus* (see p. 489 below) when the procession began to move. The Paduan producer, on the contrary, specified the singing of the entire *Magnificat* during the final procession, with the Choir in *organum* alternating verses with Mary. This solution, while satisfactory for a ceremonial and an opportunity for *organum* similar to that in the Paduan *Purification,* provides a less theatrical finale.

The play can only be fleshed out by coupling Cividale dialogue and Paduan stage directions, interspersed with narration intoned by the clergy. These last may prove an effective alternative to the modern device of prologue-reading of appropriate Biblical passages. The Paduan directions allow the play to be performed as the most liturgical of the plays in this collection, even though the original environment was a special outdoor processional ceremony.

All items except the first part of No. 16 are traditional liturgical antiphons or readings *in tono.* Item 2 is in the modern *Graduale Romanum,* p. 23, a more interesting musical treatment of Isaiah's prophecy than further intoning by the clergy; the item's assignment to the Choir is editorial. Cividale and Paduan versions of Items 6, 8, 10, 12, 14, 16, and 18 are similar, possibly because the two cathedrals are in the same northeastern section of Italy. The Paduan version of Item 12 is pitched a fifth higher than that of Cividale, probably to suit the range of the specified boy singer of the Gabriel role in Padua, the inference being that Cividale's Gabriel may have been, less typically, a man; see *Production,* pp. 14-15.

The Cast

Subdeacons (or Deacons or other Clergy)
Choir
Mary
Gabriel (boy or man)
Joseph (nonspeaking)
Elizabeth
Zacharias (nonspeaking)

    The Scene: Mary's house. Elizabeth's house. December 18, or other
              Advent date.

The Play of the Annunciation

In Annunciatione Beatae Mariae Virginis Representatio

(On Annunciation Day after the meal, at the usual hour, let
the tower bell be rung, and meanwhile let the scholars convene at
the Church, and in the sacristy let some other scholars prepare
themselves with copes and other properties needed for the procession.
And so in the sacristy also let there stand Mary, Elizabeth, Joseph,
and Ioachim [Zacharias], ready in their costumes, with a deacon and a
subdeacon carrying in their hands the silver-bound Gospel and Epistle
books. At the proper time let those persons leave the sacristy in
procession in the order listed above, and let them proceed to the
platformed area prepared for them. When they have gone, let the priests
and other scholars go in procession to the Baptistry, and there let
a choirboy be already in costume as Gabriel and be standing on the
cathedra chair. Let them pick him up and the chair, and let them
carry him from the Baptistry into the Church by the side alley, and
carry him beside the platform that is nearest the chancel. And let the
scholars stand in the middle of the Church as a Choir, and meanwhile
let the Subdeacon have begun to sing the prophecy from Isaiah:)

① SUBDEACON 1

free rhythm

Here be- gin- neth the read- ing from I- sai- ah the Pro- phet:

And the Lord spake un- to A- haz, say- ing, "Ask thee a sign of the

Lord thy God; ask it ei- ther in the depth, or in the height a-bove."

② CHOIR

Ec- ce   vir- go   con- ci- pi- et   et   pa- ri- et
Behold   a virgin   shall conceive   and   shall bear

fi- li-   um. Et vo- ca- bi- tur   no- men e-   ius
a son   And   called shall be   his   name

Em- ma- nu- el!
Immanuel!

(Then another Subdeacon sings the Gospel:)

③

SUBDEACON II

Here be- gin- neth the Gos- pel ac- cord- ing to Luke.

④

CHOIR

Glo- ry be to Thee, O Lord.

⑤

SUBDEACON II

And in the sixth month the an- gel Ga- bri- el was sent from God

un- to a ci- ty of Ga- li- lee, named Na- za- reth, to a vir-gin

e- spous- ed to a man whose name was Jo- seph, of the house of

Da- vid. And the vir- gin's name was Ma- ry. And the An- gel

came in un- to her, and said:

⑥

GABRIEL

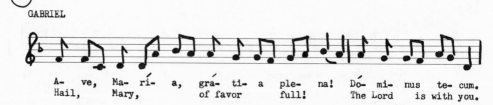

A- ve, Ma- rí- a, grá- ti- a ple- na! Dó- mi- nus te- cum.
Hail, Mary, of favor full! The Lord is with you.

(Kneeling, and holding up two fingers of his right hand)

Be- ne- di- cta tu in mu- li- é- ri- bus.
Blessed are you among women.

⑦ SUBDEACON I

And when she saw him, she was trou- bled at his say- ing, and

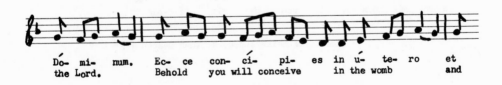

cast in her mind what man- ner of sal- u- ta- tion this should be.

(This finished, the Angel standing, raises high the two fingers of his right hand, and sings the following:)

⑧ GABRIEL

Ne ti- me- as, Ma- rí- a. In- ve- ní- sti gra- ti- am a- pud
Do not fear, Mary. You have found favor with

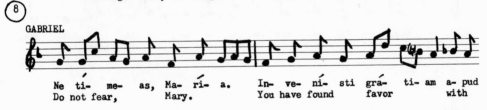

Do- mi- num. Ec- ce con- cí- pi- es in u- te- ro et
the Lord. Behold you will conceive in the womb and

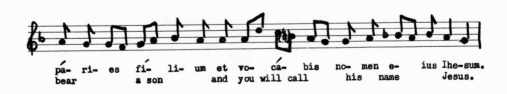

pá- ri- es fí- li- um et vo- cá- bis no- men e- ius Ihe-sum.
bear a son and you will call his name Jesus.

Hic e- rit ma- gnus, et fi- li- us Al- ti- si- mi vo- ca-
He will be great,   and son   of the Highest   will He

bi- tur. Et da- bit il- li De- us se- dem Da- vid pa- tris
be called. And God will give to him   the throne of David his ancestor,

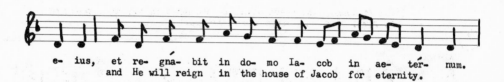

e- ius, et re- gna- bit in do- mo Ia- cob in ae- ter- num.
and He will reign in the house of Jacob for eternity.

Et re- gnum e- ius non e- rit fi- nis.
And His reign   shall have no end.

(This song being ended, another Deacon <u>says</u>:)

⑨

SUBDEACON II

Then said Ma- ry un- to the An- gel:

(10) MARY

Quo- mo- do fi- et i- stud, An- ge- le De- i, qui- a
How   can be such a thing, Angel   of God, because

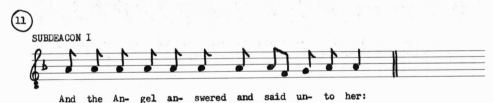

vi- rum   in con- ci- pi- en- do non per- tu- li?
a man   to be taken into me   I have not permitted?

(11) SUBDEACON I

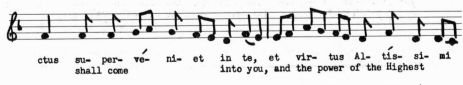

And the An- gel an- swered and said un- to her:

(12) GABRIEL

Au- di, Ma- ri- a, vir- go Chri- sti, Spi- ri- tus San-
Hear, Mary,   Virgin of Christ,   the Holy Spirit

ctus su- per- ve- ni- et in te, et vir- tus Al- tis- si- mi
shall come   into you, and the power of the Highest

(At this point let the dove be let down partway from the ceiling.)

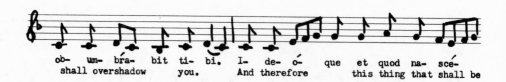

ob- um- bra- bit ti- bi. I- de- ó- que et quod na- sce-
shall overshadow   you.   And therefore   this thing that shall be

tur ex te san- ctum, vo- cá- bi- tur fí- li- us De- i.
born of you will be holy,   will be called   the son of   God.

Et ec- ce E- lí- za- beth, co- gná- ta tu- a, et ip- sa
And behold   Elizabeth,   your cousin,   shall herself

con- ce- pit fi- li- um in se- ne- ctú- te su- a. Et hic
conceive   a son   in her old age.   And this

men- sis est sex- tus il- li que vo- ca- tur ster- ster- ri- lis,
is the sixth month   for her   who was called   sterile,

qui- a   non e- rit   im- pos- si- bil- le a- pud De- um o- mne ver-bum.
for   nothing is   impossible   with God,   in all truth.

⑬

SUBDEACON II

Then   said Ma- ry   to   the   An- gel:

(This being said, let Mary stand with arms outstretched toward the dove,
and in a strong voice begin:)

⑭

MARY

Ec- ce   an- cil- la Do- mi- ni! Fi- at mi- chi   se- cun- dum
Behold   the handmaiden of the Lord! Do   with me   according to

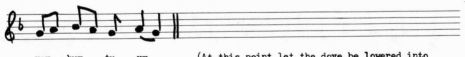

ver- bum   tu- um.   (At this point let the dove be lowered into
your word.   her arms, and let her put it under her cloak.)

⑮

SUBDEACON I

And Ma- ry a-   rose in those days, and went in- to the hill

(Let Mary descend from her platform and go to the platform of Elizabeth
and Ioachim [Zacharias] , and let both of the latter help Mary up.)

coun- try in haste, in- to a ci- ty of Ju- da, and en- tered

in- to the house of Za- cha- ri- as, and sa- lu- ted E- li-za-beth.

And it came to pass that when E- li- za- beth heard the sa- lu

ta- tion of Ma- ry the babe leaped in her womb, and E- li- za- beth

knew that she had been filled with the Ho- ly Spi- rit. And she spoke

in a loud voice and said:

(Let Elizabeth, kneeling and clasping the body of Mary with both hands, and in a humble voice, begin:)

(16)

ELIZABETH

Sal- ve, ca- ra, De- o gra- ta, Te sa- lu- to, sis be-
Hail, dear one, by God favored, You I salute, may you be

a- ta. Te- cum sit- que Do- mi- nus. (Let Elizabeth rise, and
blessed. And with you may the Lord be. standing begin:)

free rhythm

Be- ne- di- cta tu in mu- li- é- ri- bus et be- ne- di- ctus
Blessed are you among women and blessed is

fru- ctus ven- tris tu- a. Et un- de hoc mi- chi ut ve- ni-at
the fruit of your womb. And whence is this to me that comes

ma- ter Do- mi- ni me- i ad me? Ec- ce e- nim ut fa- cta
the mother of my Lord to me? Behold, as soon as was sounded

est vox sa- lu- ta- ti- o- nis tu- ae in au- ri- bus me- is
the voice of your salutation in my ears

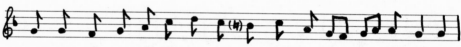

e- xul- ta- vit in gau- di- o in- fans in u- te- ro me- o.
there leaped for joy the babe in my womb.

Et be- a- ta es que cre- di- di- sti, quo- ni- am per- fi-
And blessed are you who believed, for there shall happen

ci- en- tur e- a que di- cta sunt ti- bi a Do- mi- no.
what has been said to you by the Lord.

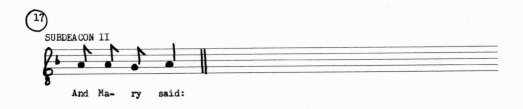

SUBDEACON II

And Ma- ry said:

MARY

Ma- gni- fi- cat a- ni- ma me- a Do- mi- num. Et e- xul- ta- vit
Magnify does my soul the Lord. And exult does

(Mary turns to the audience, and in a loud voice sings in the
eighth tone the following three verses <u>of the Magnificat:</u>)

spi- ri- tus me- us in De- o sa- lu- ta- ri me- o, qui- a
my spirit in God my savior, for

re- spe- xit hu- mi- li- ta- tem an- cil- la su- ae. Ec- ce
He has respected the humble estate of His handmaiden. Behold,

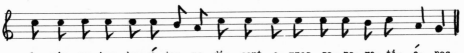

e- nim ex hoc be- a- tam me di- cent o- mnes ge- ne- ra- ti- o- nes.
henceforth blessed will call me all generations.

16. The Purification

The Purification

PURIFICATION DAY being February 2, the play risked an outdoor procession, weather or not, though less lengthy an affair than Cividale's in the piazza for *The Annunciation.* To understand the relation of the Paduan Baptistry to the Duomo and for other production concerns in *The Purification,* see *Production,* pp. 267 and 273-79.

All singing roles are taken by boys, even those of the Choir itself. The inference of the initial stage direction is that the nonsinging roles of Joseph, Mary, and the elderly Anna are also played by choirboys. The only adults in the cast are the four prophets, and they are purely ornamental.

The two items (Nos. 1 and 5) of *organum,* medieval two-part harmony, were not recognized as such by Young (II, 254), who thought the texts were repeated "to a different melody." So far as I am aware, these polyphonic compositions are here published in their intended format for the first time.

There are several apparent scribal errors in the music notation of the manuscript, from the chapter library of the Paduan Duomo (MS C. 56, fols. 14^r-16^v). In Item 1, measure 6, the d^2 is flatted unmodally, while the other part, an octave below, is not flatted. Likewise, in the fifth measure from the end of Item 1 the d^2 is flatted unmodally. In Item 5 the B-flat sign is impossibly placed on the f^1 space. Being in the everyday service books, Items 6, 7, and 8 were not written out in the manuscript. I have borrowed their melodies from the modern service book, *Graduale Romanum,* pp. 405-6, where they are in the eighth tone, not the prescribed sixth. In other respects we may assume a medieval likeness. Items 7 and 8 also are to be sung in *organum.*

The Cast

The Hosts (two choirboys in dalmatics)
The Angel Gabriel
Two Guardian Angels
Choir (boys)
Simeon
Joseph
Mary
Anna the Prophetess   } nonspeaking
Four Prophets

   The Scene: The Temple. February 2.

The Purification   *Purificatio*

(On Purification Day, immediately after the meal, let the tower
bell be rung, and while it is ringing let the scholars convene at
the Church, and in the main sacristy let the four priests robe
themselves as prophets, and two choirboys in dalmatics who as Hosts
are to sing the "Ave, gratia plena." And let these aforesaid ones,
the Prophets and Hosts, go out with cross, tapers, and other necessaries
for the procession, and let them proceed to the "Temple" platform
prepared next to the altar of Saints Fabian and Sebastian.

After that, in procession let other priests and choirboys go
to the Baptistry, and let there be in that building two choirboys
costumed as Guardian Angels; and another choirboy costumed as Mary,
with the Christchild in her arms; Joseph, carrying a wicker basket
of doves on his shoulders; and another choirboy, costumed as the
Angel Gabriel on the cathedra chair. And after Mary, let another
choirboy be dressed as the prophetess Anna with a large sheet of
parchment in her hand.

And thus let them go in procession from the Baptistry by the
side alley, and let them enter the Church: the Angels with Mary and
Anna in the lead, followed by the Angel Gabriel who is up on the
cathedra chair. Coming in the Church, let the latter Angel stay to
the chancel side of the "Temple," with two tapers and a cross. Meanwhile
let the priests and scholars stand in the middle of the Church as a
Choir, and let Mary, with the Guardian Angels and carrying the Babe
in her arms, approach the "Temple." And meanwhile let the two choirboys robed in dalmatics, the Hosts, who are already on the "Temple"
platform, begin to sing the hereinafter inscribed antiphon:)

THE HOSTS

A-   ve,   gra- ti- a   ple-   na,   De- i ge- ni- trix
Hail,   of favor   full,   of the Lord the mother

vir-   go, Ex te e- nim   or- tus   est sol Iu- sti- ci-
virginal,   from you still   rises   the sun of justice.

ae,   il- lu- mi-   nans Que in te- ne- bris sunt lae-
shining   for those who in the dark   are made

ta-   re. Tu   se- ni- or   iu- ste su-   sci- pi- ens in ul-nis
joyful.   You   the parent   rightly holding   in arms

li- be- ra-   to- rem a- ni- ma- rum no- stra- rum, Do-
the liberator   of the souls   of us,

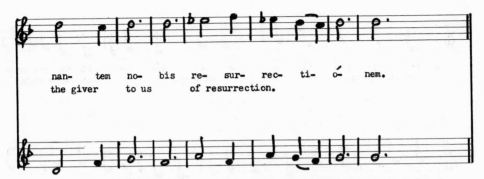

nan-   tem   no-   bis   re-   sur-   rec-   ti-   o-   nem.
the giver   to us   of resurrection.

(This being done, let Mary with her Guardian Angels; Anna; and Joseph
carrying the Boy in his arms - all climb up onto the Temple platform.
And let them, Joseph and Mary, offer up the Boy with the doves.
Meanwhile let the choirboys in the dalmatics, The Hosts, begin
the following responsory, Simeon chatting with the Boy:)

(2)

THE HOSTS   free rhythm

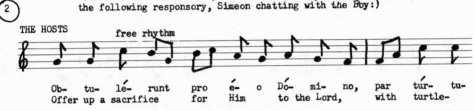

Ob-   tu-   lé-   runt   pro   é-   o   Dó-   mi-   no,   par   túr-   tu-
Offer up a sacrifice   for   Him   to the Lord,   with   turtle-

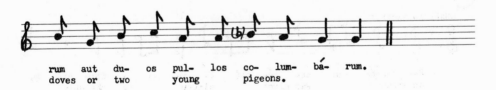

rum   aut   du-   os   pul-   los   co-   lum-   bá-   rum.
doves   or   two   young   pigeons.

(3)

THE ANGEL GABRIEL (beside the platform)

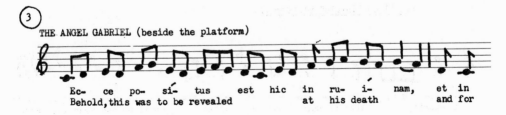

Ec-   ce   po-   si-   tus   est   hic   in   ru-   i-   nam,   et   in
Behold, this was to be revealed   at   his death   and for

re- sur- rec- ti- ó- nem mul- tó- rum. Et in si- gnum
the resurrection   of many.   And as a sign

cu- i con- tra- di- ce- tur, et tu- am ip- sí- us us
of this let it not be contradicted   or your   very

a- ni- mam per- tran- si- bit gla- di- us.
soul   will be run through by a sword.

④

GUARDIAN ANGELS

Re- spón- sum ac- cé- pit Si- me- on a Spí- ri- tu
An answer   was given   Simeon   by the Holy

(Still on "Temple" platform.)

San- cto, non vi- sú- rum se mor- tem ni- si vi- dé- ret Dó- mi- num.
Spirit,   that he should not see death   until he had seen the Lord.

Su- sci- pi- ens Si- me- on pu- e- rum Ihe- sum
Taking, as Simeon did, the boy Jesus

in ma- ni- bus, ex- cla- ma- vit di- cens:
in his hands, he cried out, saying:

SIMEON

Nunc di- mit- tis ser- vum tu- um, Do- mi- ne, se- cun- dum
Now let go your servant, Lord, according

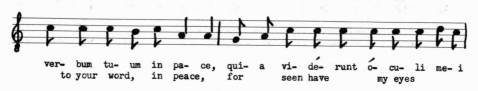

ver- bum tu- um in pa- ce, qui- a vi- de- runt o- cu- li me- i
to your word, in peace, for seen have my eyes

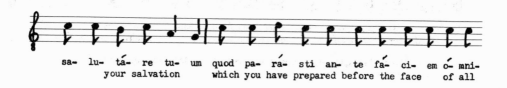

sa- lu- ta- re tu- um quod pa- ra- sti an- te fa- ci- em o- mni-
your salvation which you have prepared before the face of all

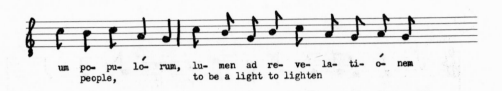

um po- pu- lo- rum, lu- men ad re- ve- la- ti- o- nem
people,   to be a light to lighten

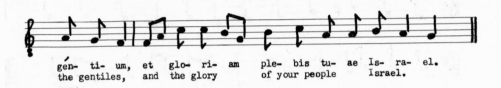

gen- ti- um, et glo- ri- am ple- bis tu- ae Is- ra- el.
the gentiles, and the glory of your people Israel.

7 GUARDIAN ANGELS

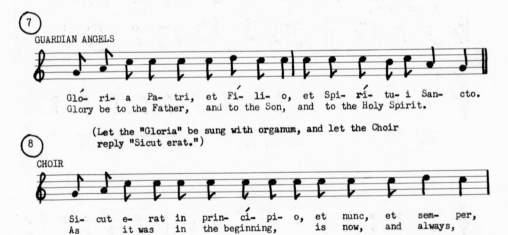

Glo- ri- a Pa- tri, et Fi- li- o, et Spi- ri- tu- i San- cto.
Glory be to the Father, and to the Son, and to the Holy Spirit.

(Let the "Gloria" be sung with organum, and let the Choir
8 reply "Sicut erat.")

CHOIR

Si- cut e- rat in prin- ci- pi- o, et nunc, et sem- per,
As   it was in the beginning,   is now, and always,

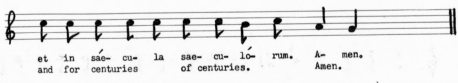

et in sae- cu- la sae- cu- lo- rum. A- men.
and for centuries of centuries.   Amen.

(Let them all, in procession, return to the main sacristy.)

Te Deum Laudamus

Te Deum Laudamus

WILLI APEL REPORTS the striking similarity of the *Te Deum* melody to that of "the oldest Yemenite *Sh'ma,* the oldest chant of the Hebrew liturgy" (*Gregorian Chant,* 1958, p. 509). The present Latin words were probably the work of Bishop Nicetus of Dacia about A.D. 400, according to Marie Pierik in *Dramatic and Symbolic Elements in Gregorian Chant* (1963), p. 26. In this form the song has spread over the Western world.

The *Te Deum* is prescribed as the conclusion of so many of the medieval church music-dramas because it is the last canticle of the Matins service, in which the medieval dramatist often found an advantageous position for theatrical troping. This coincidence provided an exalted finale for those music-dramas that were inserted in that service. In theatrical performance today, however, the *Te Deum* may sometimes prove to be the tail wagging the dog. An abbreviation with some historical sanction would conclude the hymn at "Aeterna fac... numerari," since Marie Pierik cites evidence that it ended here in its first stage.

Wherever it ends, after however much procession through the nave, there is validity and a final excitement in the choral singing of at least the last verse in *organum,* a more or less parallel harmonizing at the fourth or fifth, and sometimes third, below the plainchant melody. The only notation of *organum* in the sixteen playscripts of the present collection is found in *The Purification,* though no doubt some was improvised without acknowledgement in the manuscripts. In the same spirit the scoring of *organum* in the present edition of the *Te Deum* is left to the ingenuity of the director-conductor and group.

Te Deum Laudamus

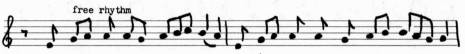

Te De- um lau- da- mus; te Do- mi- num con- fi- te- mur.
You God we praise; you the Lord we acknowledge.

Te ae- ter- num Fa- trem o- mnis ter- ra ve- ne- ra- tur.
You the everlasting Father by all the earth is worshipped.

Ti- bi o- mnes an- ge- li, ti- bi coe- li et u- ni- ver- sae
To you all angels, to you the heavens and universal

pot- e- sta- tes, Ti- bi che- ru- bim et se- ra- phim
powers, to you cherubim and seraphim

in- ces- sa- bi- li vo- çe pro- cla- mant: San- ctus, san- ctus,
continually aloud do cry: Holy, holy,

San- ctus, Do- mi- nus De- us sa- ba- oth. Ple- ni sunt
holy,   Lord   God   sabaoth.   Full   are

coe- li et ter- ra ma- ie- sta- tis glo- ri- ae tu- ae.
heaven and earth   of the majesty   of your glory.

Te glo- ri- o- sus A- po- sto- lo- rum cho- rus, Te
To you the glorious   Apostles'   chorus,   you

Pro- phe- ta- rum lau- da- bi- lis nu- me- rus. Te mar- ty-rum
the numerous prophets praise.   You the martyred

can- di- da- tus lau- dat e- xer- ci- tus. Te per or- bem
disciplined candidates praise.   You all over the globe

ter- ra- rum   san- cta con- fi- te- tur Ec- cle- si- a.
of the earth   the holy church acknowledges.

Pa-   trem, im- men- sae   ma- ie-   sta-   tis; ve- ne- ran- dum
The Father,   of an immense   majesty;   your adorable

tu- um, ve- rum, et u- ni- cum Fi- li- um; San-   ctum quo- que
     true,   and only   Son;   the Holy Ghost also,

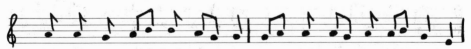

pa- ra- cli- tum Spi- ri- tum. Tu   rex glo- ri- ae, Chri- ste.
the comforter.   You are the king of glory, O Christ.

Tu Pa- tris sem- pi- ter- nus es Fi- li- us. Tu ad
You are the everlasting Father's   Son.   When you to

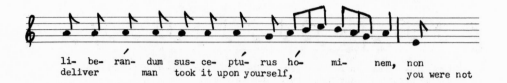

li- be- ran- dum sus- ce- ptu- rus ho- mi- nem, non
deliver   man   took it upon yourself,   you were not

hor- ru- i- sti Vir- gi- nis u- te- rum. Tu de- vi- cto
horrified   of the Virgin's womb. When you the sharpness

mor- tis a- cu- le- o, a- pe- ru- i- sti cre- den- ti- bus
of death overcame,   you opened   to believers

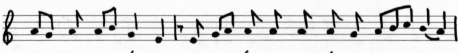

re- gna coe- lo- rum. Tu ad de- xte- ram De- i se-   des,
the kingdom of heaven. You at the right hand of God sit,

in glo- ri- a Pa- tris. Iu- dex cre- de- ris es- se
in the glory   of the Father. As judge you are believed to be

ven- tu- rus. Te er- go quae- su- mus, tu- is fa- mu- lis,
coming.   You therefore we pray, we   your   servants,

sub- ve- ni, quos pre- ti- o- so san- gui- ne re- de- mi- sti.
to help   whom with your precious blood   you have redeemed.

Ae- ter- na fac cum San- ctis tu- is in glo- ri- a
In eternity make us with the Saints   in glory

nu- me- ra- ri. Sal- vum fac po- pu- lum tu- um, Do- mi- ne,
to be numbered.   Safe   make your people,   O Lord,

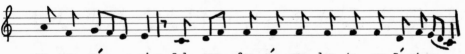

et be- ne- dic he- re- di- ta- ti tu- ae.
and bless   your heritage.

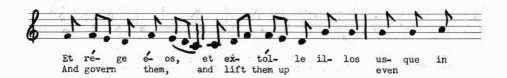

Et ré- ge é- os, et ex- tól- le il- los us- que in
And govern them, and lift them up even

ae- tér- num. Per sín- gu- los di- es, be- ne- di- ci- mus te,
forever. Through each day, we bless you,

et lau- dá- mus no- men tu- um in sáe- cu- lum, et in
and we praise your name forever, and world

sáe- cu- lum sáe- cu- li. Di- gná- re, Dó- mi- ne, dí- e
without end. Vouchsafe, O Lord, this day

i- sto sí- ne pec- cá- to nos cu- sto- dí- re.
without sin us to keep.

Mi- se- ré- re no- stri, Do- mi- ne, mi- se- ré- re
Have mercy upon us, O Lord, have mercy

no- stri. Fí- at mi- se- ri- cor- di- a tu- a, Do- mi- ne,
on us. Let your mercy, O Lord,

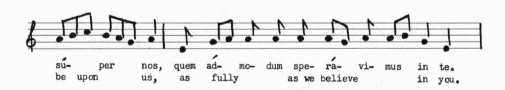

su- per nos, quem ad- mo- dum spe- ra- vi- mus in te.
be upon us, as fully as we believe in you.

In te, Do- mi- ne, spe- ra- vi; non con- fun- dar in
In you, O Lord, have I trusted; let me not be confounded

ae- ter- num.
ever.